The
MOCKING
of the
PRESIDENT

Humor in Life and Letters

SARAH BLACHER COHEN, *General Editor*

Advisory Editors

JOSEPH BOSKIN
Boston University
History and American Studies

ALAN DUNDES
University of California, Berkeley
Folklore and Anthropology

WILLIAM F. FRY, JR.
Stanford University Medical School
Psychiatry

GERALD GARDNER
Author and lecturer
Politics and Government

JEFFREY H. GOLDSTEIN
Temple University and London University
Psychology

GERALD MAST
University of Chicago
Film Studies

DON L. F. NILSEN
Arizona State University
Linguistics

JUNE SOCHEN
Northeastern Illinois University
Women's Studies

LARRY WILDE
Comedian and author

Also by Gerald Gardner

All the Presidents' Wits

The Censorship Papers

Robert Kennedy in New York

Who's in Charge Here?

The Watergate Follies

The Shining Moments

The Quotable Mr. Kennedy

News Reals

The Actor

The Back of the Incubator

Is That Seat Taken?

Miss Caroline
(with Frank Johnson)

No One's in Charge Anymore

The Tara Treasury
(with Harriet Modell Gardner)

The
MOCKING
of the
PRESIDENT

*A History of Campaign Humor
from Ike to Ronnie*

Gerald Gardner

WAYNE STATE UNIVERSITY PRESS   DETROIT   1988

Library of Congress Catalog Card Number: 88–50146.

ISBN 0–8143–2056–2 (alk.)

Typesetter: Computer Composition Corporation.
Designer: Elizabeth Hanson.

For Joanna Lee Gardner
and Henrik Perry Taubman

The Dream Ticket

Contents

Contents

Introduction

Thank heavens for America's humorists. What would we do without them during the quadrennial marathons called presidential elections?

Thank heavens for Art Buchwald, Mark Russell, Garry Trudeau, Jules Feiffer, Mort Sahl, Paul Conrad, Pal Oliphant, and Herblock, for the *National Review*, the *National Lampoon*, and *Punch*, for Johnny Carson and Bob Hope and "Saturday Night Live." And with a look over our shoulders, we can thank heavens for the creators of "Laugh-In," "The Smothers Brothers Comedy Hour," and "That Was the Week That Was."

Thanks to them, and to the journalists and entertainers who illuminate the electoral scene, Americans needn't always look at their politicians, parties, and political struggles with a sober, solemn, self-serious air.

Thanks to their satiric insights into the pretensions and posturings of our leaders, we are able to keep a sense of perspective about our presidential candidates.

Thanks to the humorists who brighten our election campaigns in the bright glare of their ironies, we can maintain our sanity, even when those who seek our votes seem most crazed with the quest for power. We can keep our senses of humor when the candidates' frailties, follies, and frauds seem most intolerable.

Bromidic as it may sound, humor is a most essential element in a democracy. Curiously, the one ingredient that totalitarian societies seem to have in common is a lack of humor. In a dictatorship the practice of satire is a jeopardous pastime indeed. This is doubtless because no public figure willingly subjects himself to the barbs of the satirist if there is some way to dispose of the troublesome fellow. In a democracy we cannot so readily eliminate our critics and iconoclasts.

As our planet becomes more autocratic, rulers tend to become more hostile to humorous reproach. This is not altogether surprising. Humor can be a wounding weapon, and a persuasive one. The witty plays of George Bernard Shaw have proselytized more theatergoers than the grim narratives of Henrik Ibsen. So humor is considered subversive by the powers that be, who often pay it the compliment of suppression.

Humor is necessary in a democracy for reasons other than serving as a device for spreading truth and attacking fools and knaves. In a free society, every few years, the populace engages in a wrenching struggle for power. Humor lets us take the issues seriously without taking *ourselves* too seriously. If we are able to laugh at ourselves as we lunge for the jugular, the process loses some of its malice.

Americans take their politics seriously—especially once the World Series is behind them. A presidential campaign could be a most divisive exercise and one that leaves scars that are slow to heal. Yet, it is essential that when the votes are counted in November, and nearly half the electorate finds their savior has been denied, the struggle cannot end in bile and bitterness, regardless of the depths of our differences. Humor helps this bonding process when the ideological battles are over. If we can laugh at the failure of our fallen hero or the feet of clay of the victor, some of the pressure is released. It is a consummation preferable to storming the palace.

If humor is valuable to the voter, it is doubly so to the candidate himself. To the president or challenger on the campaign trail, he and his staff are beset by a never ending series of problems. Acrimonious charges, venomous editorials, insidious rumors, dipping polls, rallies where the microphone unaccountably goes dead, others where the faithful do not appear in the expected numbers, a substantive speech that the press ignores and the public scorns—all of these are enough to sap the spirit of the candidate. As S. J. Perelman advised: "Go into

12

politics—earn big acrimony." Humor lends a healing balm for all this campaign travail.

Absolute power corrupts absolutely, as does the prospect of absolute power. So humor has the added merit of preventing the presidential candidate from developing messianic delusions. No man is a hero to his butler, and no man is a hero to the cartoonists and journalists who follow his campaign odyssey. To find yourself the target of these witty men is to be both humbled and freed of self-delusion. Every politician is his own best defense attorney. Each judges his opponent by his actions and himself by his motives. A heroic face stares back at him from his motel mirror. The candidate is further insulated against unpleasant truths by obsequious aides who have their eyes on a White House office. But when a presidential candidate becomes the object of the rapier wit of columnists, cartoonists, and comedians, he is not likely to ignore his own flaws.

The dissection of humor is not a promising enterprise. It is not unlike the dissection of a frog in a high school science lab. The student is permitted to take a close look at the innards of the frog, but what has he really learned? Dissecting political humor is equally unproductive, and so this book will not attempt it. However, it is useful to examine humor in the context of the presidential campaign that produced it, and this we will undertake to do, for the issues of a political battle and the personalities of the participants are magnets for the humor of observers, and they are illuminated by it. (They often provide far more illumination than the candidate might have wished.)

The humor of presidential campaigns is seldom bland. Too much is at stake, and emotions run high. When Senator Edmund Muskie was moved to tears in a New Hampshire snowstorm because a newspaper editorial had pilloried his wife, it was not long before bumper stickers appeared reading: VOTE FOR MUSKIE OR HE'LL CRY. Candidates can survive laughter but not snickers, and so it was not long before the estimable Senator Muskie withdrew from the race. Similar visceral humor was aimed at Richard Nixon, John F. Kennedy, and Hubert Humphrey. The targets, respectively, were venality, religion, and verbosity. Campaign humor is frequently caustic. Perhaps it must be strident to pierce the growing apathy of the voter. "Humor is anarchistic," said Malcolm Muggeridge, the irascible onetime editor of *Punch*, and anyone familiar with the mordant humor of Mort Sahl knows Muggeridge's meaning.

Be it mordant or antic, this book explores the sweep of presidential campaign humor and examines its relationship to the issues and personalities of the campaign. Humor is, after all, a basic form of communication through which the press, entertainers, and the candidates themselves convey their skepticism, anger, and arguments. There are many issues that are best joined with humor, many attacks that are best mounted with humor, and many subjects that are best discussed with humor. And given the unrelenting pressure of presidential campaigning, humor is a wonderful outlet for frustration. It is a release for the insiders, who are ravaged by exhaustion, and for the outsiders, who are enraged by the obfuscations of the candidates.

There is irony in the fact that the people who create our most delicious campaign humor—columnists, cartoonists, and comedians—often have a serious conflict of interest. Editorial cartoonist Jeff MacNelly of the *Chicago Tribune* expressed it well when he said that he is often torn between "what is good for my country and what is good for my business." It might be observed that Richard Nixon's fiercest foes in the comedic community would have been bereft of humor had he lost the 1972 election to George McGovern. Cartoonists and monologists found it more fruitful to have a repressed, manipulative man in the White House rather than a benign populist. If each man kills the thing he loves, as Oscar Wilde said, then each humorist loves the thing he kills.

If humor makes life more manageable for the presidential candidate, it also sustains the beleaguered staff members who travel with him and the correspondents who are forever chasing down stories and lost luggage as the candidate continues on his frantic peregrination. As a sometime participant in national political struggles, I am drawn to the unmistakable conclusion that it is impossible to endure the stresses of the campaign trail without a well-developed sense of humor. Adlai Stevenson liked to have witty people about him—on his staff and in his press entourage. Ronald Reagan loved to swap jokes with anyone within earshot. Gerald Ford thrived on funny lines and anecdotes. Jack Kennedy swapped jokes daily with the reporters who covered him. Most incumbents and challengers demand this steady infusion of humor.

As this book will make eminently clear, given the antic and satiric nature of our media and professional humorists, they are not likely to ever be without it.

Chapter 1
Campaign 1984
Acting His Age

If Reagan goes to sleep for even thirty seconds during the debate he'll be in a lot of trouble.
—ART BUCHWALD

In his march to inevitable triumph, Ronald Reagan
seemed peculiarly immune to the cuts and slashes of America's
humorists. There was something about this good-natured man
that seemed to soften the edge of humorous criticism and
make him impervious to its assaults. It was as though the country had a love affair with this aging American hero, and the
voters' sensibilities had to be respected—even by the men and
women whose preoccupation is cynical attack. Thus, though
Reagan's views were sometimes eccentric, his statements inaccurate, his friends indictable, and his ideology questionable,
the wits were surprisingly gentle. America was a very tough
room, as the comics say.

There was an irony in the Reagan campaign that was
not lost on the skeptics. Here was, as *Newsweek*'s Peter Goldman said, "an aging warrior offering a springtime of hope."
His bellicosity toward the Russians led one wag to observe, "I
always get a little nervous when a man of seventy-three says
he's ready to give his life for his country." When one counted
the millions who were dubious of his political philosophy, one
might have expected Reagan to be the target of humor that

scratched rather than tickled, that scorched rather than warmed. Instead, the doubters who had savaged Nixon, mocked Ford, and ridiculed Carter came down gently on Ronald Reagan, and the voters, in the words of Mark Russell, "swept Reagan back into office on a landslide of disapproval."

Ronald Reagan's immense popularity made his overwhelming victory a foregone conclusion. His mastery of the television medium, his genial charm and sheer likability, dismissed all criticism as somehow unpatriotic. This gave birth to the appellation, "the Teflon Presidency," a felicitous phrase coined by congresswoman Pat Shroeder. Russell illustrated this remarkable insulation with wit and cogency:

> To give you an example of how the Teflon Presidency works, and how hopeless Walter Mondale's situation is, about a month ago in Washington, a group of demonstrators gathered in front of the White House to burn President Reagan in effigy. The effigy kept blowing out the flames.

One manifestation of the Teflon presidency that was especially galling to Reagan's foes was that the numerous unethical acts of Reagan's aides failed to touch their leader. The wags had tormented Lyndon Johnson with the peccadillos of Bobby Baker; they had mocked Jimmy Carter over the bank frauds of Bert Lance; they had needled Harry Truman over the excesses of Harry Vaughan; but the humor generated by in-house flummery left Reagan untouched and unmocked. There was seldom an administration whose prominent figures had so often been trapped with their hands in the cookie jar or disdaining the public welfare. Interior Secretary James Watt had so little regard for the environment that Reagan himself joked about him "strip-mining the Rose Garden." Art Buchwald reflected that it was hard to tell when one saw Attorney General Ed Meese in court whether he was there as a prosecutor or a defendant. When Meese mounted an attack on pornography and issued a report on its dangers, Johnny Carson cracked that "Meese's next duty is to hire construction workers to sandblast the boobs off the Statue of Liberty." The number of Reagan aides who were guilty of ethical misbehavior continued to mount, but the venalities never touched Ronald

Reagan (until he found himself waist deep in the Iranamok quagmire). Walter Mondale squandered the chance to tar Reagan with the improprieties of his aides when he himself appointed the tainted Bert Lance to a lofty position in his campaign. But it is problematic whether the improprieties of Reagan's staff could have been successfully tied to him.

If Reagan had a legitimate Achilles heel, it was his age. Dwight Eisenhower had once declared that "no man over seventy should sit in the Oval Office"; the job was just too demanding. But Reagan had contrived to make his task extremely manageable by working short hours, taking numerous trips to Camp David and lengthy hibernations at his Santa Barbara ranch, and delegating more authority than any president since Warren Harding.

Much of the wit of the Washington press corps focused on Reagan's odd working hours. Said Fred Barnes of the *New Republic*, "If Ronald Reagan ever faces some terrible crisis, he'll really spend some sleepless afternoons." Recalling that Reagan had slept through a Libyan dogfight, a meeting with the Pope, and part of a cabinet meeting, Johnny Carson cracked, "There are only two reasons you wake President Reagan—World War Three and if 'Hellcats of the Navy' is on 'The Late Show.'" Reagan mocked his own light schedule by observing after a hectic week, "I've really been burning the midday oil."

What became known, in euphemistic terms, as "the disengagement problem"—and, with equal charity under the Tower Report, as Reagan's "hands-off managerial style"—was a source of much irreverent wit. Mark Russell gently inquired: "What do you get when you combine James Dean and Ronald Reagan?" and answered "Rebel without a Clue." A bruising joke that was given wide currency in the first Reagan term had the First Family at dinner. The waiter is taking their order, and the First Lady recites her wishes. "I'll have the shrimp cocktail, the trout almandine, the chocolate mousse, and espresso." "What about the vegetable?" asks the waiter. "He'll have the same," says Nancy.

The public generally laughed away the issue of Reagan's dotage. Even Mort Sahl, whose humor more often burned than singed, laughed on the side of the president on the geriatric issue. Said Sahl, "When Reagan goes to a home for the elderly and meets an 80-year-old man, he thinks, 'When I was your age I was working.'" Phyllis Diller made a virtue of Reagan's antiquity. "There is an advantage for a President being over seventy," she said. "At least he doesn't have to listen to his mother."

The runaway qualities of the Reagan campaign were impeded only once, after the first televised debate with Walter Mondale, when the president sounded bumbling and incoherent. Suddenly, the long submerged question of whether Reagan was indeed too old for the presidency reared its head. Said Mark Russell with an eloquent shrug: "He's an actor. He was acting his age." The *New Republic*'s TRB said, "We should treat the President like a college student and give him a pop quiz." Some typical questions would be: "Who is the President of Honduras?" and "Name your grandchildren." As Reagan prepared for his second TV debate, Art Buchwald said, "If he goes to sleep even for thirty seconds during the debate, he's in trouble." Said Sahl: "Truman proved anyone can be President, Eisenhower proved you don't need a President, Johnson wounded the Presidency, Nixon killed it. Carter buried it. And Ronald Reagan is trying to prove there is life after death." Said Loren Kerry-Walker: "Mr. Reagan said he would take a senility test if he was reelected. But what if he forgot?" When *The National Lampoon* raised the geriatric issue, it pointed out that Mr. Chernenko, the Soviet leader, was about the same age as Mr. Reagan. "Between the two of them," said the *Lampoon*, "they've seen Halley's Comet six times." But those who feared that Reagan had faltered fatally in his first debate by his show of debility and age did not take into account either his popularity or his resilient wit. In the final debate, he disposed of the troublesome issue with a caustic joke. He said, "I will not make age an issue in this campaign. I am not going to exploit . . . my opponent's youth and inexperience." Reagan's immense popularity did the rest. The public wanted to believe that Ronald Reagan was in tip-top shape. As Mark Russell observed:

The consensus after the first debate was that even though the President appeared to be hesitant, nervous, confused and incoherent, as long as he kept remembering to put on his pants, he would be re-elected.

Religion invaded presidential politics in the 1984 campaign. President Reagan associated himself intimately with the Reverend Jerry Falwell, the electronic preacher with special insights into American morality. Reagan announced at a prayer breakfast in Dallas, home of the GOP convention, his belief that religion and politics were intertwined. Geraldine Ferraro, stung by insinuations that she was not a very good Catholic given her dichotomous stand on abortion, questioned how good a Christian the president really was, given his indifference to the pains of poverty and his irregular attendance at church. Addressing Reagan's embrace of the evangelical right, Bob Hope remarked, "On the dashboard of his limousine, Ronald Reagan is reported to have the real Jerry Falwell sitting there." Mort Sahl grew dismayed over the infusion of religion into the secular electoral process. He said:

> Mondale says he's a preacher's kid. Ferraro says she's a Catholic. Bush says we're in Nicaragua because they won't accept God. Reagan is close to the Falwell people. Here are four people who could give God a bad name.

When Ronald Reagan declared that in appointing Supreme Court justices he would apply a litmus test of their favorable view about bringing prayer to the classroom, satirist Fran Lebowitz sniped, "My main objection to Ronald Reagan is the religious issue. He's going to want the new Supreme Court Justices to take religious tests. I'd recommend intelligence tests instead."

Though Reagan had done little to enact the programs favored by his far-right religious constituency—school prayer, antiabortion, and so forth—he sought to bond them closely with campaign rhetoric. Columnists and satirists heaped sardonic scorn on Reagan's advocacy of school prayer and its injury to the traditional separation of church and state. Noting the hypocrisy of a man who advocates the nourishment of the

21

soul but is indifferent to the nourishment of the body, one Washington scribe cracked, "Mr. Reagan has been urging prayer in the schools. And if he's successful, the first thing the kids will pray for is hot lunches."

Said Fran Lebowitz: "I've no objection to prayer in the schools if they'll put algebra in the churches." Even Robin Williams, the antic improvizational actor, had an opinion on the overheated subject. "If they vote in school prayer," said Williams, "will it be mandatory to include show tunes?"

To some, Reagan's piety comported poorly with both his irregular church attendance and his indifference to the welfare of blacks. Reagan opposed renewal of the Voting Rights Act and affirmative action programs and favored the distribution of public funds to segregated colleges. Much of Reagan's appeal—and it was handsomely embodied in his TV campaign commercials—was a nostalgic reflection of America's glowing yesterdays. It was an era of kindness and gentility, like a page out of Blanche DuBois's memory book. Some doubted whether this exercise in reminiscence did not resurrect an age only visible through the myopia of sentimental hindsight. One of these doubters was Jules Feiffer, who pictured Reagan reminiscing about the color-blind days of yore. Said Feiffer's Reagan:

> We had a black on my high school football team . . . He was a competitor. He played the game. We became friends . . . I even took him home for dinner . . . My black friend didn't ask for and he didn't receive any favors . . . The Voting Rights Act is a special favor . . . Now, special favors weaken us . . . Special favors would have divided me from my black friend . . . [cheerleading] GO–GO–GO CONGRESS! STRIKE DOWN THE VOTING RIGHTS ACT! . . . Let's win this one for the bigot.

Even after four years of revolutionary politics, during which Reagan had turned the national agenda on its head, escalated defense spending, slashed taxes, built a huge deficit, and attempted to dismantle the federal bureaucracy, there was still some residual doubt about the man's early career as an actor—whether such a background could prepare him for a position of national leadership. "This is a man," said Gore Vidal, "who used to wait for hours on a Hollywood sound stage for some director to say, 'Don't forget to hit your mark, Ronnie.'" America's humorists found it hard to shrug off the idea of a former movie actor leading the free world in its battle with "the evil empire." They were bemused by the frequency with which Reagan would appropriate scenes from movies ("State of the Union" and "Mr. Smith Goes to Washington" are two such examples) and present them as fact.

Often the jokes about Reagan's former career were benign and whimsical, as when Bob Hope said, "Ronald Reagan is not your ordinary kind of politician. He doesn't know how to lie or cheat or steal. He's always had an agent for that." Or when Johnny Carson said, "A lot of people say Mr. Reagan was in Hollywood too long. When he signed the tax bill he signed it, 'Warmest Regards, Ronald Reagan.'" Sometimes the jokes took a gentle swipe at the generally low quality of Reagan's film output, as when Phyllis Diller said, "There are a lot of Democrats who say they are voting for Reagan because they're afraid if he loses he might make another movie." Alluding to his frequent confrontations with a balky Democrat-controlled Capitol Hill, Joan Rivers said, "Reagan is getting less votes in Congress than he did when they voted for the Oscars."

Some of the anti-actor wit was a bit closer to the bone, as when political activist and TV star Ed Asner observed that Reagan was impatient with people who did not agree with his worldview. Said the star of "Lou Grant," "When I made a speech attacking his policy in Latin America, Mr. Reagan said, 'What does an actor know about foreign policy?'" But more often it was innocuous and inoffensive, as when Phyllis Diller said, "Reagan doesn't consider this a second term. To him it's a double feature." Or when Bob Hope said, with the gentleness of a leaf falling, "Ronald Reagan has discovered that the Presidency isn't as easy as he thought. In fact he's going to demand stunt pay." If presidential humor is meant to illuminate and draw blood, Reagan's chums in the entertainment world were attacking with all the ferocity of enraged gerbels. The media were no more belligerent. Looking back to Reagan's pre–movie career in radio, conservative camp follower George Will added his affectionate one-liner: "Ronald Reagan has held the two most demeaning jobs in America—President of the U.S. and radio announcer for the Chicago Cubs."

In the early days of Reagan's first term, his wife had appeared to be an autocratic woman with a taste for designer gowns and well-set tables. The day after she acquired a new set of china for the East Room, the administration published some depressing figures on poverty in America. But by the time the 1984 campaign had arrived, the magic of public relations and Mrs. Reagan's devotion to the cause of drug abuse had sweetened her image and softened the humor at her expense. By 1984 her autocracy had become a joke that she was ready to accept and even share. White House speech writer Landon Parvin, who had written jokes to enliven Reagan's first-term speeches and provide him with a reputation for wit and warmth, wrote a parody of Fanny Brice's "Second-hand Rose" called "Second-hand Clothes," which the First Lady sang at the annual dinner of the Gridiron Club. In the song, Mrs. Reagan kidded her taste for fancy raiments, and her costume was a motley mess of clothes that looked like it had been appropriated from Goodwill Industries. The laughter of the press laid the issue of Mrs. Reagan's aristocratic tastes to rest as firmly as had her husband's joke about his age landed the age issue in the dustbin of history. The theory was that if Nancy Reagan was able to laugh at the issue of designer clothes and pricey china, she could not possibly be as pretentious as her critics claimed. Others joined in the good-natured laughter. Said Phyllis Diller:

> This has been a very stylish administration. For the first time in history we have a designer deficit. Mrs. Reagan bought her fall wardrobe and we had to cancel aid to Bolivia. The Republicans say they're not waging a war in El Salvador. They're catering it.

The jokes about Nancy Reagan were so inoffensive that even Henny Youngman, that antediluvian master of mother-in-law humor, joined the panel of raillery. Said Youngman: "Nancy was in bed with Ronald Reagan. She said: 'My God, your feet are cold.' He said: 'When you're in bed you can call me Ron.'" (Like many political jokes, this one was an adaptation of an anecdote from another era and another field. The celebrated participants of the original were David O. Selznick and his wife Irene, to whom the messianic producer had said, "In bed you can call me David.") Not everyone was so forbearing of Mrs. Reagan's devotion to the good life. Her indulgences drew a sharp elbow from one Hollywood wag who said, "Mr. Reagan says his heroes are FDR and JFK, but I suspect his *real* hero is Calvin Coolidge. And Mrs. Reagan's is Calvin Klein."

Occasionally, the gibes at Nancy's expense drew blood. The well-publicized schism between the Reagans and their children was the subject of amusement and disapproval. There was a whiff of hypocrisy about a couple that was so full of conjugal warmth and filial devotion and yet had little time for their children. Reagan clearly disapproved of his son Ron writing for *Playboy* magazine or dancing in his undershorts on "Saturday Night Live." (Recalling Jimmy Carter's brother Billy and his taste for beer, Mark Russell cracked on the oddities of presidential relatives: "At least Billy kept his pants on.") It was said that Nancy Reagan, guardian of the gates of her husband's privacy, kept the children at a polite distance. Son Michael had protested that it had been eons since dad had seen his own grandchildren. George Carlin said, "I understand that Mrs. Reagan makes her grandchildren wear name tags." Others needled the First Lady for her devotion to her coiffeur, which seemed greater than her devotion to her own progeny. Said *Punch* magazine: "The Soviet decision to boycott the Los Angeles Olympics . . . was a source of great disappointment to Mrs. Reagan. She's been in training for the four hundred meter hairspray." Added Johnny Carson: "I hear Nancy Reagan fell down and broke her hair."

House Speaker Thomas P. "Tip" O'Neill, who had scant affection for Ronald Reagan (he greeted Reagan after the latter's inaugural with the condescending question, "Well, how does it feel to be in the big time?"), had an equally wounding reference for Reagan's wife. O'Neill speculated that, when Nancy left the White House, she could always become the "Queen of Beverly Hills." Johnny Carson one-upped the Speaker. Referring to the size of his own recent divorce settlement, Carson shook his head, "No, Nancy would *not* be the Queen of Beverly Hills. And I have the royal tab to prove it."

During the 1984 campaign most Americans felt sanguine about the state of the U.S. economy; Reagan had revised the tax laws in a way that benefited the affluent and which his own budget chief dismissed as trickle-down theory —help the rich and the poor will thrive on the crumbs from their table. Not everyone agreed. Conservatives applauded the new tax code. As George Bernard Shaw said, "A government that robs Peter to pay Paul can always depend on the support of Paul." Latino comedian Paul Rodriguez also had his doubts about the Reagan economic plan. Said Rodriguez: "As far as the trickle down theory, we're still waiting for the trickle." (Rodriguez expressed a polite dubiety about Walter Mondale's economic plans as well when he said, "Does this mean we won't have to sell oranges on the freeway?")

Even with as popular a candidate as Ronald Reagan, during Campaign 1984, the Republicans were at pains to shake the public perception of the GOP as the country club party. When asked the difference between Democrats and Republicans, Ann Meara replied, "100,000 dollars." Though Mort Sahl displayed an equal skepticism for liberal Democrats and affluent Republicans, he remarked with a mixture of political acumen and pop psychology, "Liberals don't believe they deserve anything they have. Conservatives believe they deserve everything they've stolen."

David Frost, cocreater of the hallmark show of television satire, "That Was the Week That Was," tried to explain the difference between the two parties by drawing analogies to the British political system. "We have a Labor Party which you in your country would call the Socialist Party, and then we have a Conservative Party, which you in your country would call the Socialist Party." Gore Vidal observed that there is really only one political party in America—the Property party. And Jason Epstein, erudite editor of Random House, pointed out that all issues really boil down to two protagonists —people and property. Columnist Russell Baker came down on the side of the angels when he praised the neutron bomb as the perfect Republican weapon in that it "killed people while leaving the mortgages intact."

The bloated federal deficit and the gargantuan budget were issues that left the electorate unmoved, despite the attention they received from the nation's wits. Said Mark Russell: "Think of a $1.5 trillion budget. If you stood on top of the payment book, you'd experience weightlessness." Bob Hope said of the mammoth deficit, "The President is a showman. He has props for his next economic speech. A hat and a rabbit."

Many voters were uneasy with Reagan's pugnacious attitude toward the Soviets and the fact that in four years in the White House he had never met with any Russian official with a higher position than ambassador. His open-mike gaffe about falling bombs troubled the faithful, and Reagan's staff knew that in the course of the 1984 campaign there would be, well, *something*. They were uneasy about the president. He was prone to mishap when the script had not been carefully rehearsed. As Jeff Davis said, "Reagan is the Fred Astaire of foot-and-mouth disease." Reagan's aides knew that some sort of gaffe was inevitable. And indeed it was.

The president was sitting before an open mike at his Santa Barbara ranch, doing a voice test for his weekly radio address to the nation, when a carefree attitude overtook him. "My fellow Americans," he purred, "I am pleased to tell you today that I have signed legislation that will outlaw Russia forever. We begin bombing in five minutes." Later, Mort Sahl said, "I heard one delegate at the GOP convention say, 'I hope this isn't just another empty campaign promise.'" Said Argus Hamilton: "I covered the Republican convention when the President made his joke about bombing Russia in five minutes. The New York delegates thought he'd flipped his lid. The California delegates thought he ought to, like, apologize and deal with it. The Texas delegates couldn't believe he'd give them five minutes."

Lyndon Johnson had painted Barry Goldwater as indifferent to the needy. Walter Mondale had a more difficult time painting Ronald Reagan with the same brush. Though Reagan's policies were as indifferent to the poor as Goldwater's, Reagan seemed like too decent a man to embody such callous views. Scathing gibes about his myopic attitude to the poor never really stuck. Yet they appeared. Said an editor for *Mother Jones* magazine, "I don't think Mr. Reagan has the proper attitude toward the unemployed. He just thinks they have the wrong agent." And one political wag said, "Mr. Reagan said yesterday that this nation can no longer ignore the suffering of the needy. People started cheering in Watts, but then they discovered he meant Nicaragua."

Reagan campaigned on the formidable achievements of bringing down inflation and interest rates, and, since those twin towers had torpedoed Jimmy Carter four years before, it was no mean achievement. But critics claimed that Reagan had broken inflation on the backs of the poor, producing a recession that had brought pain to the elderly and the working class. Jules Feiffer mocked the Reagan process of gain through selective pain in a cartoon strip in which Reagan is explaining his economic philosophy to a doubting voter. "Recession has its good points," says the president cheerfully. "Recession brings down Inflation. Recession lowers interest rates. Recession will make life more bearable for the middle class." The voter is unmoved. She responds, "But what do we do about the old, the poor, and the unemployed?" Reagan shrugs: "The old die. The poor starve. The unemployed go into the military . . . Not perfect maybe, but it's a beginning."

Reagan's triumph was personal and profound. It seemed to reflect the truth of Edward Bennett Williams's observation about the secret of presidential campaigning and the basic rule for getting reelected. "Politics," said Williams, "is the gentle art of getting votes from the poor and campaign contributions from the rich by promising to protect each from the other."

Chapter 2
Campaign 1984
Walter over the Bridge

Mr. Mondale has said that God doesn't belong in politics, and apparently God feels the same way about
Mr. Mondale.

—MARK RUSSELL

The motto of the Washington press corps is "If you
don't have anything nice to say—let's hear it," which may account for the fact that a decent, intelligent, stalwart man like
Walter Mondale became an object of raillery and humor in his
campaign for the U.S. presidency. It was not the press alone
that found him a figure of fun. The comedians, cartoonists,
and voters also shared in the bruising merriment. With Ronald Reagan, the wags made sport of his ideological excesses.
But in Mondale's case, the target was most often his ineffectuality. The most amusing thing about Mondale's candidacy was
the curious fact that no one seemed to want him to be president. He was not a victim of the anger he provoked but rather
of the apathy.

Many of the people who laughed most loudly at the anti-
Mondale humor would have liked to see a liberal Democrat in
the White House rather than an aging Republican. They un-
doubtedly liked Mondale's dignity and determination, his
stamina and sobriety. They respected his campaign, which was
encrusted with concrete issues, and were equally dubious of

Reagan's carnival of opiates and free-floating Americanism. But the fact was that, rather than stimulate enthusiasm, Mondale generated ennui and was vulnerable to ridicule for his gray eminence. Fritz Mondale drove Gary Hart from the race with the commercial gag line, "Where's the beef?" but he himself was nullified by the unspoken question, "Where's the spice?"

Mondale did not enjoy the humor he ignited; candidates seldom do. But those who seek the presidency are supposed to be thick-skinned. The gibes and slanders of the professional wits are supposed to roll off their backs. "If you can't stand the heat, get out of the kitchen," admonished Harry Truman. And yet, presidential candidates are all too human, and mockery and scorn are painful. "Thank God I don't read the newspapers," snapped Bobby Kennedy, as he scaled a copy of the *New York Post* across his Hotel Carlyle livingroom. But he *did* read the papers and fumed. "How can they do this to me!" barked John F. Kennedy, as he flung a copy of *Time* magazine across the Oval Office, and Hugh Sidey looked on in discomfort. "I bit the stem off many a pipe," recalled Gerald Ford, thinking of the calumnies of "Saturday Night Live" that ridiculed his clumsiness. "And my own children thought it was funny!"

And so Walter Mondale, that fine and decent man—son of a minister, married to the daughter of a minister—fumed and fretted at the campaign humor that was leveled at him from virtually all quarters—even from his own supporters and from sympathetic journalists. And despite his suffering, the rain of humor continued. Epithets might have been easier to bear than the drumbeat of caustic wit.

One of the basic themes of these attacks was Mondale's purported dullness. On his monthly PBS farrago, Mark Russell said, "Walter Mondale's charisma falls somewhere between a Presbyterian minister and a tree." Mocking Mondale's humorlessness, columnist Marc Shields cracked about the candidate's Scandinavian ancestry: "The three thinnest books in the world are the books on humble politicians, modest anchormen, and Norwegians with a sense of humor."

Mondale's dullness did not escape the attention of Pat Paulsen, the saturnine wit who ran a mock presidential campaign of his own on "The Smothers Brothers Comedy Hour" and is currently resurrecting it. Said Paulsen at the Gerald Ford Symposium on Humor & the Presidency: "Whenever I saw Walter Mondale on television, I thought I had lost the color."

The Mondale grayness was dutifully reported to those members of the British public who developed a taste for following American presidential contests. The Washington correspondent for the London *Times* said, "Walter Mondale is stirring up apathy all over this country."

Early in Mondale's campaign for the presidency, he had communicated with a Hollywood comedy writer to ask if the scribe could provide him with humorous material with which to bloody Ronald Reagan. The writer obliged but discovered to his dismay that Mondale used little of the material that was supplied him. When it was revealed that a Reagan mole had filched President Carter's briefing book to help Reagan prepare for his TV debate with Jimmy Carter, the Hollywood wit sent an assortment of gibes to Mondale, only to have the candidate solemnly respond: "I don't feel that thievery is a proper subject for humor." (Mondale's opponent, on the other hand, felt that nuclear war and farmers' bankruptcies were suitable subjects for humor, and the public seemed to agree with him.)

When Fritz Mondale chose a woman to run for the vice presidency for the first time in American history, even this act of audacity was used as a stick with which to beat the Minnesotan. Said Mort Sahl: "So Geraldine Ferraro will run with Walter Mondale. Women keep getting the crummy jobs." The audience howled, and Sahl went on to reflect on the fate of the distaff entry into presidential politics. "As for women," said Sahl, "running with Walter Mondale is a way to keep them *out* of government."

The perception was always that Walter Mondale was a passive cipher and that Mrs. Ferraro was a ball of fire. One Washington newsman remarked, "Mrs. Ferraro is the perfect running mate for Walter Mondale. She will add a little macho to the ticket." And Robert Klein made a similar point when he cracked, "I'm a little dubious about Walter Mondale. Even if he's elected, I'm not sure Mrs. Ferraro will find enough for him to do." Bob Hope reflected fancifully that Mondale had hired James Cagney as his new campaign manager and that Cagney had advised the candidate to get tough. "Cagney told him the way to look tough was to slap some women around," said Hope. "Mondale tried that and Geraldine Ferraro decked him." Hope dismissed the Ferraro nomination as a trifling threat to the Ronald Reagan steamroller and tossed it aside with a quip. "Mrs. Ferraro's nomination really affected Reagan's strategy," said Hope. "He's fitting George Bush for a dress."

The disorganization of Mondale's campaign was another object of humorous attack. Reagan's campaign seemed serene and effortless, while Mondale's stumbled along in fits and starts. Mondale had been savaged by Gary Hart as the candidates fought through the endless primary process.

Political humorists zeroed in on the logistics and strategies of the Mondale campaign. Reviewing the opening days of the campaign, Mark Russell observed, "Mondale started slowly . . . then he tapered off." Mondale seemed to lack the savvy of Reagan's strategists; he never quite got his operation on track. Eyes twinkling, Russell observed that Mondale's staff handled the candidate somewhat badly. Labor Day is the kick-off date for presidential election campaigns in America. Employing the hyperbole that is the stock in trade of the satirist, Russell said:

> The Labor Day Parade in New York begins at noon. So at 8:00 A.M. they had Mondale riding down Fifth Avenue on a garbage truck. Waving at the winos.

The Mondale campaign, with all its glitches and foulups, triggered the wit of professional gagsters who are accustomed to a better sense of organization when you take a show on the road. Said Phyllis Diller: "I admire the Democrats. Here it is a week into the campaign and they're off and stumbling."

Premier attorney Edward Bennett Williams was more sympathetic to the snafus of the Mondale organization. He reminded the candidate that, try as he might to avoid the workings of Murphy's Law, it would inevitably prevail. "Remember," admonished Williams, "in 1895 there were only two automobiles in the entire state of Ohio, and they collided." Williams added another example of the inescapability of Murphy's Law to the hapless campaigner. He reminded Mondale that "the chance of the peanut butter and jelly sandwich landing with the jelly side down is in direct correlation to the value of the carpet."

Fritz Mondale found himself increasingly irritated by hecklers. Of course, hecklers are a traditional part of presidential campaigning, and some candidates learn to deal with them deftly. Anti-heckler tactics call for a strong stomach and a quick wit, which may account for John Kennedy's adroitness with ruffians in the crowd. But Walter Mondale lacked the spontaneity needed to answer them with humor and the staff to arm him with canned responses. Hence, he was rattled by the hecklers who dogged his trail. Art Buchwald noted this painful phenomenon that plagued Mondale and chose to see the curse as a blessing. Said Buchwald:

Heckling has played an important role in the Mondale campaign. If you get heckled, you get covered by the press. With heckling you get on the evening news. The staffs know this. The more hecklers the better it is. Reagan's people are going to bring out their own hecklers to have Reagan heckled. Then Reagan will have some of these great rejoinders to the hecklers which will give him standing ovations. Right now the Republicans are hiring hecklers to heckle Reagan to make him look good. They're holding auditions right now.

Mondale's liberalism was also good for a laugh. His compassion for the poor made for some good punch lines, however decent its inspiration. One might say, with Shakespeare, that "he jests at scars who never felt a wound," but Mondale's compassion made him a tempting target to observers less touched by those in the shadows of life. Said Ronald Reagan, "I just received a Valentine Card from Walter Mondale. I know it was from him because the heart was bleeding."

Mondale's social conscience became a bull's-eye for lampooning. Orson Bean remarked, "At his best, John F. Kennedy made us feel we had class. At his best, Ronald Reagan makes us feel everything's all right. At his best, Walter Mondale makes us feel guilty."

Others mocked Mondale's devotion to heartwrenching causes, as though Roosevelt, Kennedy, and Johnson's similar devotion to the needy was merely quixotic. Said Phyllis Diller:

> The Democrats have a lock on social issues. They're pushing welfare for unemployed whales who suffer the effects of pollution while participating in anti-nuclear demonstrations.

Some lashed back at Reagan's apparent callousness, mocking his selective concern for the "truly needy." Reagan's heart seldom seemed to bleed for the unemployed. His humorous repertoire was full of anecdotes about welfare queens who used food stamps to buy a fifth of vodka at Safeway. On balance, Walter Mondale suffered more for his compassion than Reagan did for his self-absorbtion.

Some compared Mondale scathingly to another bombastic liberal Democrat who was no longer around to resent the comparison. "Mondale is the reincarnation of Hubert Humphrey," said Mort Sahl. Then, after a moment's reflection, Sahl added, "Maybe you have to be reincarnated to displace Ronald Reagan."

Religion became a measurable element of the Mondale-Reagan campaign. It was the first time religion had been a major ingredient in a presidential election since the scurrilous underground attacks on Jack Kennedy's Catholicism. The dais of the Republican convention in 1984 became a resounding pulpit for Jerry Falwell and other television divinities, preaching in support of compulsory morality for the sinners of the electorate. Walter Mondale, in his innocence, did not feel that religion and politics were linked. Here, too, Mondale invited raillery and was whipped by the nation's wits. Mark Russell said, "Mr. Mondale has said that God doesn't belong in politics. And apparently God feels the same way about Mr. Mondale."

When the Democratic candidate took the courageous step of promising to raise taxes as a way to lower the crushing deficit—a step that Reagan mocked but came to embrace after the 1987 stock market crash—he made himself a magnet for jocosity. One White House wag, reflecting on Mondale's opposition to a linkage of church and state and his proposal for increased taxes to retire the deficit, exclaimed: "Mondale has done pretty well so far. He's come out for taxes and against God."

Mondale suffered both ways for his groundbreaking choice to have a female running mate. There were scathing comments that contrasted his passivity with her feistiness. And Mrs. Ferraro was far from immune to humorous attack based on her gender. It was not always tasteful or kind, but perhaps, as Malcolm Muggeridge affirmed, satiric humor must be harsh to penetrate the cynicism of the voter. If so, the antifeminist humor leveled at Geraldine Ferraro satisfied the requirements of political satire.

At first Gerry Ferraro's sex insulated her to insult, serious or comic. Her selection had jarred the political traditions. The GOP was disoriented by a female adversary, and some Republicans reacted with tasteless overkill. Ed Rollins, Reagan's savvy campaign manager, who should have known better, prophesied, "Mrs. Ferraro will end up being the biggest bust in politics." Even the genial Ronald Reagan was unsettled by the blue note of this comment, and when reporters at his next press conference queried him on it—this was back in the days when Reagan used to hold press conferences on occasion —he shrugged his eyebrows and put himself a country mile from the sexist remark.

Barbara Bush, wife of the vice presidential candidate, showed something less than the generosity of spirit we tend to expect from our First and Second Ladies, when the subject of Mrs. Ferraro arose. Asked her assessment of George's opponent in the Veep sweepstakes, Mrs. Bush declined to characterize the lady, except to say that the relevant adjective "rhymes with witch." One did not need the help of the Stephen Sondheim rhyming dictionary to divine the adjective Mrs. Bush had in mind.

When Mrs. Ferraro's personal problems—or, more accurately, her husband's personal problems—burst upon the public press, a good deal of the luster was rubbed off the attractive candidate. Reagan's aides knew all the juiciest tidbits of her financial torment almost as soon as she did and were joyous at the details. No longer would Mrs. Ferraro be in on a pass. Now she was vulnerable to the most scathing attack, and

America's comics found the facts of Ferraro's case equally nourishing. "Geraldine Ferraro has been named woman of the Year," said one wag. "By H. & R. Block."

Gender alone made Geraldine Ferraro a subject of lampoonery for Bob Hope, which must have set Gloria Steinem to grinding her teeth. Said Hope:

> Geraldine Ferraro is having her problems. She is married and has some children. That is undoubtedly why she agreed to run for Vice President. Right now she can only handle a part time job.

Then, employing a familiar slogan for a woman's hair coloring, Hope added: "I've always known that blondes have more fun. Mondale wants to find out if they can get more votes."

Phyllis Diller put a knife in about the candidate's rapid rise from obscurity, ostensibly on the strength of her gender, and by implication her lack of qualifications, for the office she sought. "Until last Tuesday," laughed Diller, "I thought Ferraro was a car."

There was no question that Geraldine Ferraro was chosen as Mondale's running mate because of her sex rather than because of her political experience. Henry Morgan observed that it might be more responsible to have only one criterion in selecting the vice presidential candidate. "It should be the person who would make the best President. . . . Some day we may even choose our *Presidents* that way," smiled Morgan.

Ms. Ferraro was fond of referring to the humble roots of her immigrant parents, and the satirists targeted this for critical attention. At the Democratic convention, Gerry Ferraro was not the only one to boast of her progenitors. Mario Cuomo praised his Italian-born parents, and Jesse Jackson lauded his African heritage. Mort Sahl took a swipe at the pretensions of the New York governor, the minister, and the vice presidential nominee when he said:

> The Democrats had a convention of immigrants. Governor Cuomo said, "My parents came from Sardinia." Jesse Jackson said, "My parents came from Nigeria." Mrs. Ferraro said, "My parents came from Naples." We've been here two hundred years. You would think it's time to unpack.

When Geraldine Ferraro debated George Bush on television in Philadelphia, her Ivy League opponent managed to suppress any humor at her expense. (The next day he was not so successful. A ubiquitous microphone picked up his comment to a labor leader: "I really kicked a little ass last night!") But if George Bush was not sarcastic on camera, he was patronizing, which may in fact have been worse. When the discussion turned to the problems of the Middle East, Gerry Ferraro criticized administration policy. Bush turned an admonitory glance on her—the sort one reserves for backward children and drunken workmen. "Let me help you, Mrs. Ferraro," said Bush with a patient sigh. "Let me help you with the difference between Iran and Lebanon." Mark Russell caught the aroma of condescension in the vice president's tone and cracked:

> You know what he was really saying. You know what the translation was. "Don't you worry your pretty little head about such things. And I believe I'll have some more of those nifty brownies."

At about the time that George Bush was patronizing Ms. Ferraro, Joan Rivers had abandoned her role as stand-in for "Tonight Show" host Johnny Carson to sign a lucrative contract with Fox Broadcasting to host a competing talk show. Carson joked about the new "Talk Show War" and observed that Ronald Reagan was out of the country and Vice President Bush was in charge. Said Carson: "Bush said this would be his last week as guest president, he was starring in his own presidency soon."

Geraldine Ferraro suffered a good deal of sexist slights, comic or sarcastic. If Mondale won, she would be one heartbeat away from the presidency, and Robin Williams speculated on the dubious virtues of a woman president. "We'd never go to war," he said, "and every twenty-eight days we'd have severe negotiations."

Of course, the irony of Bush's insults to Mrs. Ferraro were not lost on the Washington press corps. One White House correspondent observed, "The ultimate slur against a woman vice president is that she would be hysterical, illogical, and highly emotional. Which to my mind rules out George Bush."

There were some limits, of course. No one referred to a romance between Mrs. Ferraro and Mr. Mondale. The days of Gary Hart's reckless liaisons with a Miami model were still a few years away. In the waning days of the campaign, however, as the polls showed calamity ahead, David Steinberg remarked:

Walter Mondale is getting increasingly desperate. He knows he's in trouble. He just announced that if elected he will marry Geraldine Ferraro. Or, if the people of San Francisco prefer, Gary Hart.

Mondale joined Barry Goldwater, Alf Landon, and George McGovern as victims of the greatest electoral landslides of the century. America's love affair with the genial Californian flattened Mondale and his special interest politics. It was a spectacular victory for Mr. Reagan and his feel-good magic.

But much of the blame must rest with Mondale's dullness and his prosaic style, which were the topics of most of the humor of the 1984 campaign. Mondale would have done better had he employed more humor in his campaign of the sort he displayed the day after it ended. On that solemn postelection morning, Mondale said, "All my life I've wanted to run for the Presidency in the worst way. And that's what I did."

Chapter 3
Campaign 1980
The Easy Target

Sometimes when I look at my children I say to myself, "Lillian, you should have stayed a virgin."
—LILLIAN CARTER

When the campaign of 1980 began, the presidential
incumbent, James Earl Carter, was painfully vulnerable to
humorous attack, despite his rectitudinous posture, or perhaps
because of it. Inflation raged at 20 percent, the prime rate approached the record set in the Great Crash of 1929, the stock
market limped along, the bond market was anemic, the housing business was in shambles, the auto industry was asthmatic,
and the trade deficit was at an all-time high. Voters recalled
the long lines at gasoline pumps and raged at American impotence in the face of Iranian hostage-takers, and when Ronald
Reagan asked, "Are you better off today than you were four
years ago?" he provoked a resounding chorus of No's. And
Jimmy Carter was history.

Inflation, recession, hostages, unemployment—they
combined in a truly beatable combination. It seemed to the
electorate that Jimmy Carter was a lackluster president who
was over his head in the responsibilities of the Oval Office.

By the time the 1980 campaign began, inflation was so
high and Jimmy Carter's standing so low that one member of
the Washington press corps joked, "Carter is the first president with poll ratings lower than the prime interest rate."

Carter responded with a bitter humor of his own. Everywhere he went, Carter encountered cool to hostile audiences. His performance had generated scant approval; there was an obvious estrangement between Carter and the public he served, and this manifested itself in crowds that were not shy in showing their disapproval. Carter responded with a sardonic humor that bordered on sarcasm and often stepped across the line of taste. On one rare occasion when Carter was greeted by an exuberant, cheering crowd—"He must have given the city a grant the week before," said an aide—he appeared stunned by the sounds of unaccustomed affection. Carter said to the throng: "It's a pleasure to see people waving at me with all five fingers."

The general perception of Carter's as a failed presidency unleashed a flow of wounding wit from all points of the media spectrum—comedians, satirists, reporters, cartoonists, and even his own aides, who resented his arrogance and sardonic humor at their expense. An editorial cartoonist in the Los Angeles *Herald-Examiner* pictured California governor Jerry Brown speaking to President Carter. "No one thinks more highly of you than I do, sir," Brown is saying, "and I think you're a disaster."

In *Who's In Charge Here?* I made use of a photo of Carter speaking to ABC broadcaster Frank Reynolds. I had them discussing Carter's television advertising campaign:

CARTER. All my TV commercials will present me as an intelligent, efficient person.

REYNOLDS. You going to use a double?

By the time the 1980 election campaign began, the public seemed to have lost confidence in Carter and was willing to embrace almost any alternative. Edward Bennett Williams was clearly referring to Jimmy Carter, the loner from Plains, Georgia, when he observed:

Satchel Paige warned never to look over your shoulder because they might be gaining on you. As President, you've got to look over your shoulder every once in a while, to make sure someone is following you.

Appraisals of Jimmy Carter were so depreciative early in the 1980 campaign that one Washington wag was reminded of Clarence Darrow's acerbic comment—"When I was a boy I was told that anybody could become President. I'm beginning to believe it." Another Potomac wit said that Jimmy Carter's performance brought to mind Mark Twain's line, "Suppose you were an idiot and suppose you were the President of the United States. But I repeat myself."

Carter had made a speech in which he blamed public indignation on a "general malaise." It was not a well-conceived rationale. Ronald Reagan would use that phrase as a stick with which to whack his opponent all through the fall. Comedienne Lily Tomlin referred to public disaffection for Carter when she said, "Ninety-eight percent of the adults in this country are decent, hardworking, honest Americans. It's the other lousy two percent that get all the publicity. But then—*we elected them.*"

Editorial cartoonist Mike Gorrell zeroed in on the Carter record with an illustration in the *Charlotte News* of the White House Situation Room. A map of the world is labeled: CRISIS ZONES—DOTS INDICATE PROBLEM AREAS. The map is pocked with a plague of black dots. Next to the map is a portrait of President Carter—with a black dot on his nose.

The *National Review*, William F. Buckley's irreverent political weekly, was often abrasively witty in its campaign attacks on Carter. When former president Gerald Ford announced he was no longer contesting for the Republican nomination, leaving the path to the presidency open for Ronald Reagan, the *National Review* tucked its tongue firmly in cheek and said, "Jerry Ford's withdrawal from the presidential race severely diminishes the likelihood of a pardon for Jimmy Carter."

As the polls turned against President Carter and the hostages remained unreleased, Carter's frustrations increased. Some thought his attacks on Ronald Reagan grew intemperate and excessive. Carter portrayed his genial opponent as a mad bomber who would surely propel us into nuclear war. This strategy closely resembled that of Lyndon Johnson in his attacks on Barry Goldwater—except in its success. Carter's rhetorical excesses generated what the media came to call The Meanness Issue. Thus, the understated, gentle Georgian suddenly seemed to show a vicious side. A man who heretofore had an image of decency, honesty, and sincerity was exposing a quality of petulance and malice that was not at all flattering. Said one White House press aide who pleaded anonymity: "Some say Jimmy Carter is mean and vindictive. But I work for him and I know he's just the opposite. Vindictive and mean."

Jeff MacNelly, the Pulitzer Prize-winning editorial cartoonist whose work appears in the *Chicago Tribune* and hundreds of other newspapers, focused on Carter's surprising "mean side," as shown by his intemperate attacks on Ronald Reagan. In the midst of the campaign, with Reagan showing strength and Carter desperation, MacNelly pictured Carter in a series of cartoon panels. Carter is saying:

PANEL 1. (calmly) I am disappointed in my opponent . . .

PANEL 2. (calmly) I had hoped that by now we would be engaged in a useful discussion of the issues. But instead, Governor Reagan . . .

PANEL 3. (shouting) WHO HATES POOR FOLKS, AND WANTS TO . . .

PANEL 4. (screaming) ENSLAVE BLACKS AND HISPANICS AND BLOW UP THE WORLD . . .

PANEL 5. (calmly) has resorted to a campaign of slurs and innuendos which insults the intelligence of all Americans.

Carter was stung by the mockery of his vindictiveness. Perhaps he could be forgiven for his growing sense of frustration; he was learning what Walter Mondale would discover four years later—that intemperate attacks on the agreeable Reagan had the habit of rolling off his back in what congresswoman Pat Schroeder called a Teflon effect. Carter saw that he had gone too far with his rage. Here was no Barry Goldwater, to be immobilized by charges of saber rattling and social blindness. Carter was quick to apologize and promised to moderate his comments. The *National Review* responded with its customary wit:

Mr. Carter promises to be very, very good and says he'll try "to be sure that we do not have a lowering of the tone of the campaign." Whether it's possible for him to lower the campaign at this point is far from clear.

Some thought there was method in Carter's meanness—that he was trying to draw attention away from the faltering economy with his vitriolic attacks on Reagan. One of these observers was cartoonist Jeff MacNelly. He pictured Carter as an engineer in the cab of a locomotive that has crashed. The train is a shambles and is labeled THE ECONOMY. Carter is saying: "Uh, not to change the subject or anything, but did you know Reagan is a HATE-MONGERING RACIST?"

As the campaign unfolded, many Democrats viewed Jimmy Carter as unelectable, and they turned their attention to Senator Edward "Ted" Kennedy, the attractive young senator from Massachusetts, whose name evoked the evergreen memory of his martyred brothers. But when Teddy entered the race, encouraged by early polls that showed him devastating Carter, he found himself hounded by the accident at Chappaquiddick, in which a girl had died and Kennedy's behavior seemed less than heroic. The tragic events at Chappaquiddick had triggered a repertoire of wounding jokes that were disinterred when Teddy announced his candidacy on Labor Day of 1979. Said the *National Lampoon:* "Teddy says he regrets the accident but that's all water over the dam." In *Who's In Charge Here? 1980,* I made use of a campaign photo of Teddy pointing down the street and had him saying, "You go down two blocks and drive off the dock." Teddy's hunger for the White House proved abortive, so in another photo I had him remarking to a group of children: "Sometimes I wonder what my brothers would have done." A youngster replies: "They would have won." Said one Washington wag: "Teddy has his eye on the presidential seat, but Mr. Carter has something better on it." In his short-lived, ill-fated campaign to wrest the Democratic nomination from Jimmy Carter, Teddy damaged his chances with a disastrous interview with Roger Mudd in which Kennedy faltered and rambled incoherently on such topics as why he wanted to be president and what had happened at Chappaquiddick, two questions for which one would have thought he could have formulated reasonable answers. As Kennedy fumbled Mudd's questions on CBS, the ABC network was running the Steven Spielberg thriller, *Jaws*. Said Senator Bob Dole, the Kansas senator whose virulent wit had tarnished the campaign of running mate Gerald Ford in 1976 and helped put Jimmy Carter in the White House: "Seventy-five percent of the country watched *Jaws*, twenty-five percent watched Teddy, and half couldn't tell the difference." The famous slogan of *Jaws II* was "Just when you thought it was safe to go back in the water. . . ." After watching Kennedy's embarrassingly inept performance, a Carter aide cracked, "Just when Teddy thought it was safe to go back into politics. . . ."

Teddy's fumbles on CBS recalled the Zeke Bonura Theory of Government, as wittily enunciated by Edward Bennett Williams. Bonura was the clumsy first baseman for the Washington Senators, who each year contrived to end the season with the best fielding average in the majors. He did so by recognizing the baseball rule that you cannot be charged with an error *unless you touch the ball*. Hence, Bonura avoided touching anything that looked the least bit difficult. This, said Williams, was a rule that had been respected by most politicians of our century. Teddy fumbled the two sharp grounders from Roger Mudd that he might have been better off not touching at all.

Kennedy's critics also found him too liberal by half. These preoccupations, they nagged, had become tiresome and predictable. His speeches focused on the sick, the black, the old, and the poor. One reporter, returning from a trip to Capitol Hill to interview the Massachusetts senator, joked about the futility of the assignment. "It was useless," he said. "Whatever I asked him, he answered the same way. If I had asked him about the weather, he would have said, 'When I think about the weather, I think first about the sick, the black, the old, and the poor.'"

The Kennedy brothers had always been adept at joking about their vaunting ambitions. In politics, said Will Rogers, it is essential to be ambitious but fatal to appear so. Bobby had decried his own ambitions for the presidency when Lyndon Johnson occupied the White House. He said, "I have no de-

signs on the presidency and neither does my wife, Ethel Bird."
And so, when Teddy stood in for President Carter at a labor
rally, he said, "Mr. Carter phoned me early this morning and
asked me to fill in for him. I told him, 'I've been trying to do
that for a year.'"

Teddy's campaign to unseat Jimmy Carter for the 1980
nomination was ultimately fruitless, producing some slighting
humor at the senator's expense. In one Second City sketch, a
morose Teddy is commiserating with his mother about his inability to seize the nomination from Carter.

TEDDY. I lost, Mama.

ROSE. Maybe you're adopted.

In his failed attempt to take the nomination from a sitting president of his own party, Teddy's philandering and his
failed marriage drew some ridicule. His wife Joan had joined
her husband on the campaign trail and had done yeoman service in trying to paper over their split. (The efforts of Lee Hart
to camouflage the ruptures in her marriage to husband Gary
seemed a rerun of the Adventures of Joan and Teddy, and
equally doomed. Said Billy Crystal of Gary Hart's reentry into
the 1988 race: "If he's elected, will Donna Rice be the First
Chick?") As Teddy and Joan sought to put a happy face on
their marital hemorrhage, a reporter bluntly asked Rose Kennedy why Joan lived in Boston and Teddy lived in Virginia.
Rose answered, "Who's Virginia?"

During the week of the Democratic National Convention in New York City, the *National Review* puckishly ran a
photo of Carter and Kennedy embracing, wearing transparent
grins. In the balloon captions, Teddy is saying: "What Carter
is saying is that the country is getting better because it's getting sicker at a slower rate." And Carter is saying, in a replay
of his well-publicized prophecy: "I'll whip his ass!" At the apex
of Kennedy's threat to Carter's nomination, the president had
issued this prediction. When he fulfilled it by savaging Kennedy in the primaries, one Washington columnist cracked: "In
whipping Senator Kennedy's ass, President Carter has finally
managed to keep a campaign promise."

Curiously, much of the humor generated by Ted Kennedy's candidacy had nothing whatever to do with either liberalism or Chappaquiddick but with the senator's weight. Kennedy's decision to seek the nomination was a vacillating one. Capital reporters noted that you could tell whether Teddy was running or not on any given week by whether his weight was going up or down. If it was going down, it meant he was running and wanted to be more telegenic. If he was leaning toward beefiness, it meant he cared little about voter image and was not running for president. The insight was a dead giveaway when Teddy decided to make his assault on the Democratic nomination. Several jokes were given wide currency by the Washington press corps about Teddy's tendency toward flab. A reporter for the *Boston Globe* said, "You know where Teddy stands because there's a dent in the ground." Another reporter said he liked to watch Kennedy go into McDonald's and watch the numbers change. Another asserted that Teddy's campaign motto, in a gloss from Truman's famous line, was: "If you can't take the heat in the kitchen, then eat the cookies in the living room." Another media member referred to Teddy as "the Senator from Pizza Hut." Still another said, "There's no getting around Ted Kennedy—except with a high mileage car." And still another gibed, "Watching Ted Kennedy get out of a leather chair is like watching the Russians get out of Afghanistan." Johnny Carson has often expressed his comedic theory that it is perilous to do more than three jokes on the same subject in his monologue. It will be noted that the Washington press corps displayed no such sense of proportion.

To any student of dissembling in government—such as the duplicities of Vietnam, Watergate, and Iranscam—Jimmy Carter's habit of fudging the facts will not seem particularly reprehensible. Like the vicuna coat that Ike's White House chief of staff, Sherman Adams, accepted from a wealthy industrialist, Carter's delinquencies with the truth seem like small beer when compared with scenes of bugging the Oval Office and diverting funds from ransom to rebels. Yet, at the time, Carter's tendency toward what the press called "misstatements" and "disinformation" (but which those with less discretion call "lying") was worthy of satiric attack.

Mike Peters, the talented young political cartoonist for the *Dayton Daily News*, recalls his attitude toward Carter's campaign fibs. "I didn't want to call him a liar," explained Peters slyly. "And so I drew a cartoon of three presidents. Washington was saying, 'I cannot tell a lie.' Nixon was saying 'I cannot tell the truth.' And Carter was saying 'I cannot tell the difference.'"

President Gerald Ford had once referred to Carter's carelessness with the truth. Speaking at a Gridiron Club banquet at which Carter was also a guest, Ford pointed to the Georgia governor who would oppose him in the 1976 election and said, "Governor Carter is sitting over there. You can always tell where he's sitting. But it's hard to figure out where he stands." Ford was deprecating Carter's habit of changing his views to suit his audience.

Referring to Carter's propensity for obfuscation and selective memory, the *National Review* needled candidate Carter in 1980 with an invented news items. Said the *NR*:

President Carter promised a "complete investigation" when reporters questioned his statement that "I do not have a younger brother." A White House clarification the next day stated that what the President meant to say was that he "had no recollection" of having a younger brother.

Carter's strategic vacillations on substantive matters brought a funny broadside from cartoonist Jeff MacNelly. When Carter and Reagan were scheduled to debate on television, third party candidate, John Anderson, sought to join the debate, but Carter rebelled. Cartoonist MacNelly brought his wit to bear on the situation. He showed the TV debate in progress. There were three participants: Ronald Reagan and *two* Jimmy Carters. In front of one of the Carters were papers marked, CANCEL B-1, NO TAX CUT, DELAY MX, CUT DEFENSE and NO DRAFT REGISTRATION. But in front of the second Jimmy Carter were papers labeled BUILD MX, DRAFT REGISTRATION, NEW BOMBER, and $25 BILLION TAX CUT. In the MacNelly drawing, one of the Carters is saying to third party candidate Anderson: "We've already *got* three candidates."

Carter's vulnerability was increased by his reaction to the Soviet invasion of Afghanistan. He expressed incredulity at the Russians' aggression, which led some to mock his naivete. MacNelly showed Carter as a rube in the big city, holding a deed to the Brooklyn Bridge that is signed by Leonid Brezhnev. The shocked Carter is saying, "You mean he *lied* to me?" To show American anger at the Soviet invasion, Carter cancelled American participation in the upcoming Moscow Olympics, which led some to ridicule the president. His reaction seemed tepid and timid to White House watchers. A cartoon in the *Christian Science Monitor* showed an overweight mother serving dinner to her obese son and admonishing him, "How do you expect to make the Olympic Team and boycott the 1992 Olympics if you don't eat your vegetables?"

When the Iranians seized American hostages, the immediate effect on Carter's candidacy was positive—Americans stand behind their president in moments of international distress. But with the passage of time, they stood even further behind him. As the weeks and months slipped by, and with it the failure of a helicopter rescue mission, the public came to blame and mock Carter for his seeming impotence. The Ayatollah Khomeini became a target for caustic humor across the United States. Ballantine Books published *The Green Book*, a paperback containing the eccentric social and sexual philosophies of the ayatollah. His attitude toward women, for example, would have been laughable were it not so venomously sexist. (Speaking at a symposium on Humor & the Presidency sponsored by former President Ford, Pat Paulsen cracked, "The Gerald Ford Symposium on Humor is like the Ayatollah Khomeini symposium on the Sexual Revolution.") With American hostages imprisoned in Tehran, Khomeini announced by way of extenuation that Iran was in "a state of chaos." One columnist cracked, "The Ayatollah was then brought before a Revolutionary Court where he presided as judge, and sentenced himself to execution."

The utter failure of Carter's helicopter raid to rescue our hostages made Carter a target for mockery. When the president called the Republican convention "a debacle," one conservative wag said, "That's high praise from our Country's *Debacler-in-Chief*. Jimmy Carter says the GOP Convention was a 'debacle.' What did he expect—a helicopter rescue mission?" The *New Republic* pointed to the disarray of the Carter administration on the hostage nightmare, citing two headlines it found on the same day in the *Washington Post*: CARTER VOICES OPTIMISM IN HOSTAGE CRISIS and, elsewhere on the page, CARTER OFFICIAL CAUTIONS AGAINST PREMATURE OPTIMISM ON HOSTAGES.

Most presidents offer up their families as hostages to the wit of their detractors and the country's clowns and, frequently, use their kin as subjects for their own humor. Jack Kennedy joked affectionately about the beauteous Jacqueline, his daughter Caroline, his aggressive brother Bobby, his affluent father, and the sheer numbers and naked ambition of the Kennedys. (He once praised astronaut John Glenn by saying, "You're doing pretty well for someone who isn't in the family.") Lyndon Johnson got about as much comic mileage out of his wife and daughters as the comedians who were paid to do it. But Jimmy Carter's family offered even more food for satire than the Kennedy clan or the assorted Birds of the Johnson White House. Most of the humor was produced by the Washington onlookers and considerably less by the president himself. Art Buchwald, who accomplishes the extraordinary feat of being hilarious and relevant three times a week, observed that the Carter family would make a spectacular TV sitcom. He pictured himself proposing the comedy series to a television producer. "It's about a peanut farmer who's also a nuclear engineer and a naval officer and wants to be President. His mother is a member of the Peace Corps, his kid brother runs a gas station, one of his sisters rides a motorcycle, and the other is a faith healer." Concluded Buchwald, "You know what the producer is going to say, don't you? 'Kill the faith healer and we've got a show!'"

Billy Carter, Jimmy's ebullient younger brother, was the butt of most of the jokes, benign and destructive, that were leveled at the president's family. In a revelation that the press predictably labeled "Billygate," it was learned that brother Billy had received $200,000 from the government of Libya to lobby his big brother on their behalf. Congress convened an investigation, and Jimmy mumbled something about having used Billy as a conduit to free the hostages—which stood somewhere near the zenith of diplomatic folly until Ronald Reagan shipped arms to the Iranians for the same purpose. Comedians found humor in Billy Carter, who on one occasion appeared resplendent in a costume made entirely of beer can openers to help promote a brew opportunistically called Billy Beer. Billy's lobbying efforts on behalf of the Libyan regime provoked Bob Hope to remark, "The difference between Jimmy Carter and his brother is that Billy has a foreign policy." Billy remained an embarrassment to his brother throughout the 1975 campaign. In *Who's In Charge Here?* published in that year, I printed a photo of Billy staring perplexedly out of a hot air balloon. He is plaintively asking, "Can I come down after the election?"

Rosalynn Carter invited mirth of a different stripe. She was an intelligent, assertive woman who was the only First Lady to commonly attend her husband's cabinet meetings. Even Nancy Reagan, whose detractors deplore her influence over government policies and personnel, never appropriated a seat at the cabinet table. Nor did Jacqueline Kennedy so directly involve herself in her husband's plans. Jack Kennedy once quipped, "At least I know that Jackie will never greet me at the end of the day by saying, 'What's new in Vietnam?'" I kidded this shared power in the Carter White House in my *Who's In Charge* volume. Two voices were heard from an upstairs White House window:

VOICE NO. 1. Am I or am I not the leader of the Free World?

VOICE NO. 2. You are, Rosalynn.

Jimmy's mother, Lillian Carter, was a feisty, white-haired woman whom America took to its heart. Her unsentimental candor was immensely appealing. On one occasion, when she was more than usually dismayed by the behavior of her sons, she said, "Sometimes when I look at my children I say to myself, 'Lillian, you should have stayed a virgin.'" If Billy was sometimes an embarrassment to the president, Jimmy's daughter Amy did little to enhance his stature. Certainly, she did not bring her father the outpouring of affection that the three-year-old Caroline brought to the New Frontier. The

UPI and Wide World photo libraries abound with shots of little Amy yawning vigorously as her father orates before a variety of campaign audiences. Once she lent unintended levity on the stump. A wire service reporter asked Amy, "Have you any message for the children of America?" to which Amy promptly responded, "No."

If Jimmy Carter was a target for the malicious humor of others—cartoonists, columnists, comics, and his opponent—he was adept at employing humor as a weapon himself. Ted Sorensen, who wrote both speeches and humor for John F. Kennedy told me, "Carter's sense of humor was very much like that of Kennedy's. It was dry and understated." Unfortunately for Carter, his sense of humor was also rather sarcastic, reflecting his hostility to the Washington establishment, which had failed to accept him, and to the Washington press corps, which found him bucolic and unsophisticated. Carter's propensity for mordant, sardonic humor damaged him—unlike Kennedy's ironies and Reagan's anecdotes, which were upbeat and ingratiating.

This sardonic tone was evident on the eve of Reagan's inauguration, when Carter still sat in the White House, bloodied by electoral defeat. Carter called Reagan to brief him on the state of the hostage negotiations, which were ongoing. Carter was thorough in his report to his successor, and when he hung up the phone, Hamilton Jordan asked, "What did Reagan say, Mr. President?" Without cracking a smile, Carter replied, "Well, I briefed him on what was happening to the hostages. He just listened. Then when I finished he said, 'What hostages?'" This nasty little gibe, which implied Reagan's ignorance of worldly matters, typified Carter's humor. It also suggested that even before Ronald Reagan had spent a day at work in the Oval Office, his predecessor suspected he would exercise power in a decidedly hands-off manner. Carter's preconception may have been confirmed by the Tower Commission, as the Iran-*contra* affair unraveled.

A sarcastic wit is not the ideal tone for a presidential candidate. Though it may serve a cabaret entertainer or a moviemaker who seeks to cut and slash his targets, sarcasm is a chancy weapon for a political incumbent or challenger. Robert Dole learned this to his grief as Gerald Ford's running mate and, in the process, helped hand the presidency to Jimmy Carter. (Interestingly, in the 1988 presidential primaries, Dole, who was easily the wittiest of the Republican hopefuls, was careful to suppress his native humor to keep from promoting the appearance of malice.) But though Carter profited from Dole's vicious humor, he did not seem to profit from Dole's example. If experience is the name we give to our mistakes, Jimmy Carter left the White House with abundant experience on the subject of the nuances of campaign humor. All through his four years in office, White House aides had been waving red flags, if Carter chose to see them. They referred in hushed conversations to the chief's "borderline sarcasm." Carter's chief speech writer, Jim Fallows (now a contributing editor for the *Atlantic Monthly*), complained about the draft of a speech that Carter had sent back to him marked simply "A-minus." Joe Califano, Carter's secretary of health, education and welfare, also felt the flick of Carter's sarcastic wit. When Califano brought a group of charts headlined CARTER WELFARE REFORM into the Oval Office to brief the president, Carter twitted his cabinet officer for his well-known egotism. He said "Joe, when you come in here with cards that say CALIFANO WELFARE REFORM then I'll know we're on the right track."

Carter's aides grew gun-shy of the boss's cracks at their expense. When he completed some gentle wheezes to a press dinner that drew scant response, Carter glanced at his chief speech writer and said, "I told my staff I wanted them to prepare a talk for me to make tonight that was funny, but they didn't get around to it." One chastened member of Carter's staff repaid the president for his slights with the comment: "It used to be said that Jimmy Carter was a generous man who, on the occasion of a friend's birthday, would always send a modest gift. And so in time, Jimmy Carter became known as a man of modest gifts."

Carter's cutting wit was so deeply ingrained in his personality that he did not use it merely to singe the people who worked for him. He often directed it at those who supported him with their money and their celebrity. Warren Beatty had assembled a group of cinematic notables at his Beverly Hills home to raise money for the 1980 Carter campaign. To many southern censors and Bible Belt reformers, Hollywood had always been a Sodom with modern plumbing, a hotbed of sex, drugs, and poor table manners. Carter no doubt was reflecting this cultural suspicion when he said to the assembled stars: "It's a real thrill to meet the famous people here tonight. I hope I don't get to know too much about you."

Every candidate who has ever struggled through the exhausting travail of a presidential election campaign knows that the most efficacious kind of wit for a candidate's use is a self-deprecating humor. The public likes a "good Joe" who can mock his own flaws and frailties. Jimmy Carter's performance in the 1980 campaign, however, was quite another matter. In the course of the reelection campaign, one senior aide said, "Jimmy's idea of self-deprecating humor is to insult his staff." Despite the substantial power of the press during an election campaign, Carter did little to ingratiate himself with the reporters who covered his campaign. It was as though Carter felt his superior morality and intellect were such that he need not stoop to conquer the correspondents who had little respect for his gifts. Hence, the Carter campaign humor was sarcastic in its contacts with the press as well. At one briefing along the campaign trail, the president sighed, "I don't have very much for you today, so you can just put away your crayons."

Carter's hostility toward the reporters who covered his campaign was well known. At a White House dinner late in his presidency, Carter concluded his remarks to the assembled journalists by saying, "I want to thank all of you who make my job so easy and enjoyable." Then he turned to his wife and said, "Thank you, Rosalynn." Carter turned his sardonic wit on *New York Times* correspondent Jim Wooten who had often been critical of Carter's policies. "In the White House environment," said Carter, "it is difficult to separate fact from fiction, which reminds me of my friend Jim Wooten here—the Erica Jong of the *New York Times*." His vitriolic humor reached a new plateau when, near the completion of his abortive 1980 campaign, Carter said to an assemblage of newsmen, "I've had a lot of setbacks and a lot of troubles, as you know, and you reporters have been kind enough to make them clear to the

American people." What Carter and so many of his predecessors in the Oval Office failed to perceive was that this is precisely the function of the Washington press corps—to report the travesties along with the triumphs, not to behave as though criticism was a subtle form of sedition.

Even Carter's running mate, Walter Mondale, was not immune to Carter's glancing wit. In one campaign speech, Carter turned to his vice president, who sat beside him on the dais, and said, "I am very grateful that my associate, Walter Mondale, is here. I've done the best I could to find something for him to do." Not content with that remark—since Veeps are notoriously sensitive about their inactivity and impotence —Carter continued:

> I would like to ask you to keep Walter Mondale from getting lonesome in the White House. . . . If you have any questions about the Concorde, Northern Ireland, abortion, gay rights, downtown parking. . . .

In *Of Thee I Sing*, George S. Kaufman created the prototypical vice president, Alexander Throttlebottom—underworked, ignored, and sent out for sandwiches. At one point, when someone observes that Throttlebottom doesn't look well, he says, "I'm having a breakdown. Underwork." Walter Mondale, Hubert Humphrey, Lyndon Johnson, George Bush —all the good and worthy men who have occupied the vice presidential office—have known the agony of that empty position. But only Jimmy Carter would ridicule the vacuum of the vice presidency to the man who held it.

Carter's critics in the 1980 campaign taxed him as a president who knew the words but not the music—if his pronouncements had the ring of action, too often they failed to produce any meaningful change. Mr. Outsider was now on the inside, but he had failed to augment his cadre of Good Ole Boys with any of the establishment types he loathed. Hence, Carter seldom seemed able to turn good intentions into good works. (Ironically, President Kennedy was often unable to turn his soaring rhetoric into the hard currency of legislation. It took Mr. Insider, Lyndon Johnson, to transmute JFK's sterling rhetoric into law.) Carter's inability to match words with deeds led political cartoonist Jules Feiffer to pillory him with his syndicated strip. Said a ruminative Carter:

> I give a strong talk on the environment. And do nothing about it . . . I deliver an innovative speech on disarmament. And do nothing about it . . . I issue a clarion-call on energy. And do nothing about it . . . I may not be much of a President . . . But I am a hell of a political columnist.

Carter's born-again rectitude brought him close to arrogance. But it also gave him a calm, cool demeanor that the public found particularly welcome, especially after the overheated atmosphere generated by such activists as Kennedy and Johnson and the corruption fostered by Richard Nixon. The soft southern drawl, the sly, understated humor, the gentle smile that bore no relation to the solemn message of his words —all this provided a gentling air that the electorate welcomed —at least until the gas lines stretched to the horizon and America was held hostage by Iranian terrorists. Jules Feiffer gave Carter's coolness one-handed applause in a memorable series of panels during the 1980 campaign. Said a placid Carter:

> I do not panic in crisis . . . I use statements in a crisis . . . I preach normality in a crisis . . . I hide out in Camp David in a crisis . . . I act passive in a crisis . . . And after a while, the crisis goes away . . . Or would you prefer the Bay of Pigs [and] Vietnam? . . .

President Lyndon Johnson's mixture of liberalism and conservatism was vexing to many of his supporters and invited charges of hypocrisy. President Carter produced similar angry humor as he ran for reelection against Ronald Reagan. The former actor was quite clear about his position and his principles, while Carter was ambivalent and calculatedly imprecise. Feiffer pinpointed this tendency in a strip that pictured a man wearing a hood over his face. The cartoonist offered RIDDLE:

> "I am smiling . . ."
> "I am crying . . ."

"I am weak . . ."
"I am strong . . ."
"I am liberal . . ."
"I am conservative . . ."
"I am leaving . . ."
"I was never here . . ."
"Who am I?"

Whereupon the man whips off his hood, revealing himself to be Jimmy Carter. "I am a political cartoonist's nightmare," he concludes.

The 1980 campaign ended with Jimmy Carter rejected by the public he sought to serve. Inflation, recession, hostages, and unemployment had led to popular disenchantment with James Earl Carter. During the frantic week that followed Election Day 1980, the Associated Press reported that Carter was planning to write his memoirs. "Fine," chirped the *National Review*. "We'd rather he write than be President."

Chapter 4
Campaign 1980
The Actor

There was a fire in Ronald Reagan's library and
both books were destroyed.
                        —PAUL KRASSNER

Running for president, said Garry Wills, is a delicious wound inflicted on willing sufferers. And much of the
pain derives from the insights of humorists. Nineteen-eighty
proved a painful race and a fast track for those who sought the
GOP presidential nomination. There was Howard Baker, the
bantam media star whose easy eloquence had dominated the
Senate Watergate hearings. There was Bob Dole, who had
made an indelible if not altogether positive impression as Jerry
Ford's running mate with his abrasive wit. There was George
Bush, with a resume as long as Chile and memorable indict-
ments ("voodoo economics," for example) that he would later
have to swallow when he joined the ticket of the target of his
contempt. There was John Connolly, the charismatic Texan
who took a bullet from the rifle that killed John F. Kennedy
and who poured a fortune into a campaign that would bring
him a thimbleful of votes. And then there was the husky-
voiced star of three dozen B-pictures on the Warner Brothers
lot and a forgettable Western TV series. The outcome of this
colorfully casted contest is history.

57

When Ronald Reagan took on incumbent Jimmy Carter, it was natural for America's chorus of wits and clowns to focus on his former career in films. If there is any profession that Americans view with more disdain than politics it is acting. It seems like such a trivial way for grown-ups to spend their time. After all, how could the electorate decide that a former movie actor was a "serious person"? Reagan was not a luminescent star in the tradition of Gregory Peck or James Cagney. As Jack Warner smirked when he first heard that Ronald Reagan was contesting for governor of California, "No no, that's all wrong. It's Jimmy Stewart for Governor and Ronald Reagan for Best Friend."

Reagan had made a career out of being the best friend to his cinematic betters in an array of Hollywood second features. Yet, jokes about his former calling had as little effect on his candidacy as rain on the ocean. Like the Teflon presidency that would later make him immune to the misdeeds of his administration, jokes about his thespian beginnings simply failed to stick. Most such jokes were more friendly than malign. Indeed, comedians and humorists who sought to make light of Reagan's film career found that the candidate had cut them off at the pass. Reagan skillfully co-opted the issue, defusing whatever problems it contained by laughing away his Hollywood years with good-natured aplomb. But on occasion, Reagan's critics were able to invoke his celluloid beginnings by linking them to his approach to affairs of state. Jules Feiffer turned his acid pen to the task in one series of panels in which Reagan is speaking to the public. In Feiffer's strips, Reagan never opened his speeches in the mandatory political idiom, "My fellow Americans. . . ." In the world of Feiffer, Reagan began his orations, "My fellow audience. . . ." After that he becomes a walking trailer for a new superproduction, saying,

> We are about to release "MOVIE-AMERICA" . . . As the producer of "MOVIE-AMERICA" let me lay out the story line. Boy meets girl. Girl gets marriage and family . . . Father gets a new job and a tax cut. Mother gets a drop in grocery prices . . . Children pray and go to church socials. Business sky-rockets. Russia can't keep up in the arms race and unconditionally surrenders . . . Black and white, yellow and brown, young and old, mend their differences and go to the prom . . .

[An explosion of lights illuminates the White House like a Hollywood premiere.]
Watch for "MOVIE-AMERICA." Coming soon to the White House.

If any of the gibes about Reagan's palmy days before the movie camera should draw blood—which was most unlikely—his loyal advocates on the right were prepared to dismiss the derision as irrelevant, immaterial, and left-wing. W. H. von Dreele, the sardonic poet laureate of the *National Review* wrote:

Now watch the Walter Cronkite types
And every last detractor
Remind the folks that Reagan is
A former movie actor.

Reagan's other target of vulnerability was his ultraconservative message. Like Barry Goldwater in 1964, Reagan ran against the government he sought to lead. He would get the government off the people's backs. He would dismantle the social machinery of the New Deal, the New Frontier, and the Great Society. That message had been an irresistible target for America's humorists when Goldwater articulated it. It had produced a landslide victory for Lyndon Johnson. But Jimmy Carter was not Lyndon Johnson, and Ronald Reagan was not Barry Goldwater.

For one thing, it was Reagan, not America's professional humorists, who was the most visible joke teller, and they were *his* gibes that were engaging the public's funny bone. Oppressive, bloated government became the target for Reagan's humor, and Reagan was much more adroit in attacking the bureaucracy than America's funny men were at attacking Reagan's message. This should not be surprising to political junkies who have long known that, next to the media, the government is the favorite target for angry humor. When Reagan ridiculed the excesses and stupidities of government, he found a most receptive audience. Many laughed so hard that they lost sight of the support and security that these "bloated" government agencies offered them.

Reagan had a huge repertoire of scathing jokes and anecdotes that pictured congressmen and bureaucrats as a pack of mendacious prodigals and government as the original evil empire, an institution berserk in a blizzard of paper. The quality of Reagan's anti-Washington humor, as expressed in the 1980 campaign, had been honed during a thousand roasts, when he acted as spokesman for the General Electric Corporation. There was little subtlety to this government-bashing humor. Some of his one-liners and anecdotes sounded like retreads of ancient wheezes from the *Reader's Digest*. Some of it had the aroma of Hollywood, which was not surprising, since throughout his primary and election campaigns, Reagan was fed a steady stream of jokes by the premier gagsters of Hollywood. But all of it, vintage or fresh, was delivered with the impeccable timing and genuine humility of Reagan the performer. Adlai Stevenson spent an inordinate amount of time *writing* his own speeches. Ronald Reagan was more astute. He spent an inordinate amount of it *rehearsing* his speeches—particularly the jokes that were crafted for his campaign and his ideology. (His opponent, President Carter, made the lethal mistake, according to his top White House aides, of spending virtually no time at all in writing, reading, rehearsing, or embellishing his campaign speeches or in guiding his speech writers.)

In targeting government for his humorous attacks, Reagan was doing much the same thing that his opponent had done four years before in riding a wave of antibureaucratic loathing to power. Carter was as much an outsider in 1976 as Reagan was in 1980, but when they met at the turn of the decade, the former actor was the master of the game. After all, Reagan was still an outsider, while Carter had been on the inside for four years.

The popular contempt for government is regularly fueled by well-publicized scandals. Politicians themselves attack the government that they are meant to serve. Senator Eugene McCarthy, between naps and effete pontificating, said, "The only thing that saves us from the bureaucracy is its inefficiency." The brilliant curmudgeon H. L. Mencken observed, "It is inaccurate to say I hate everything. I am strongly in favor of common decency. This makes me forever ineligible for any public office." Said Edward Langley; "What this country needs is more unemployed politicians." Given the slanderous things that witty men have been saying about it for centuries, government makes an irresistible target for public figures like Ronald Reagan who want to reach the White House.

Reagan's witty antibureaucratic one-liners in 1980 included the following:

> Where else but in Washington would they call the department in charge of everything outdoors the Department of the Interior?

> There are two ways of doing things—the right way and the way they do it in Washington.

> When you mention common sense in Washington, you cause traumatic shock.

> The Washington establishment believes that the only good dollar is one taken from a taxpayer's pocket.

> In Washington the economists have a Phi Beta Kappa key at one end of the watch chain and no watch at the other.

> Washington is the only city where sound travels faster than light.

> Washington didn't have the same problems other cities did. . . . They grabbed hold of the fastest growing industry in America.

Much of Ronald Reagan's antigovernment wit pandered to the popular repugnance to the income tax. Running in favor of motherhood is no more secure a position than running against taxes. Reagan's joke book of antitaxation gibes served him well in 1980 and led him to a solemn vow never to raise taxes—a vow that he would reluctantly abandon after the stock market crashed in 1987. To imply that taxes are excessive is as unassailable a position as recommending that a starving man eat more.

Humorous one-liners are the ideal instrument for discrediting taxes—if somewhat more irresponsible than reasoned debate. When laughter is engaged and the emotions are aroused, there is little opportunity to assess the merit of the programs that the taxes fuel. Indeed, there is not a little irony in the fact that Reagan and his tax-blasting repertoire won him major support from the people who benefited most from the programs the taxes financed. Reagan's grab bag of antitax levity included the following:

To paraphrase Will Rogers, in government they have never met a tax they didn't like.

There is an old saying: In levying taxes as in shearing sheep, it's best to stop when you get to the skin.

The big spenders in Washington would have been right at home with Oscar Wilde. He's the one who said that the only way to destroy a temptation is to yield to it.

Government is like a baby—an alimentary canal with an appetite at one end and no sense of responsibility at the other.

Balancing the budget is a little like protecting your virtue. You just have to learn to say "no."

Feeding tax dollars to government is like feeding a stray pup. It just follows you home and sits on your doorstep asking for more.

The enormous outpouring of affection that Ronald Reagan generated among the public outraged his opponents. Barry Goldwater and his antediluvian policies drew a small army of adherents who could be disdainfully dismissed by liberal members of the media and the public. But this fellow Reagan was adored—not because of his views but despite them. Thus, Reagan was a magnet for good-natured insult. But the effect of the humor on Reagan's mounting popularity was practically nil.

The Republican convention met in Detroit in 1980. Reagan had swept to victory over his numerous rivals in the primaries—Dole, Baker, Connolly, and Bush had all tasted his dust. His nomination on the first ballot was as secure as the Oscars for *Gone With the Wind*. The one question mark centered on Reagan's running mate, and the other candidates could foresee his choice's value in Reagan's electability. The spot meant becoming heir to the Oval Office in eight years or, given the vagaries of health and age, in four. For a moment former President Ford seemed "a definite possible," as Sam Goldwyn used to say. It would be a dream ticket, said the cigar-wielding power brokers. "Terrific," said Mort Sahl—"the Gipper and the Tripper." But the romance was a brief one, and after Ford was briefly hustled between the microphones of Walter Cronkite and Barbara Walters, and the clamorous talk of increased responsibility for the former president ("a co-presidency" they called it), Reagan decided that there would be no Ford in his future. Jerry Ford, who never entirely got along with Ronald Reagan, slipped out of the picture, and the cameras focused on George Bush, who quickly laundered his positions to blend with the man at the top of the ticket. Bush's moderate perceptions on economics and abortion underwent a quick convention conversion, and he happily took up the mantle of running mate. Editorial cartoonist Paul Conrad of the *Los Angeles Times* showed a supplicative Bush on his knees, gripping Reagan about the calves with ardor. Bush is saying: "By golly, gee whiz, it's sure good to serve this President!" (Bush never quite shook this image of subservience and genuflection. Eight years later he was still fighting the look of an obedient cheerleader, as he sought to win the presidential nomination in his own right—without the explicit endorsement of the man he had served so long.)

One of Reagan's primary rivals, John Anderson, formed a third party to run against Reagan and Carter in the general election. Anderson was a witty, intelligent man, cruelly hampered by lack of funds, staff, and hope, yet he was not entirely without assets. He stung his opponents with humor, as when he referred to Ronald Reagan, his Hollywood past and conservative views, as "a product of Eighteenth-Century Fox." Anderson derided Reagan's plan to balance the budget while cutting taxes and increasing defense spending. "How do you do that?" asked Anderson rhetorically. "It's very simple. With mirrors." When critics called Anderson a spoiler for running against his fellow Republicans, he smiled, "What's to spoil?

Spoil the chances of two men at least half the country doesn't want?" Anderson's caveats were prescient, as were George Bush's, who called Reagan's monetary program "voodoo economics." The combination of a substantial tax cut and greatly increased Pentagon spending failed to balance the budget; indeed, it created a gargantuan deficit that helped precipitate a market crash. But in the euphoric days of 1980, the plan seemed entirely plausible and Anderson's gibes the querulous carpings of a loser.

When Jimmy Carter learned that the TV debate planned by the League of Women Voters would include John Anderson, he refused to participate, and he was mocked by the press for his decision. They suggested he was afraid to face the articulate Anderson, but the president stuck by his guns. When League president Ruth Himerfeld reported, "There will probably be an empty chair in Mr. Carter's place," Pat Oliphant, editorial cartoonist for the *Washington Star*, drew a telling picture of the debate in progress, with a baby's high chair in place of Carter to illustrate the president's infantile pique. Responding to the possibility of an empty chair, Johnny Carson quipped, "What if the chair wins the debate?" Another wag described President Carter's arrival at the debate: "An empty car will pull up to the station and Carter will get out." Given the hectic atmosphere of the debate and the uncertainties as to who would be debating whom, Ronald Reagan cracked, "A funny thing happened on the way to the studio." Ultimately, Reagan debated Anderson sans an empty chair.

When President Carter finally debated challenger Reagan, he doubtless thought that Reagan's controversial positions opposing programs like Social Security would make him easy pickings. The script didn't quite unfold that way. George Kaufman used to mock the traditional Hollywood story line thusly: "Boy meets girl, girl gets boy in pickle, boy gets pickle in girl." The Reagan-Carter story line was also an unexpected twist on the traditional story. Part of the cause of this unexpected turn of events was not revealed until three years later, when it was learned that just before the debate, a Reagan mole had stolen a copy of Carter's briefing book and passed it on to Ronald Reagan. Thus, the challenger knew every point the president planned to make and could prepare a seemingly spontaneous counterpoint. An editorial cartoon in the *Milwaukee Journal* showed the two candidates in the TV studio at their respective podiums. Carter is about to speak when Reagan interrupts, "I know exactly what you're going to say."

To those innocents who find this thievery analogous to Nixon's "dirty tricks" and wonder why the public did not reproach Reagan for this deplorable strategy, it should be recalled that Nixon never possessed a fraction of Reagan's immense likability. The pilfered papers were considered a tempest in a teapot. Ron Zeigler called the Watergate break-in "a third rate burglary" without too much success. Reagan's press secretary dismissed the theft of Carter's briefing book as much ado about nothing, and the voting public seemed to concur. Reagan had cooked the books and gotten away with it. He even had columnist George Will coach him for the debate; Will then appeared on TV in a postdebate analysis without disclosing his partisan role and solemnly declared Reagan the winner. But it is doubtful whether the stolen briefing book or the secret Will assist was crucial to Reagan's triumph in the debate. Reagan's polemic victory was the product of his charm and Carter's sanctimony. Whenever Carter glared furiously at Ronald Reagan ("he looked like he was going to slug him," said one observer), Reagan was affable and agreeable. When Carter reached a shrill crescendo of attack on Reagan's past positions, Reagan simply chuckled and said, "There you go again." The audience laughter seemed to wash away Carter's argument and mock his wrath. This lighthearted reaction disarmed the audience, which burst into laughter—as four years later Reagan would disarm Walter Mondale with irrelevant humor on the issue of Reagan's age.

Carter's humor during the debate was mainly unintentional. Late in the confrontation the subject turned to arms control, a field where Carter could properly have felt he held an advantage over the Russophobic Reagan. Carter's aides stared dumbfounded and reporters laughed as President Carter suddenly said, "I was talking to my daughter Amy the other day, to ask her what the most important issue was. She said she thought it was nuclear weapons and the control of nuclear arms." The image of the nine-year-old Amy, stifling a yawn and pontificating on nuclear proliferation, was laughable

—an example of unintended campaign humor that damaged Carter beyond remedy.

Despite Reagan's easy affability with audiences of all kinds—he always seemed to have an anecdote that was felicitous and flattering to the group he was addressing—Reagan tended to commit unfortunate gaffes when answering questions of the press. When the scenario was not carefully scripted, Reagan was likely to produce a howler that sent his aides rushing for their typewriters to produce an explanation. (As the campaign progressed, reporters were kept further and further away from the candidate to prevent these calamitous misstatements. One correspondent, quoting the famous line from the film *Love Story*, said, "Covering Ronald Reagan is never having to say you've seen him.")

Reagan's chief ally in the campaign of 1980 was the TV camera. It was no secret that in the Age of Television, the personality of a presidential candidate had become more important than his positions, a dangerous triumph of matter over mind and image over issues. (In the seventh year of the Reagan era, screenwriter/director James Brooks would display the dangers of cosmetics over facts in his film, *Broadcast News*. But, by the time it appeared, the battle between substance and aesthetics had become a cliche; seven years of Ronald Reagan had schooled even the most primitive voter in the power of personality over program on TV.) Television had given fame to Lucille Ball, Jackie Gleason, and Johnny Carson. It would now give ultimate power to Ronald Reagan. In what other presidential campaign would a Republican aide run up to a campaign manager (in this case Bill Casey) after the candidate had made a substantive policy statement, and exclaim, "My God, Bill—he was wearing a white shirt!"

Image was important to Ronald Reagan, and President Jimmy Carter quite properly felt flummoxed by the ineffable warmth and charm of his opponent. Cartoonist Jeff MacNelly took careful aim at the image issue. He showed Carter looking like Herbert Hoover, wearing a prim Hoover collar and a Hoover/Carter button, and looking at a poster of Ronald Reagan who wears an FDR grin and holds an FDR cigarette holder at a jaunty angle. The poster reads: HAPPY DAYS ARE HERE AGAIN, Roosevelt's old campaign slogan. And the Hoo-

veresque Carter is moaning, "WOULD SOMEBODY PLEASE EX-
PLAIN WHAT'S GOING ON? . . . ."

Ronald Reagan generated a great many jokes about his
intellectual deficiencies. It was said he did not read books and
had little taste for the study of history. The books in his library were chosen for their color, said the wags. It was bruited
about the beltway that reports on policy matters had to be
compressed into one-page memos (a slur that was retailed
about President Eisenhower before him). Said satirist Paul
Krassner: "There was a fire in Ronald Reagan's library and
both books were destroyed." And author/editor Vic Navasky
said, "There's a side to Ronald Reagan that people don't
know. When he was a young man, Reagan read the complete
works of William Shakespeare. Of course, when Reagan was
young, Shakespeare hadn't written all that much." Ted Sorensen told a story that also called Reagan's cerebral gifts into
question. In it, Reagan asks his barber to place a black dot on
his forehead. The barber protests that a dot on one's forehead
is a decoration in India, but Reagan is insistent. "I just met the
Indian ambassador," says Reagan, "and after our conversation
he turned to a friend, tapped his forehead, and said 'Nothing
there.'"

Reagan laughed away the question of his meager intellectual qualities. He deflected the matter as deftly as he dealt
with matters of age—by acknowledging it. Visiting a grammar
school during his campaign, he told a classroom full of children, "I thought you asked me here to a remedial English
class because you heard my speeches." Returning to Eureka
College where he had earned his sheepskin by way of the pig-
skin, he kidded his modest academic record by saying, "I only
came back to clean out my gym locker. . . . But I am excited to
receive this honorary degree. I had always figured the *first* one
was honorary."

Ronald Reagan had created a rocky road for Gerald
Ford when the latter sought the presidential nomination in
1976. But in 1980 Reagan would not be denied. The former
governor's assets were daunting. He had enormous charm,
was an able public speaker, and the camera was kind to his

face. The Goldwater circle comprised his loyal clique. On occasion a liberal Democrat, outraged by Reagan's artful simplicities, would protest, as did Hubert Humphrey: "Ronald Reagan is George Wallace with eau de cologne." But these quibbles were drowned in a chorus of cheers.

In the election campaign of 1980, political observers were aware of what has since become known as Ronald Reagan's hands-off management style. In the blunt lexicon of the Washington press corps, this was referred to as "Reagan's tough four-hour-days." Newsmen grinned that, if he ever faced a really formidable crisis, "Reagan will have to spend some sleepless afternoons." Or the derisive suggestion, on the occasion of a visit from a chief of state; "Reagan is taking a working nap." By 1987, *Time* magazine was emblazoning its cover with the rude question, WHO'S IN CHARGE? as the stock market collapsed and the Congress rejected Reagan's Supreme Court nominee; a vacuum seemed to cry out for the filling in the West Wing. But in 1980, as Reagan ran for the presidency against a chief executive in whom the public had lost faith, the disengagement issue was not widely observable. Of course, a few perceptive satirists noticed something. Jules Feiffer pointed a finger at Reagan's tendency to delegate too much authority as he cleared brush on the ranch. In one series of pen-and-ink panels, Feiffer showed Reagan speaking to a vast unseen electorate:

My fellow audience, I'm gonna run a committee-style government . . . With me in the Oval Office supervising lotsa little governments . . . We're gonna have a State Department Government . . . An' a Defense Department Government . . . An' a CIA Government . . . An' a Budget Bureau Government . . . An' they're all gonna run themselves an' leave the President alone . . . Go, Go, GOVERNMENT FELLAS! [Reagan falls back into his chair in an ecstacy of withdrawal] . . . I'm gonna take a nap.

The humorists who had been laughing at Reagan's Hollywood beginnings and Carter's waist-high administration had expected a lame contest, reflecting their doubts about both candidates. But Mae West, that padded temptress of the twenties, had called the turn when she murmured, "If I have

to choose between two evils, I pick the one I haven't tried."
That advice portended trouble for Carter. The American people picked the man they hadn't tried. Ronald Reagan was swept into office. His plurality was eight million votes, and he garnered 489 electoral votes, while Carter won a scant forty-nine. It was a humbling defeat for a sitting president, the worst since Herbert Hoover bowed to another charismatic charmer fifty years before. It was an arresting change of direction for the U.S. government, since Ronald Reagan articulated the views of the far right, stating quite clearly that he planned to dismantle the welfare state of Roosevelt, Truman, Kennedy, and the rest. He would cut taxes for the rich and be more scrutinous of welfare cheaters; in short, he was adopting the agenda of the conservatives at a time when the nation was moving inexorably rightward. The *National Review* greeted Reagan's election with the joyous impudence that had long characterized its conservative voice in the wilderness and that of its coruscating founder, William F. Buckley. Suppressing a chuckle and a cheer, it wrote:

With the election of Ronald Reagan, The National Review assumes a new importance in American life. We become, as it were, an establishment organ. . . . This is therefore the last issue in which we shall indulge in levity. Connoisseurs of humor will have to get their yuks elsewhere. We have a nation to run.

Chapter 5
Campaign 1976
"No Problem!"

I feel rather embarrassed about the way I treated
you on "Saturday Night Live" and I'd like you to
pardon me . . . Oops!
                          —CHEVY CHASE

It was said that Jerry Ford gave America three years
of good government and eight years of comedy material. This
was doubtless the result of Ford's singular vulnerabilities to
humor. In the presidential election of 1976—when Ford first
wrested victory from Ronald Reagan in the primaries and
then lost the general election to a grinning Georgian named
Jimmy Carter—Gerald R. Ford was a perennial target for the
wit of satirists. Ford squirmed under much of the mockery.
Ten years later, when he convened a symposium on Humor &
the Presidency at his presidential museum in Grand Rapids,
the outpouring of affectionate mirth at Ford's deficiencies was
still at torrent strength, though his sensitivity to it seemed to
have lessened.

The chief flaw that America's wits, journalists, and cartoonists found in Ford's persona was clumsiness. Ford's pedes-
trian mind and phlegmatic ways were other targets for raillery. In his incisive book, *A Ford, Not a Lincoln*, Richard Reeves
quotes a *Washington Post* poll that revealed Ford's friends characterized him as "slow, plodding, unimaginative, poorly

staffed, out of touch and inarticulate." Said one comic, after reading the *Post* results: "Ford has his friends and he has his enemies. Some think he's dull, slow, and boring. And those are his friends." The qualities elicited by the *Post* questionnaire made Ford a lightning rod for deprecatory wit. During the 1976 presidential campaign, these uncharitable gibes led Ford, as he told it, to bite the stem off many of his favorite pipes. When Ford prematurely freed the Polish people in a famous gaffe during a TV debate with Jimmy Carter, the mistake became the topic of another outpouring of caustic humor. Ford's full pardon of the sins of Richard Nixon also produced ample humor, somewhat less benign than that produced by Ford's clumsiness or intellectual lethargy.

Ford's perceived clumsiness was a target for humor, both amusing and destructive. Week after week, "Saturday Night Live's" youthful audience—most of whom were of voting age—observed Chevy Chase aping Ford, crashing through doors, falling down stairs, knocking over tables, collapsing on the floor, disappearing from view behind a podium, and promptly reappearing to purr, "No problem, no problem!" Not only did the public find the humor hilarious, but President Ford's own teenage children were vastly amused. In one of the show's most famous sketches, Ford's press secretary (played by Buck Henry) explains to the president (portrayed by Chevy Chase) that they have devised a fresh tactic for fighting the perception of Ford's clumsiness. The strategy is called "Operation Stumblebum," and the plan is brilliant in its simplicity. Each time the president stumbles, all his aides will stumble too. Thus, the president's stumbling will appear to be the sort of thing that could happen to anyone. As the skit unfolded, the presidential aides and Secret Service men are bumbling about the Oval Office like drunks and spastics, crashing into the furniture and one another.

There is some humor that strokes its object—one thinks of the humor directed at Kennedy's clan, Reagan's Hollywood roots, and Johnson's steers. There is other humor that diminishes its target by making him the object of sneers and ridicule. One thinks of Gary Hart's philandering and Joe Biden's plagiarism. The gaggery about Ford's clumsiness was of the latter variety. Ford was powerless to either ignore or to laugh away the clumsiness issue. The unshakable image of oafishness was particularly galling to Ford and his advocates since it was basically "a bum rap." Richard Nixon and Jack Kennedy had ridden the bench at Whittier and Harvard football games, but Jerry Ford had been a legitimate gridiron star. He had led his team to the Rose Bowl with regularity. This suggested an extremely well-coordinated man, not the awkward, bumbling fellow of the comedian's image. But satire is a matter of exaggeration. Humor does not always reflect the truth; sometimes it feeds on it for humorous effect. "You would sacrifice anyone for an epigram," a friend once said to Oscar Wilde. And the humorist *would* sacrifice anyone for a laugh. If truth is the first casualty of war, it is also the first casualty of comedy. Whether Jerry Ford was actually a cluster of aberrant motor reflexes is somewhat irrelevant. The comics and cartoonists had found a "schtick" that could assure laughter, like Nixon's jowls and Jack Benny's pusillanimity. Though Ford did not relish this mockery, he realized that it came with the territory. He also recognized that one cannot protest such indignities without irrigating them.

Editorial cartoonists thrived on the Ford clumsiness. Mike Peters of the *Dayton Daily News* pictured him with a ubiquitous band-aid on his forehead. Pat Oliphant showed him in constant disarray from some recent calamity. The cruel canard all began when Ford fell down the ramp as he and Betty were emerging from an airliner in Munich; then he gilded the lily by butting his head on a helicopter door. Both events occurred before a phalanx of photographers and TV cameramen, who were quick to register the happenings on film and tape for the amusement of posterity.

It was not only the editorial cartoonists who mocked Ford's clumsiness—though Peters, Oliphant, Paul Conrad, and Jeff MacNelly were in the forefront of the attackers. Cartoonist Garry Trudeau relied on the Ford palsy for his laughter. One Trudeau strip pictured Ford at the White House indoor pool. President Kennedy swam daily with his pal, Dave Powers, exchanging bawdy stories as he did laps to ease his aching back. President Johnson swam naked with uptight establishment types to shock their prim sensibilities. President Nixon had the pool covered and turned into a commodious press room, ostensibly for the reporters' convenience, but more likely to keep them a greater distance from the Oval Office. President Ford opened the pool again, and this in turn opened the door to Garry Trudeau:

PRESS SECRETARY. Mr. President, the workmen have finished reconverting the press room back into a pool.

FORD. Oh, good, good! Let's try it out!

PRESS SECRETARY. Ladies and gentlemen, the President of the United States!

[We see a volcanic SPLASH! The final panel shows a group of eager correspondents brandishing microphones.]

REPORTERS. Mr. President! . . . Mr. President! . . . Wow! Didja see that gainer?!

Ford tried to laugh along with the comics who were kidding his disorientation. To the Washington Press Club he said, "I don't agree with those who have called me the Evel Knievel of politics." He even invited Chevy Chase, his chief tormentor, to the annual dinner of the Radio and Television Correspondents Association. Then, when Ford was introduced, he "accidentally" caught the tablecloth in his trousers and tumbled a ton of silverware into Chase's lap. "Oops!" said the president in mock chagrin—"Oh, by golly. . . ." As Ford approached the microphone at the center of the dais, he pretended to trip, and his fifteen-page speech went flying over the audience. Dan Rather, Walter Cronkite, and the rest went rushing to retrieve the speech. Havoc reigned and laughter exploded. When the audience stopped roaring its delight, the president produced the real script from his breast pocket, pinned his celebrated guest with a sharp eye and said: "Good evening. I'm Gerald Ford and you're not!" The inspired sight gag was the product of Don Penny, the former TV actor/director who was brought to the White House to enliven the president's oratory. Penny overcame the opposition of the West Wing traditionalists in promoting this buffoonery and

endeared himself to both Ford and the Washington journalists. Of course, the amusing antidote failed to work entirely,
and the mockery of Ford's clumsiness, justified or not, acted as
a brake on his hopes for election in 1976.

The power of campaign humor is such that Ford and his
aides spent a fair amount of time trying to defuse this particular target for ridicule. Ron Nessen, Ford's amiable press secretary and a former TV journalist, developed the idea of appearing on "Saturday Night Live" as a guest host. His aim: to show
that the president didn't take their mockery very seriously and
neither should the voters. After all, went the rationale, Jack
Kennedy had laughed away the ticklish subject of his religion
and his father's wealth in winning the 1960 election. Why
couldn't Ford laugh away an issue that was far less cosmic than
God and money? So Ron Nessen appeared on "Saturday
Night" in one of the most memorable episodes of that iconoclastic series. Nessen played along with the stumbling mys-
tique, telling the audience that his work as presidential press
secretary had been an invaluable training ground. He had
learned, for example, to remove the president's necktie from
the helicopter blade, while Mr. Ford was still wearing it. He
smiled indulgently as Chevy Chase impersonated Ford by
stumbling around the set, talking to a stuffed animal, stapling
his ear, and signing his hand instead of the tax bill. Nessen's
appearance tended to disprove the maxim, "If you can't beat
'em, join 'em." The president of NBC and numerous columnists all thought Nessen's appearance on the show was ill-
advised and insulting to the president. Some senior White
House aides went so far as to suggest that Nessen resign.

If Ron Nessen was trying to defuse a destructive issue in
the midst of an election campaign, it was counterproductive at
best. The *Washington Post* printed a letter to its editor that carried a chilling message. Ford, after all, had granted permission
to his press secretary to participate in the unseemly farrago.
Wrote an irate *Post* reader: "I don't know how I can vote for a
man who could be so dumb."

Another vulnerability that generated campaign humor
was Gerald Ford's general lack of charisma and imagination.
Ford's own minister had said of the most distinguished mem-

ber of his congregation: "Gerald Ford is a normal, decent, God-fearing man, but you can say that about a lot of people." This is known as damning with faint praise, or in the case of a minister, praising with faint damns. Lyndon Johnson was less gentle in his attack on Ford's modest cerebral powers. Said Johnson, in a splendid example of the mean spirit and barnyard aroma that characterized the Johnsonian wit: "Jerry Ford couldn't fart and chew gum at the same time." Ford did little to dispel the image of an intellectual lightweight. He even acknowledged it. On one occasion he joked, "If Lincoln were alive today, he'd roll over in his grave." If Jack Kennedy brought poetry to politics with his rhetorical flourishes, Jerry Ford brought a sort of dull blank verse. He displayed his deafness to the glory of words when he named his campaign organization, which would joust with Jimmy Carter. He named his election team "The President Ford Committee"—PFC—one of the lowlier ranks in the U.S. military.

In 1976 members of the Republican electorate had to choose between two men who no one was ready to acknowledge as intellectual Goliaths. Both Gerald Ford and Ronald Reagan, who fought for the GOP nomination, were not renowned for their mastery of history, biography, economics, or the complex issues that informed the final third of the twentieth century. Ford declared that his favorite TV program was a shoot-em-up detective series called "Cannon," and Reagan was a fervent fan of "Mission: Impossible."

Ford's gaffes were dismaying to his staff to a degree that has seldom been approached within the beltway and that would not be seen again until Ronald Reagan moved into the White House. (Reagan's howlers were more blatant and more numerous than Ford's and led his aides to keep him away from any microphone or TV camera unless the script had been well rehearsed and the backdrop carefully selected. But curiously, owing perhaps to Reagan's personal appeal, the blunders that tarred Ford merely rolled off Reagan's well-tailored back.)

Ford had a problem with names—a curious failing in a politician—and this too brought gibes from the gallery. Campaigning for Dr. S. I. Hayakawa, the GOP candidate for the U.S. Senate in California, President Ford referred to him as "Dr. Haya-kama." A Ford aide grimaced at the error but then looked at the matter in a more cheerful light. "It was better than what he called Hayakawa when they met privately. Then he called him 'Hiawatha.'"

Ford's occasional vacuity was pricked by Garry Trudeau in a "Doonesbury" strip that tightened jaws in the West Wing on the eve of the TV debates with Jimmy Carter. Trudeau has the president consulting his chief of staff, Dick Cheney:

FORD. Dick, how do you think I should handle that opening statement tomorrow [in the TV debate]?

CHENEY. Well, sir, I certainly think you want to touch as many bases as possible . . . It's important that you underscore the considerable progress made by the Administration, particularly in restoring trust in government and faith in the economy.

FORD (weighing the advice). Maybe I should give my Acceptance Speech again.

During the late 1970s Johnny Carson turned the force of his wit more and more to politics. It was a lamentable turn of events for Jerry Ford, who more than once felt the sting of a Carson one-liner in "The Tonight Show's" opening monologue. The political zingers were most often the product of the cool, wry wit of Hal Goodwin, Larry Klein, and Ray Siller, Carson's top writers. Through the medium of their comic perceptions and Carson's impeccable delivery, the comedian had become middle America's contemporary Will Rogers. During the Ford-Carter campaign of 1976, Carson regularly riddled the foibles of both candidates. To Carson, President Ford looked like "the guy at Safeway who okays your checks."

There was no question that Gerald Ford was boring, bland, and somewhat limited in his perspicacity. In the words of one political columnist, he was "giving decency a bad name." Ford was not clever like Kennedy or cunning like Johnson. David Steinberg suggested that Ford seemed destined to join Jimmy Carter and Richard Nixon on "a Mount Rushmore of Mediocrity." Thus, in that peculiar autumn of 1976, satirists and cartoonists alike found Ford's passivity fed their funnybones if it did not stimulate their cerebrums. They were amused by the gap between the good guy character and bad guy programs (much as they would react to the same dichotomy in Ronald Reagan). Comics were nourished by his bumbling good nature and his mental lassitude. He was like a soothing Valium after the evil prodigies of Nixon and Johnson.

Jules Feiffer said of Ford: "He fills spaces like a vacuum." For three decades, Feiffer has been exposing us to the political inanities of our times. He always illustrated Ford with a tin can on his head and drew him as Happy Hooligan, the lunkhead hero of the turn-of-the-century comic strip character. "Another creation he closely resembled was the Frankenstein monster," said Feiffer with more mirth than malice. Feiffer had begun his career under the benign aegis of Harvey Kurtzman, the creator of *Mad Magazine*, but he found his true forte in his incisive mockery of America's presidents, from Eisenhower to Reagan. Ford must have often squirmed at the Feiffer panels that flowed from the President's TV debates with Jimmy Carter. The cartoonist once showed Ford behind his lectern, a sign proclaiming: GREAT DEBATE.

QUESTIONER. Mr. President, critics claim you don't care about the poor.

FORD. The who?

QUESTIONER. The victims of rising unemployment.

FORD (alarmed). The unemployed are rising? Call out the guard!

QUESTIONER. Describe your views on civil rights.

FORD (puzzled). Who's Sibyl Rice??

QUESTIONER. Describe your views on civil liberties.

FORD (brightening). On individual liberties? I know that one! Any corporation has the right of free choice to make as much profit as they want as cheaply as they can . . .

MODERATOR. This ends our rehearsal, Mr. President. Two minutes to air time.

FORD (ecstatic). HOORAY! BRING ON JIMMY CARSON.

Bob Orben, the premier comedy writer for Red Skelton and Jack Paar, who President Ford brought to the White House to enliven his often soporific speeches with crisp, relevant one-liners, had equal reason to blanch at Ford's wayward way with words. On the campaign trail in 1976, Orben would often find that his presidential patron had inadvertently substituted the wrong word at a critical point in the punch line. The *New Republic* called the candidate "Jerry the Joke Killer," as the president trashed the humor of a well-turned phrase. Here is an example of Ford at work in dismantling the wit of an anecdote:

> As I was walking through the lobby a friendly lady came up to me, shook my hand and said, "I know you from somewhere, but I can't remember your name." So in a friendly way I tried to help her out. I said, "I'm Jerry Ford." She said "No, but you're closer." [The proper punch line: "No, but you're close."]

Ford again undermined his own humor on the campaign trail when he addressed the National Athletic Association, an organization comprising athletic directors from the most prestigious colleges in America. Said Ford:

> I feel very much at home here today, because the athletic director of any college and the President of the United States have a great deal in common. We both need the talent, we both need the cooperation of others, and we both have a certain lack of performance in our jobs. [Proper punch line: "We both have a certain lack of permanence in our jobs."]

If the voters of America viewed Gerald Ford as less knowledgeable than Kennedy or Johnson or Nixon, and if columnists and cartoonists focused joyous attention on his shortcomings, Ford tried manfully to shrug aside the petty slanders. He appeared at the annual Alfred E. Smith Memorial dinner in New York City. It was a propitious platform. It was at this dinner in 1960 that John F. Kennedy had used his delicious wit to turn a political embarrassment into a popular triumph. Ford tried to replicate the Kennedy trick at this famous Manhattan banquet, when he said:

> Let me say first how busy it is, running the country and the campaign at the same time. We seem to go from one place to another without pausing. Sometimes it gets confusing, but it is always nice to come back here to Philadelphia.

Kennedy's and Roosevelt's intellectual fire exploded in their oratorical skill, but even Ford's staunchest advocates admitted that he was not an exceptional speaker. He would often flub his lines during a critical campaign speech. These misadventures in the text occurred so often that Bob Orben pasted a 3X5 card on the inside cover of the presidential speech binder. It bore a line to be used by Ford on those occasions when he blew a line. It read:

> I told my wife I knew this speech backwards, and that's how I'm delivering it.

In show business, such a line is called "a saver," and no comedian is without one. Ford found that it invariably brought laughter and applause from his audience; it carried a measure of modesty that was most appealing. Ford grew to like the line so much that he would purposely flub his lines in order to use it.

Ford's use of a professional comedy writer within the White House drew its share of ridicule. Though Kennedy and Johnson both pressed their regular speech writers into service as gag writers (Ted Sorensen for JFK, Ben Wattenberg and Liz Carpenter for LBJ), only Ford hired a writer exclusively for these comic creations. This seemed to many like excess in image making. Barry Goldwater had said that extremism in the defense of liberty was no sin. Ford seemed to be saying that extremism in the promotion of humor was no sin either. Not everyone was so forbearing. Garry Trudeau found the hiring of a presidential comedy writer a phenomenon worthy of his attention. In one of Trudeau's strips, President Ford is reading a letter inscribed in the unformed handwriting of a child. It reads:

> Dear Mr. President . . . I read that you pay a man to write your jokes for you. So I made up a joke. Here it is. You say, "I'm a Ford, not a Lincoln, and Ford has a better idea." Please send me $10.00 for this joke. Your friend, Billy R.

Not every public figure need be a Cicero or Demosthenes. Indeed, there are some who say the era of rhetoric is leaving us. If so, Gerald Ford anticipated the change. As even his best friends would attest, Ford was not a terribly moving speaker. An election campaign makes demands on the nominee's stamina and judgment, but it makes its maximum demands on his oratorical skill, and Ford's were modest. Don Penny, who doubled as Ford's speech coach, told of training the president in delivering his acceptance speech to the GOP convention, and Penny's description stands as one of the funniest monologues in the history of presidential life. "I played Bugs Bunny to his Brer Bear," said Penny, who had brought a videotape camera into the Oval Office. Ford improved under Penny's tutelage and his convention address was splendid. But on the campaign trail, with Bob Orben consigned to editing speeches and removed from his job of writing humor, Ford's speeches once again had the ability to empty arenas faster than the Chicago Cubs on a bad day. Ford acknowledged his own rhetoric deficiencies with engaging humor. He told of giving a speech in Omaha during the campaign, after which he was taken to a reception elsewhere in town. Said Ford: "At the reception a sweet little old lady came up to me, put her gloved hand in mine, and said, 'I heard you spoke here tonight.' And I said, 'Oh, it was nothing,' and she said, 'Yes, that's what I heard.'"

As Gerald Ford prepared to debate Jimmy Carter on TV, his oratorical shortcomings came into the gunsights of Garry Trudeau. Like Al Capp and Walt Kelly before him, Trudeau has managed to turn his daily strip into an entertaining battleground for frauds, fools, and ideologues of all colorations. (Most recently he has been featuring an invisible George

Bush). The public figures savaged by the insightful Trudeau seldom appreciate this form of recognition, though they often have the wit to importune him for the original artwork. In spotlighting Ford's rhetorical flaws, Trudeau pictured the president behind his desk in the Oval Office. He buzzes his secretary on the intercom:

FORD. Call Dick Cheney [White House chief of staff] and tell him I want to have my debate briefing at noon . . . And has my speech coach arrived yet?

SPEECH COACH (entering). Hi, Chief! Ready to run through some warm-up drills?

[Ford tells his secretary to forget it.]

SPEECH COACH. After me, Chief! The RAINS . . . in PLAINS . . . fall MAINLY on . . .

FORD (interrupting). Hold on. I gotta loosen my tie . . .

The televised debate with challenger Jimmy Carter was doubtless the turning point of the 1976 campaign and sealed the fate of Jerry Ford. His memorable declaration that Poland was free of Soviet domination was one of the Great Moments in Unintentional Humor and a gaffe from which Ford never recovered. Said Art Buchwald, in reflecting on his profession as a political humorist: "Are American Presidents providing us with enough humor? Well, just when I think they aren't, Richard Nixon says 'I am not a crook.' And Jimmy Carter says, 'I have lusted after women, but God has always forgiven me.' Or Jerry Ford says, 'I have just freed the Polish people retroactively.'"

It was the second Ford-Carter debate, and Ford's misstatement was triggered by a question from Max Frankel of the *New York Times*. Frankel asked the president about Soviet influence in Eastern Europe, and Ford blundered into an answer that would feed a hundred comedy writers from downtown Burbank to Rockefeller Center. Said Ford with the solemnity of a grandfather clock striking the hour fifteen minutes late: "There is no Soviet domination of Eastern Europe, and there never will be under a Ford administration." As aides winced, reporters gasped, and viewers rubbed their eyes, Ford plunged on, like Al Campanis explaining why blacks "lack the necessities." "I don't believe, Mr. Frankel," continued Ford, "that the Poles consider themselves dominated by the Soviet Union." Said one political observer: "If Ford believes the Poles are free, there's a bridge I want to show him in Brooklyn."

If the Ford campaign caught a cold with his Polish gaffe, his pardon of Richard Nixon gave him pneumonia. It haunted him throughout the debates and the entire campaign. In an editorial cartoon in the *Boston Globe*, Paul Szep showed a laughing Jimmy Carter and a grim-faced Jerry Ford before the television cameras. A relaxed Carter is sitting in a rocking chair, while a tense Ford is dressed in convict's stripes that recall Nixon's felonies and his possible fate, had it not been for Ford's pardon. In the cartoon, Carter is saying: "I'LL BE JACK KENNEDY. WHO DO YOU WANT TO BE??"

Paul Conrad, the Pulitzer Prize–winning cartoonist for the *Los Angeles Times*, tweaked the confusion and ambiguity of Ford's political statements. Conrad showed two Jerry Fords standing behind their respective lecterns at the debate. The first Ford is pointing indignantly at the second and shouting: "MY OPPONENT IS DELIBERATELY DISTORTING MY POSITION!"

If Garry Trudeau kidded Ford and his performance at the great debate, he had little taste for the satiric attacks that "Saturday Night Live" mounted on the president. Trudeau characterized the NBC show as "screw you" humor and "slash-and-burn" comedy. To Trudeau, "Saturday Night" reflected "a sort of callousness" and might lead, he said, to a society that is "intolerant of failure and uncompassionate in the face of suffering." Certainly, "Saturday Night" was intolerant of Ford's failure and indifferent to his suffering at their hands. There is some evidence that even Chevy Chase, the chief purveyor of this slash-and-burn humor at Ford's expense, felt twinges of guilt at his mockery of the president. When he met Ford ten years later, Chase said, "Mr. President, I feel rather embarrassed about the way I treated you when you were president, and I'd like you to pardon me . . .Oops!"

Trudeau did not stoop to slash-and-burn tactics after the Ford-Carter debate. He brought to it his gentle ironies, which were more effective for their understatement. In the Trudeau strip, the debate is in progress, and a viewer is watching it on his livingroom TV. The announcer is saying,

> Direct from Philadelphia—THE PRESIDENTIAL DEBATE! Tonight's debate is being broadcast live from the Walnut Street Theater, which has been chilled to a previously agreed upon temperature of 68 degrees Fahrenheit! In the interests of fairness, both candidates have been made up and lit exactly the same way. They're also sitting behind matching lecterns, and are wearing identical blue suits . . . Now, then, which of you is Governor Carter?"

In 1976, the hearts of many conservative Republicans were betrothed not to Jerry Ford but to the charismatic governor of California, Ronald Wilson Reagan. The popular former actor was seeking the Republican nomination in 1976, and, despite his incumbency, Ford found Reagan a formidable rival. The usually amiable Ford turned bilious where Reagan was concerned. He said on one occasion, "There is a rumor to the effect that Ronald Reagan dyes his hair. That is ridiculous. He's just prematurely orange."

Ford had his hands full with Reagan in the Republican primaries. Reagan was armed with a covey of conservative gag writers in his old Hollywood home, so it was at this moment in history that Ford summoned Don Penny to his campaign train to feed him strategic anecdotes and one-liners. One of these tried to puncture the cinematic gloss of the California challenger. Said Ford: "Governor Reagan and I *do* have one thing in common. We both played football. I played in Michigan. He played for Warner Brothers."

Reagan's assets were, paradoxically, similar to those of Democrat Jimmy Carter's; he had never served in the nation's capital and so could attack the government and the bureaucracy with vigor, and he had no links, as did Ford, to the scorned Nixon team. As John Dean, the whistleblower of the Watergate scandal, said of Ford: "[He was] the unquestioning soldier and servant of the Nixon White House." Dean was maximizing his exposure by covering the GOP convention for *Rolling Stone*. As the *National Review* observed, mocking the self-promoting former Nixon aide, "John Dean's own story will be told in the forthcoming book, *Profiles in Chutzpah*." But *NR* was not always supportive of Ford; generally, they came down on the side of the genial former governor of California. Ford had been far too tolerant, they felt, in permitting the growth of government during his watch, and that rankled the opinion makers at the *National Review*. Said the *NR* in their witty "This Week" review of recent events:

> President Ford last week opened a Centennial safe containing among other nostalgic mementoes, a list of all the federal employees in 1876—80,000 of them, presumably ancestors of the 2,800,000-strong swarms of them in 1976, and if that doesn't confirm your worst fears about bureaucratic breeding habits, get out the calculator.

If Carter and Reagan were outsiders, attacking from the woods, Ford was the insider, firing from the dubious safety of the wagon train. Like the middle-aged movie actor who became an overnight political success after two decades on the Hollywood sound stages, Ford's political career took a meteoric leap as well. His surge came in the mid-seventies with Nixon's flummery. From House minority leader, Ford became, in a rapid series of escalations, first an instant vice president, then an instant president, both without the messy requirements of a general election. Ford joked about his hasty ascendency, saying: "The Marine Corps Band is a little confused. They don't know whether to play 'Hail to the Chief' or 'You've Come a Long Way, Baby.'" As Ford sought the presidency in his own right—as had LBJ in 1964, after reaching the Oval Office adventitiously—he looked back on his early indifference to his office. As congressman from Grand Rapids (where rumor had it a sign reads, "Gerald Ford Slipped Here") he had often protested that he had no interest in the presidency. He had a safe seat, a handsome family, a loving wife, and that was enough. When pressed on the subject, Ford would say, "I must admit that late at night, when I'm driving home to Virginia and I pass the White House, I sometimes say to myself, 'If I lived here, I'd be home by now.'" But Ford seemed sincere in the modesty of his ambitions.

It was said by Washington wags that the reason Nixon chose Ford as his vice president was that Nixon couldn't believe the American people would impeach him since it meant handing power to Jerry Ford. Nixon's calculation was faulty, as was his decision not to burn the tapes. But shortly after Ford redecorated the Oval Office, bringing "an end to our long national nightmare," he issued a full, free pardon to his predecessor "for any and all crimes he may have committed in office." Many Americans felt they were not prepared to have their national nightmare ended so abruptly and turned on Ford as though he were the network programmer who had cancelled "Star Trek." Watergate had, indeed, taken on the appeal of a long-running TV series, and its abrupt cancellation by Jerry Ford injured our sense of theater as well as our sense of justice. The public uproar was deafening, and it says something of Ford's political antenna that the firestorm profoundly surprised him. If much of the public screamed in reproach, America's satirists reacted with a mixture of hostility and mirth. In the edition of *Who's In Charge Here?* for 1976, I showed a photo of President Ford at his Oval Office desk reading a letter. It said: "DEAR JERRY, THANKS FOR THE PARDON. BY THE WAY, I HAVE JUST RECEIVED THE ENCLOSED PARKING TICKET. . . ."

Garry Trudeau pictured Ford on the phone:

FORD. Get me Mr. Nixon on the line! . . . Dick? This is the President.

NIXON. Jerry! How thoughtful of you to call. How's everything at the Oval Office?

FORD. Not all that it could be, Dick . . . Quite frankly your pardon has turned out to be quite a headache!

NIXON. Oh, now you mustn't mind what people say! I never did!

FORD. Well, I probably wouldn't, Dick, if you had gone the contrition route. But you didn't—even after massive incriminating evidence!

NIXON. Well, that's the way it has to be . . .

FORD. How so, Dick?

NIXON. Jerry, you've got to try to understand—for me to apologize would simply be inappropriate! It would set a precedent that would *compromise* the office of the former President.

FORD. Huh?

NIXON. You see, it's not *me* I'm thinking of, Jer—it's *future* Presidents!

Jules Feiffer zeroed in on the pardon with telling effect. In the midst of the 1976 campaign, Feiffer pictured a grim, befuddled Ford, head in hands, behind his Oval Office desk, ruminating:

I was right on federal spending . . . I was right on inflation . . . I was far right on busing . . . Where did I go wrong? . . . THE PARDON! . . . [In the next panel, Nixon's bedside phone rings, awakening him. He seizes it, listens, slams down the receiver]

PAT NIXON. Who was that, Dick?

NIXON. An obscene call.

As the 1976 campaign unfolded, the public seemed particularly ambivalent about Jerry Ford. It liked his obvious decency and disliked his policies. It was the good cop–bad cop within the same uniform. Feiffer addressed this dichotomous dilemma by showing Ford staring at his image in a mirror and pausing to reflect.

FORD. Mirror, mirror on the wall, who is the best candidate of them all?

[The reply summed up two years of the Ford presidency with pith and perception.]

MIRROR IMAGE. Well, you couldn't care less about the unemployed but you're candid . . . You bomb Cambodians but you're humane . . . You're for ravaging the environment but you're decent . . . You have an 18th Century view of economics but you're honest . . . You have a liking for dictators but you're good natured . . . You think secrecy in government is nobody's business but you're open about it . . . You think civil rights is wrong but you're a terrific dancer . . . Accordingly *you're* not so hot but I, your image, am the best candidate of them all.

For a candidate who, in the words of his chief confidant and speech writer, Bob Hartmann, "was tone deaf to humor," Jerry Ford tried hard throughout his 1976 campaign to bear the gaggery of others with grace and respond to it with humor. He used the surrogate whimsy that Bob Orben created for him in the time-honored way. Politicians from Cromwell to Churchill have sought public office with self-deprecating wit, sensing that voters like the man who can mock his own flaws. So Ford kidded himself about everything from his paunch to his golf game. About the latter, he said,

Arnold Palmer has asked me not to wear his slacks except under an assumed name . . . They say you can tell a good golfer by the number of people in the gallery. You've heard of Arnie's Army. My group is called Ford's Few . . . My problem is that I have a wild swing. Back home on my home course, they don't yell "Fore," they yell "Ford" . . . The Secret Service Men you see around me today—when I play golf, they qualify for combat pay . . . In Washington I'm known as the President of the United States, and in golf I'm known as the Jinx of the Links.

As Gerald Ford's campaign train wound across the map of America, his humor of self-depreciation reached new heights, or rather, depths. To a convention of skiers, he said, "I can ski for hours on end." To an assembly of recreational sailors, he said, "Is there any correlation between the fact that sailing needs a great deal of wind, and your invitation to me? . . ." At Ohio State, he said, "I met Woody Hayes at the airport. We had our picture taken . . . and the caption read: 'Woody Hayes and Friend.'" Of his awkwardness on the dance floor, he said of the days he was dating Betty: "We had a problem. Betty had studied modern dance and I was a football player . . . She had a theory as to why I played center rather than quarterback. She said it was one of the few positions where you don't have to move your feet." To a Rose Garden gathering, he modestly averred: "I told the Republicans I had a safe seat in Grand Rapids—and look what happened." To another group, he protested, "You don't need to have a pool at the White House to get in deep water." And to a fund-raising dinner, he announced, "I didn't know the honeymoon was over until the [subway] started to build a new station in the Oval Office."

Beyond the lacerating damage done by Ford's pardon of Richard Nixon, his campaign suffered from his controversial secretary of agriculture, Earl Butz. Butz had resigned in embarrassment after telling a particularly repellent joke that was offensive not only to the blacks it ridiculed, but to a great many nonblacks as well. The joke, if it may be so dignified, dealt with the evacuative and sexual pleasures of the black man. The fact that Ford took an inordinate amount of time to ask for Butz's resignation was taken as a sign of his insensitivity. Butz had given the president fair warning that his humor was an accident waiting to happen. On an earlier occasion, Butz's untethered wit brought long faces to the White House staff. Commenting on the Pope's restrictive views on birth control, Butz affected a broad Italian accent and cracked, "You no playa the game, you know maka the rules."

Ford tried to laugh away Butz's corrosive wit during a speech to the Radio and TV Commentators Association, where he shared the dais with Bob Hope. Said Ford: "I have only one thing to say about a program that calls for me to follow Bob Hope—it's ridiculous. Bob Hope has stage presence, comedy timing, and the finest writers in the business. I'm standing here in a rented tuxedo—with three jokes from Earl Butz!"

Washington cartoonist Pat Oliphant found Ford too forgiving in his toleration of Butz's comic offenses and drew a pattern of behavior that went beyond forbearance to callousness. In the first panel, Ford is pinning a FORGIVEN button on Richard Nixon; in the second, on Earl Butz; and, in the third, on himself. Many voters felt that none of the three deserved absolution from the consequences of their mistakes.

CAMPAIGN 1976

Ford was not forgiven for his—the Nixon pardon, the Poland gaffe—and on Election Day 1976, the born-again Georgian they called "Jimmy Who?" took a four year lease on the impressive public housing on Pennsylvania Avenue.

Chapter 6
Campaign 1976
"Jimmy Who?"

That's Governor Carter over there. It's easy to see
where he sits. Now if we could only figure out where
he stands.
                                    —JERRY FORD

Could George S. Kaufman and Moss Hart have cre-
ated a more lovably eccentric clan in *You Can't Take It With You*
than Jimmy Carter's family? Probably not. And it was small
wonder that as Jimmy Carter emerged from the Democratic
pack in the primaries of 1976, America's wits emerged from
their hibernation. They had not really reveled in a First Family since the Kennedy years. Of course, there was some humor
to be found in the Johnson ménage—all those birds, the jokes
about the cattle grazing on the White House lawn, Lyndon
baring his surgical scar to his secretaries, Lyndon roaring
through the Texas hills in his Lincoln Continental. But there
was scant humor in the Nixon household, except for the irony
of daughter Trish marrying one of Nader's Raiders. And
daughter Julie wedding Ike's jug-eared grandson. Or, for
those with a taste for black humor, the stricken president beg-
ging Henry Kissinger to kneel with him in prayer for an unlikely salvation. The Ford family had been a source of occasional merriment. Betty Ford's outspoken advocacy of
premarital sex produced snickers from the Hollywood crowd,

and so did Jerry's battles with the law of gravity. Official White House photographer David Hume Kennerly produced some brazen wit. On the day Saigon fell, Kennerly scurried into the Oval Office to declare, "The good news is the war is over. The bad news is we lost." There was also the canned laughter that Bob Orben brought to Ford's speeches and the indiscreet appearance of press secretary Ron Nessen on "Saturday Night Live." But not since the Kennedy years had a First Family been so ripe for the scalpels of America's wits as when the Carters emerged from the obscurity of Plains, Georgia.

Carter's southern accent spawned its share of humor as he took to the campaign trail. Kennedy's Boston twang and Lyndon Johnson's Texas drawl had both lent themselves to the impressionists, giving Vaughan Meader and Rich Little food for fun. Indeed, so had Nixon's harsh vibrato. But when Kennedy spoke of "Cuber," the electorate at least knew the subject of discussion. The Carter drawl was so thick that two separate books were published in the form of mock dictionaries to help the citizenry know what the gentleman from Georgia was saying.

In *The Jimmy Carter Dictionary*, written by William Maloney and published by Playboy Press, the author presents various familiar words and the meaning that Carter attributed to each of them:

HAR: a growth covering the skull.

STOW: an establishment with goods for sale.

PIN: a writing instrument using ink.

MILE: letters or items sent via the post office.

JEW: the second person pronoun.

TAIL: to relate, narrate, recount.

TOAD: past tense of the verb "to tell."

RETCH: having a great deal of money.

Carter joked about his drawl in many of the speeches he delivered throughout the south. In Atlanta, Birmingham, and Biloxi, he smiled, "Isn't it time we had a president without an accent?"

After all, Jimmy Carter was the only man from the Deep South to be nominated for the presidency by one of the two principal parties in the past century. He displayed the modesty of the obscure outsider with a nice mixture of humor and humility. When he received the Democratic nomination, he opened his remarks with a wry line that he had often used in the bruising primary battles. "My name is Jimmy Carter," he said, "and I'm running for president."

Garry Trudeau addressed the Carter drawl with amusement while drawing a bead on Jerry Ford, as both candidates prepared for their first TV debate. In the "Doonesbury" version, an aide is briefing President Ford on the ground rules:

AIDE: Sir, the debate will last 90 minutes. Each of you will first make a statement, and then field questions. You will be permitted to rebut . . . On your opening statement, sir, just try to be yourself and play it as presidential as possible. When Carter's up, be sure to make hard eye contact.

FORD: And in my rebuttals?

AIDE: Take charge. Flaunt your superior command of facts. Use classified information if you have to.

FORD: Can I do that?

AIDE: Uh-huh. And don't be afraid to *make fun of his accent.*

Carter's principles and policies seemed unsettlingly flexible; they changed with his audience. The GOP castigated Carter's chameleon views by asking: "Why not a debate between Carter in New York and Carter in Atlanta?" Once Carter reached the White House, Jules Feiffer showed the new president rationalizing his vacillating views. Said Feiffer's Carter:

Originally I campaigned against a tax cut. But my experts are for it, so I'm for it . . . I campaigned in favor of wage and price guidelines. But my experts oppose it, so I oppose it . . . I campaigned against the B-1 bomber. But my experts want it, so I may want it . . . If these decisions turn out to be wrong don't blame me—I'm the President, not an expert . . . It's not as if I'm qualified.

On the heels of the corruption and cynicism of Watergate, Carter seemed to protest too much about his own probity. "I will never lie to you," he insisted at hundreds of campaign stops throughout the primaries and the campaign. Carter aide Jody Powell saw some of the humor of this insistence when he cracked, "We're going to lose the liar vote!" Carter's mother snapped, "Well, I lie all the time. I have to—to balance the family ticket."

The uncertainty of who and what Jimmy Carter represented was sardonically limned by cartoonist Herblock. He pictured a grinning Carter as the groom in a wedding ceremony. The apprehensive bride, her gown labeled "Democrats 1976," hovers outside the chapel, chattering to her bridesmaids as she eyes the groom waiting at the altar. "But I don't think I *know* him!" she gasps.

Like Reagan in 1980, Carter won his way into America's heart in 1976 by attacking Washington. After the tragedy of Vietnam and the travesty of Watergate, Washington was the ideal joke for a candidate's campaign humor; Carter realized that attacking Washington was the best way to get a job there. In traveling about the country, he perceived the dismay and disgust the voters felt toward the capital, the bureaucracy, the Congress, and the White House. Hence, like George Wallace and Ronald Reagan, Carter developed a repertoire of Washington-bashing jokes. His mocking humor carried the southerner through the primary battles. Carter launched his speeches by proposing to catalog his assets and liabilities. He would smile his toothpaste grin and say, "Well, my assets are all in my campaign literature. So perhaps I'd better start with my liabilities. [The crowd tittered] I'm not from Washington. [Laughter from the crowd] I'm not a member of Congress. [Hoots of derision] I've never been part of the national government. [Laughter turning to applause]." Jody Powell recognized the wisdom of ridiculing the capital. "In most of the primary campaigns," he said, "we benefited from being able to joke about Washington."

Carter's gaffe in *Playboy* magazine generated abundant campaign humor. Since sex and politics are said to be America's two greatest focuses of interest, a story that combined the two—as would Gary Hart's escapades in the 1980s—created a geyser of printer's ink. Though the public likes its leaders to be religious, it does not like them to be *too* religious. And Carter was anxious to persuade the mainstream voter that this born-again Christian was not a sanctimonious fundamentalist. Thus, in his interview with *Playboy's* Robert Scheer, Carter was open-minded to a fault. As the interview concluded and reporter Scheer packed up his tape recorder and headed for the door, the candidate seemed to feel he had not laid to rest the electorate's view of him as a pious, narrow-minded fellow. He stopped Scheer and continued the conversation in an unexpected direction that produced snickers across the country. Said the candidate: "I've looked on a lot of women with lust. I've committed adultery in my heart many times. This is something that God recognizes I will do—and I have done it—and God forgives me for it." Carter was swept along by his ruminations, and Scheer's tape recorder gobbled up the confessional. "That doesn't mean I condemn someone who not only looks on a woman with lust but who leaves his wife and shacks up with somebody out of wedlock." (Carter may have had in mind certain members of his own staff of whose sensual excesses he was said to disapprove.) "Christ says, 'Don't consider yourself better than someone else because one guy screws a whole bunch of women while the other guy is loyal to his wife.'" Carter's views on sex produced laughter and mockery —as did Ford's on the freedom of Poland.

If Carter regretted his *Playboy* remarks, America's comics did not. The bumper sticker manufacturers prospered as well. Recalling the famous Barry Goldwater slogan of a dozen years before, IN YOUR HEART YOU KNOW HE'S RIGHT, luminous stickers started appearing on bumpers that read, IN YOUR HEART HE KNOWS YOUR WIFE. A rhapsodic female supporter at a New Orleans rally waved a placard at the candidate that read: I LUST AFTER JIMMY CARTER FOR PRESIDENT. Ford exploited the episode with understated irony. When Jerry Ford's face appeared on the cover of *Newsweek*, his supporters ran a newspaper ad juxtaposing the *Newsweek* cover with the one of *Playboy* that had hyped the Carter interview. Said the ad's headline: ONE GOOD WAY TO DECIDE THE ELECTION— READ LAST WEEK'S *Newsweek*. READ THIS MONTH'S *Playboy*. SEX, SIN, TEMPTATION—CARTER'S CANDID VIEW headlined the *Chicago Sun-Times*. CARTER ON SIN AND LUST screamed the *Washington Star*. The individual members of the press were more ribald than the city editors who wrote the headlines. Some members of the media covering the Carter campaign sang a parody of "Heart of My Heart" that amused their listeners more than it did the candidate. It went:

Lust in my heart, how I love adultery.
Lust in my heart, it's my theology.
When I was young, at the Plains First Baptist Church,
I would preach and sermonize
But oh how I would fantasize.

Oh, lust in my heart, who cares if it's a sin?
Leching's a noble art.
It's okay if you shack up
'Cause I won't get my back up,
I've got mine
I've got lust in my heart.

The Carter lechery story brought out the best and brightest in editorial cartoonist Paul Conrad. Conrad has the uncanny ability to express outrage and humor with a minimum of symbols and a minimum of text. When *Playboy* hit the stand, spreading the Carter sexual philosophy across America's newsstands, Conrad captured the humor of the situation in a cartoon in which a grinning Jimmy Carter is mentally undressing the Statue of Liberty. In Carter's fantasy, the old girl is bereft of her robes and in voluptuous form. Carter's reference to lusting after other people's wives provided a wag at the *National Review* to remark: "We'd trust Jimmy Carter with our wives any time. What we don't like is the way he eyes our

paychecks." Then as public attention passed on to other issues, the *NR* cracked, "Well, maybe he's weathered this one.
But wait for the *Hustler* interview." Carter tried to laugh away
the *Playboy* storm, with scant success. Introducing Andrew
Young, who was actively supporting him in his election campaign and who had also been the subject of a *Playboy* interview,
Carter said: "Andy Young has helped me a lot. He made it
clear that I was not the only one that gave a *Playboy* interview.
And he pointed out to the *Playboy* people that I still was filled
with lust, but I didn't discriminate."

On balance, Carter's *Playboy* declaration probably
helped him more than it hurt, in allowing the candidate to display a refreshing honesty to Americans who feared his excessive piety. In 1988 the American public would be confronted
by minister candidates in both parties—Pat Robertson and
Jesse Jackson—and both carried the albatross of religiosity
and the confusion of church and state. Carter's born-again
Christianity carried this same risk, and his *Playboy* interview,
while generating abundant ribald humor, may have relieved
the doubts of many.

Carter revealed another insight into his secular tastes
when he met Elizabeth Taylor at a dinner party. "I couldn't
take my eyes off her," he acknowledged. When she asked the
candidate a question, he failed to respond, continuing to stare
fixedly at the glamorous star. When she repeated the question, Carter finally replied. "I'm sorry, Miss Taylor," he said.
"I'm sure you were talking to me, but I didn't hear a word you
said." Neither history nor journalism reveal whether Elizabeth Taylor was undergoing the same fanciful inspection that
Paul Conrad showed Carter giving to the Statue of Liberty.

Billy Carter was the target of humorous attention
throughout the campaign. He was a corpulent, gimlet-eyed,
fun-loving young fellow who ran a gas station in Plains, Georgia, while sharing responsibilities at his older brother's peanut
farm and factory. Billy parlayed his fifteen minutes of fame—
in the jargon of Andy Warhol—into a product called Billy
Beer, and promoted it assiduously. He posed for news photographers in a costume made entirely of the rings from beer
cans, cradling a six-pack in his arms. Billy relished the eccen-

tricities that ran rampant in the Carter family. Said Billy to a fascinated pack of reporters as the 1976 campaign began: "I got a mamma who joined the Peace Corps and went to India when she was sixty-eight. I got one sister who's a Holy Roller preacher. I got another sister who wears a helmet and rides a motorcycle. And I got a brother who thinks he's going to be president. So that makes me the only sane person in the family."

If Jimmy Carter sometimes found his kid brother to be something of an embarrassment, he managed to conceal his irritation. And if the elder Carter's jokes at his brother's expense seemed at times to be somewhat close to the bone—questioning Billy's mendacity as well as his intellect—that was Jimmy's cautious form of reprisal. Speaking of plans to reorganize the government, Jimmy said, "I'd like to involve Billy in the government. I've been thinking of reorganizing and putting the CIA and the FBI together. But Billy said he wouldn't head up any agency he couldn't spell."

Some Washington observers dismissed Billy as a bumpkin; others called him "a loose cannon." This latter appraisal was prophetic. When Carter moved into the White House, Billy embarrassed his brother by accepting a $200,000 fee from the Libyan government to lobby his brother on their behalf. When influential Jews objected to Billy's behavior, he declared that "the Jews can kiss my ass." This was nearly as offensive as Jesse Jackson's reference to the "Hymies in Hymietown" (that is, the Jews of New York) that raised a ministorm during the 1984 campaign. But as Carter's popularity declined in the later years of his presidency, he ruefully observed, "A lot of people criticize Billy, but his standing in the public opinion polls is substantially above my own." And, as the election campaign unfolded, Billy Carter was a reliable source of humor for his candidate brother. On one occasion, when Billy's beer interests were reaching a head, the elder Carter observed, "Billy is doing his share for the nation's economy. He's put the beer industry back on its feet." When Billy was invited to Montreal to help publicize a new public swimming pool, the candidate remarked, "My brother has found another way to make a living other than growing peanuts. He can go to Canada and do a belly-buster in the swimming pool and make more money than he made all year on the farm. . . . When I mentioned that to Billy, he said, 'Well, you forget, Jimmy, that I don't know how to swim.'"

Students of sibling rivalry find little odd in Billy Carter's resentment of his older brother's achievements. So Billy's response was unsurprising when a reporter asked him on election eve how he would be changed if his older brother became president. Billy weighed the proposition and said, "If Jimmy becomes President tonight, I'm gonna make everybody call me *Mister* Carter for the first twenty-four hours." When Ford made his concession announcement late on election night, Jimmy Carter approached the podium, eyed his brother and declared, "*Mister* Carter, I want to thank you for waiting up all night to greet me." The day before Jimmy Carter took the inaugural oath the following January, Billy Carter kidded his brother's religious ties, saying, "I hear it's gonna be forty degrees here in Washington tomorrow for the inauguration. Jimmy must've been talkin' to the Lord again."

The Jimmy Carter grin produced a great deal of campaign mirth in 1976. Recalling the toothy grin of a famous First Lady of an earlier era, one irreverent wit cracked that Jimmy Carter looked like "the illegitimate son of Eleanor Roosevelt." Carter himself mocked his expansive smile with its rows and rows of gleaming teeth when he said, "My tax audit is coming out okay. The only thing they questioned so far is a six hundred dollar bill for toothpaste." Paul Conrad took a page out of *Alice in Wonderland* in his editorial cartoon in the *Los Angeles Times*. Twitting Carter's frequent avoidance of the issues, he pictured the huge, toothy, disembodied smile of Jimmy Carter poised overhead in the foliage of a tree, and a perplexed Alice studying it from below. "WELL! I'VE OFTEN SEEN A CAT WITHOUT A GRIN," THOUGHT ALICE. "BUT A GRIN WITHOUT A CAT! IT'S THE MOST CURIOUS THING I EVER SAW!"

Carter's splay-toothed grin became famous during the primary and election campaigns of 1976. Perhaps Teddy Roosevelt's tombstone teeth, as Gore Vidal called them, could approach the Carter smile, but no other presidential candidate of this century could compare. Of course, the hard-driven aides who took Carter's orders and who were often subjected to his icy stares of disapproval could tell that there was a distinction to be drawn "between Jimmy's good smiles and his bad smiles."

When the campaign struggle of 1976 concluded with Jimmy Carter the victor, the White House took on a new look. Carter put the imperial pretensions of Richard Nixon and the country club resonance of the Republican party far behind him, taking care to be photographed carrying his own suit bag and addressing the nation in a cardigan sweater. Mike Peters in the *Dayton Daily News* pictured the government in transition most effectively by showing the famous facade of the White House, and in place of the familiar portico were the huge, gleaming teeth of Jimmy Carter.

Chapter 7
Campaign 1972
So I Made a Mistake

> Where does Richard Nixon stand on the great issues
> of our time? Aside.
> —DAVID FROST

Richard Nixon has always provided an irresistible target for the malicious humor of American satirists, playwrights, novelists, essayists, and monologists. Other presidents have inspired the benign laughter of the one-liners of Bob Hope and Johnny Carson. But only Nixon has become the nemesis of America's counterculture, providing an opportunity for millions of Nixon-haters to ridicule his remarkable career. Given the controversial aspects of his long political struggle—his "Six Crises" plus one—Nixon has generated a spectacular outpouring of toxic humor.

If Nixon had the crackling wit of a Jack Kennedy or the genuine humility of a Ronald Reagan, he could have responded to these libelous attacks by slipping many of their punches. But he lacked the gift of humor that so many of his assailants possessed. He was cursed, in the words of Theodore Sorensen, by "a bitter mind-set" that ill-equipped him to fight fire with fire or humor with humor. Hence, as the satire of his detractors reached its zenith in the 1972 campaign, Nixon could do little more than crouch in the imperial cocoon of the West Wing, displaying a solemn mien, his shoulders hunched and his jowls waggling in self-pity.

101

The siege mentality that developed in the Nixon White House was irrigated to a large extent by the steady stream of mocking humor that issued forth from the media and the entertainment world. Nixon was its perennial target, and if the eye sees itself but by reflection, as Shakespeare tells us, Nixon must have grown bitter at the image his tormentors threw back at him. He was quick to protest that "you can't let your enemies defeat you [with slander and ridicule]." But can any man withstand the steady onslaught of caustic wit?

Richard Nixon's lack of humor made him a perfect butt for the wounding humor of others. His paucity of wit was exemplified by Lou Cannon, venerable White House correspondent for the *Washington Post*. Cannon told a story of a congressman who had been a cohort of Nixon when the latter had been in the House of Representatives. When Nixon reached the White House, a number of legislators wanted to throw a party to laud the former friend who had risen so high. They needed some funny stories to brighten their lauditory speeches. So the congressmen phoned Nixon's private secretary, Rose Mary Woods, telling her, "Rose Mary, we'd like some funny stories about Mr. Nixon." There was a lengthy pause on the line. Finally Rose Mary Woods spoke. "There *are* no funny stories about Mr. Nixon," she said.

The humor of John F. Kennedy was laconic and elegant. The humor of Lyndon B. Johnson was earthy and anecdotal. But the humor of Richard Nixon was largely unintentional. And this obliviousness to humor inspired Nixon's critics to prodigies of ridicule. Comics had a field day with Nixon's desire to act the "good Joe." The most famous such display was when Nixon greeted David Frost, the journalist/satirist who was interviewing him for a series of syndicated interviews in his post–Watergate days. Nixon greeted Frost with a one-of-the-boys question: "Well, David, did you do any fornicating this weekend?" A less familiar display of Nixon's forced humor occurred during the 1972 campaign when a motorcade was carrying Nixon through the streets of Denver. The motorcycle of the lead policeman overturned, breaking the officer's arm and leg. As he lay on the pavement writhing in pain, awaiting the arrival of the ambulance, Nixon leaned over the stricken officer and said: "How do you like your job?"

Nixon's lack of humor invited scathing wit from his political opponents, to which he was unable to respond in kind. Jack Kennedy's alter ego Ted Sorensen, in an address before the National Press Club, fabricated a display of Nixonian wit that, though clearly apocryphal, was accepted as fact by a credulous reporter from *Time* magazine. It was reported in that magazine as evidence that Mr. Nixon "had not lost his sense of humor." Said Sorensen:

> I ran into Richard Nixon last week and he said to me, "I watched the Kennedy Inaugural and I have to admit that there were some words he said that I wish *I* had said." And I said to him, "Well, thank you, sir. I guess you mean the part about 'Ask not what your country can do for you.' And Nixon said, 'No, I mean the part about I do solemnly swear.'"

Just as Barry Goldwater was a target for malicious humor in 1964, Richard Nixon proved an inviting target for caustic wit in 1972. The difference lay in the outcome of the two campaigns. In 1964 the target was swept away in a humbling defeat, but in 1972 the target was swept back into office on a seeming landslide of ridicule. In effect, Nixon laughed all the way to the White House. If their boss was the subject of scathing wit—from Buchwald, Russell, Baker, Oliphant, Feiffer, and the rest—Nixon's aides could not have cared less, as the candidate continued his triumphal march to reelection. With the polls showing Nixon running far ahead of the hapless George McGovern, a Nixon aide laughed, "We're running scared . . . for about an inch." It was doubtless the shortest run of panic in electoral history. Joked Bob Dole, then the chairman of the GOP campaign committee, and already the repository of the most brutal wit in public life: "We aren't saying we'll win all fifty states, but we aren't conceding anything." Even Nixon's buttoned-down, uptight press secretary, former Disneyland guide Ron Ziegler, could laugh at the prospects for a Nixon runaway. Mixing his humor with his antimedia animus, Ziegler reflected on how the Nixon-hating press would handle the McGovern debacle that unmistakably lay ahead. "I can picture the headline in the *Washington Post*," cracked Ziegler. "McGOVERN SWEEPS D.C., with the sub-head NIXON CARRIES NATION."

(Ziegler was the source of unintentional humor a year later when he reviewed the accomplishments of Nixon's presidency in the year 1973 for a White House reporter. It was an impressive list of achievements. Ziegler concluded the list by saying, "So it was a really terrific year except for the downside." "What downside?" asked the reporter. "Watergate," said Ziegler.)

Certainly the 1972 campaign between Richard Nixon and George McGovern was one of the most bizarre contests of the century. Johnson v. Goldwater was incongruous, and Eisenhower v. Stevenson was anomalous, but the contest between Nixon and McGovern exceeded all others in its offering of contrasting candidates. The point was not lost on America's wits. Never had two men more diametrically different sought the White House. Nixon was suspicious and paranoid, McGovern was forthright and accessible. Nixon was hostile to the young, while McGovern rode to prominence on the shoulders of youth. Nixon sought honor in Southeast Asia, while McGovern wanted us out as quickly as possible.

Much of the humor at Nixon's expense flowered from his perceived character. He was a loner, humorless and manipulative. Many remembered with distaste the pink circulars he used to discredit his opponent in his race for the Senate. They recalled the secret slush fund that nearly got him jettisoned from the Eisenhower ticket and the maudlin speech about his wife's cloth coat and his little dog Checkers that retrieved his career. They remembered his tears on that occasion and the vitriolic comment after his loss of the California governorship, "You won't have Nixon to kick around anymore." And so, fifteen years before the so-called character issue decimated the ranks of presidential candidates in 1987—with Biden's plagiarism and Hart's adultery—the character issue plagued Richard Nixon and generated a campaign of particularly nasty humor.

Said one Washington correspondent of Nixon's maudlin sentimentality: "When Nixon read an article on his boyhood years, he cried for two hours. They spelt his name wrong." Reflecting on his sore loser speech after the gubernatorial loss, one reporter cracked, "Nixon sent a very sportsmanlike message to Kennedy conceding the '60 election. He wrote,

'WARMLY CONGRATULATE YOU ON YOUR WELL-EARNED VIC-TORY AND CHARGE FRAUD IN ILLINOIS, MARYLAND, AND TEXAS.'" A wire service reporter said he had heard how Nixon deals with pressure. "He has a little trick when the tension is too great. He closes his eyes and people can't see him." To protestations that power had mellowed the old campaigner and there was a "new Nixon," the correspondent for a British daily remarked, "Is there a new Nixon? Absolutely. The old Nixon was sly and opportunistic. The new Nixon is just the opposite. Opportunistic and sly." The view of Nixon as a loner spawned other jokes. Said one San Francisco monologist: "I hear a lot of talk that Nixon doesn't have any friends. That's absurd. He has a lot of friends. In fact, he recently went on a lengthy tour visiting all his friends. And since the weather was good, he walked." Mocking the imperial adornments that Nixon had brought to the White House during his first term, a correspondent, looking ahead to 1976, said, "One wonders whether Nixon will make Agnew his successor. Probably not. White House insiders say that when Nixon leaves office, he's planning to take the United States with him." David Frost summed up Nixon's personality problems with the sardonic observation: "President Kennedy proved that a man could not be prevented from being President simply because he was a Catholic. Nixon went him one better. He proved that a man could not be prevented from becoming president simply because he was Richard Nixon."

Nixon ran for reelection by citing the accomplishments of his first term, and none had more luster than his opening to Red China. Inevitably, some American president would have recognized the reality of China and established relations with that most populous state, but to his credit, that president was Richard Nixon. It was a laudable achievement, especially for a man who had spent a lifetime vilifying the communist Chinese and slandering the opposition party for "losing China." But even this extraordinary icebreaking brought laughter in certain circles. Roy Kammerman created a book of captioned photos that kidded Nixon's China trip unmercifully. Said another humorist: "What is Nixon's position on Red China? He is opposed to their admission to the Diners Club. And what is his position on the Great Wall? No handball playing."

Given his lifetime of exertions as a professional Communist-hater, it was hard for the public to accept Nixon's conversion to detente—just as Reagan's infatuation with Mikhail Gorbachev was a crash cut from his "evil empire" orations. The voters of 1972 asked with strained credulity: Does Richard Nixon really want improved relations with the Russians? Sometimes the answer was sardonic. Said a Manhattan nightclub comedian: "I believe Nixon does want better relations with the Russians. I hear he's planning a trip to the Soviet Union to cement relations. The State Department has worked out an extremely fair exchange with the Russians. The Soviets say that if we send Nixon there, they'll send him back."

There was a whiff of arrogance about Richard Nixon that triggered campaign attack. A correspondent wrote to *Ramparts* magazine: "I hear that Mr. Nixon is deeply sympathetic to Israel's national aspirations. I understand he is planning to provide Israel with an important new irrigation project. He'll shortly go to Tel Aviv to smite a rock with a rod."

Another allusion to the Nixon pomposity zeroed in on his work habits. It was said that the presidency had not made him the least bit pretentious. His workday was just what it had always been. "For example," said one White House wag, "this past week he worked at his desk for six days, and on the seventh day he rested."

Others thought Nixon had little to be arrogant about. Said novelist Peter De Vries: "I used to think that Nixon was deep. But now I see that deep down he's shallow." There was a cold quality about Nixon. His apparent remoteness to the needy prompted the witticism: "'What are the things closest to Nixon's heart?' 'His lungs.'" Nixon's political foes assumed that he was indifferent to the plight of the poor, in America and elsewhere around the globe—despite the fact that he had certainly not grown up in affluence. Said TV commentator Lindsay Gardner: "Nixon is deeply concerned about the area of the world where the streets are crowded with teeming masses and where men struggle to escape the bonds of misery and ignorance. San Clemente."

Hubert Humphrey said that a government must be judged by how it treats those in the dawn of life, its children; those in the twilight of life, its elderly; and those in the shadows of life, its poor and disabled. Nixon's fancied callousness, said some, extended to those in the twilight of life. The preoccupation of Kennedy, Johnson, and Humphrey with the aged was well documented. George McGovern had spoken passionately about his plans for the elderly. But Nixon had been mute. One D.C. satirist cracked: "Have you heard about Nixon's amendment to the Medicare Act? If you're over sixty-five and you need an operation but you can't afford it, the doctors retouch your X-rays."

If Richard Nixon was perceived to be indifferent to the plight of the poor, the homeless, and the elderly, his attitude toward the jobless was also in question in the campaign of 1972. Said one Democratic critic: "Oh yes, Nixon cares about the unemployed. He's put hundreds of computers to work to analyze the data and find a solution to the problem of five million unemployed. In a few weeks, these computers can do the work of five million men working for years."

Nixon had taken office in 1969 with a pledge that he had a "secret plan" to end the war in Vietnam, but four years later, as American campuses and cities continued to explode with fury, the war ground on. McGovern called for the instant withdrawal of U.S. forces from Southeast Asia, while Nixon and his secretary of state, Dr. Henry Kissinger, continued to seek an elusive "peace with honor." This situation spawned a black humor among the country's satirists. The following exchange brought gallows laughter at a cabaret in Los Angeles:

"Nixon failed to fulfill his election pledge to stop the war, end the killing, suspend the draft, and bring peace to America. What excuse does he have for this?"
"He didn't say positively."

A west coast improvisational group picked repeatedly at the scab of American dismay at the Vienam War. In one sardonic sketch, two citizens discuss their views:

"Do you think Nixon really wants to get out of Vietnam?"
"Absolutely. He's seen this war first hand. He's been a witness to the dirtiest kind of guerilla warfare imaginable—

107

sniping, stabbing, and sadistic barbarism. So now he's ready for the 1972 election campaign."

The chief instrument of Nixon's peace-seeking efforts was Henry Kissinger, a man with all the sparkling wit that Nixon and the Haldeman-Ehrlichman team lacked. On one of his trips to Southeast Asia that sought a negotiated peace, Kissinger's security escort picked up rumors of a plot to kidnap the secretary of state and hold him for ransom. Kissinger's favorite Secret Service man was Walter Busby. Speaking of the feared kidnapping attempt to the head of the Secret Service, Kissinger said in his ripe German accent: "I love Valter. I asked Valter vat he vould do in the event they tried to kidnap me. And Valter said, 'Don't vorry, Mr. Secretary, ve von't let them take you alive.'"

Nixon's detractors often found food for mockery in his frequent invocations of his wife, Pat. There was something unctuous and manipulative in his cloying proclamations on her virtue and loyalty and the perennial pluralizing of the president ("Pat and I are happy to be here in Cleveland," for example). Alluding to the president's apparent waffling on a certain issue, one comic said, "They say Nixon is vacillating. It's not true. Nixon doesn't vacillate. He has been standing pat . . . There's the children to consider." Referring to Nixon's propensity for trumpeting the achievements of his administration, one McGovern aide cracked, "Pat Nixon doesn't want any more children. With Nixon around, she can always hear the patter of little feats." And comedy writer George Foster said, "Nixon has hedged against defeat in 1972. He just put the White House in Pat's name." Reflecting on Mrs. Nixon's contribution to her husband's success, one political observer wrote, "Pat Nixon proves the truth of the old saying that behind every successful man is a very surprised woman."

Nixon made his wife the object of some of his awkward attempts at spontaneous humor. When a crowd of supporters at the GOP convention began to chant, "We want Pat!" Nixon grinned and said, "You can't have her. I've got to keep her." Keep her he did, and often he used her in a uxorious fashion that set one's teeth on edge. In greeting the convention in Miami that was more like a coronation, he said, "Mr. President and Pat—because she is the First Lady of the land, but I think in the hearts of all of us she is 'Pat,' and we are just going to take advantage of it and keep it that way." In a speech at San Diego airport, Nixon thanked Art Linkletter, who was campaigning with him, and made Pat Nixon the subject of some atypical ribald humor. Said Nixon: "When Art Linkletter talks about having breakfast . . . with Pat, I just want to keep the record straight. He has slept in the White House. He slept in the Queen's Room. When Pat's room is being painted, she sleeps in there, so you could say that Art Linkletter has slept in Pat's bed."

The campaign of 1972 also saw a healthy outpouring of humor at the expense of Nixon's running mate, Vice President Spiro Agnew. If there was talk of a "new Nixon" and an "old Nixon," almost as dramatic was the political restyling of Spiro Agnew for the 1972 campaign. The new, refurbished Agnew had undergone a dramatic transformation. Gone were the alliterations and personal epithets that had brought rage from the media and the liberals at whom they were directed all through the first Nixon-Agnew term. Jeff MacNelly, the witty editorial cartoonist of the *Richmond News-Leader*, mocked the Agnew metamorphosis by picturing the Veep's tombstone. On it were some of the scathing words with which he had excoriated his enemies: EFFETE SNOBS, NATTERING NABOBS OF NEGATIVISM, VICARS OF VACILLATION, RADICLIBS, TROGLO-DYTE LEFTISTS, HOPELESS, HYSTERICAL HYPOCHONDRIACS OF HISTORY. That was the preelection year wit of Spiro Agnew, entombed for the duration of the campaign.

Agnew still drew his share of gibes from the press he had so often wounded. One reporter reflected on the way Nixon had chosen Agnew as his running mate. "I don't know exactly how Nixon chose Agnew, but it certainly cured him of making decisions during a total eclipse." A reporter for the *Miami Herald* reflected wryly that Agnew had a dedicated following in the southern and western states. "If something happens to Agnew, Georgia and Arizona light up." One TV network adviser, musing on Agnew's use of invective, remarked that the candidate's televised speeches should be followed by a half hour of tetanus shots. A Manhattan cabaret comedian took a swipe at Agnew by declaring, fictitiously of course, that First Lady Pat Nixon had led a committee to beautify America. "She went about Washington planting tulips and hollyhocks. And Agnew provided the fertilizer." Some of the Veep's detractors focused on his modest intellectual gifts. Said one member of the press corps, paying sarcastic tribute to the onetime Maryland governor: "Agnew has a quick mind. He can seize the nub of a complex problem immediately. He recently attended a Cabinet meeting where a thorny problem of defense planning was being discussed. It took Agnew only thirty seconds to see a solution, and three hours to find his way back to his office."

If Agnew abandoned his inflammatory rhetoric during the 1972 campaign, he did not abandon his corrosive wit altogether. The more restrained Agnew twitted Sargent Shriver, the Democratic candidate in the Veepstakes, on his personal wealth. Shriver was Jack Kennedy's brother-in-law, and between his own wealth and that of his wife, Eunice Kennedy Shriver, his affluence was considerable. Said Agnew: "My opponent says he knows what it means to be poor. He says 'When I was a kid, my father had eight hungry mouths to feed. My mother and me and six polo ponies.'" Agnew returned to the theme of Shriver's wealth with a fictional story of Agnew and Shriver growing up together in Maryland. "I have vivid memories," said Agnew, "of little Sarge when we'd play hide-and-seek. I'd hide and he'd put a private detective on retainer to go out and find me." There has been a long-standing argument between those who favor finding our presidents among the rich and those who would look for them among the poor. Say the cynics: "Why let the rich run the country? It's enough that they *own* the country." The activism of wealthy presidents like Franklin Roosevelt and John F. Kennedy argues for the virtue of wealth. Richard Nixon's and Spiro Agnew's histories do not support the values of a humble boyhood; one resigned in disgrace, and the other stood accused of accepting bribes in the vice presidential office.

On occasion, the combative Agnew wit would surface under the provocation of the campaign trail. In Tampa hecklers interrupted his standard stump speech. "I'll wait a minute," said Agnew acidly, "to see whether some sort of catatonic reaction will set in—or a freezing of the vocal cords."

Editorial cartoonists had a field day with the pompous, posturing Agnew. Chief among his tormentors was Pat Oliphant, one of America's premier political artists, who came to America from Australia in 1964 to replace Paul Conrad at the *Denver Post*, when Conrad moved on to the *Los Angeles Times*. Art Buchwald called Oliphant "a threat to the American political system. His irreverent cartoons . . . are dangerous because they make people think while they make them laugh." Buchwald's praise was a splendid definition of all the best of America's political writers and cartoonists, preeminently Buchwald himself.

When Richard Nixon announced that Agnew was his choice for vice president, Oliphant pictured Agnew as a complacent lap dog being stroked by Richard Nixon. In his portrayal, the dog's neck is circled by a spiked collar, and on its face reflects obedience and adoration for its master. (The lap dog metaphor seemed felicitous for a vice president. Fifteen years later, in a scathing column excoriating Vice President George Bush's cheerleader image, George Will compared him to a lap dog. Bush confirmed the metaphor by praising George Will as a man whose opinion he respected!) Seizing on the campaign conversion of Agnew from vitriol to gentility, Pat Oliphant showed him in flowing robes, a dove in his hand, a halo atop his head. A disturbed Nixon is watching "the New Agnew" and saying, "Are you trying to make me look shabby?" And Oliphant's ubiquitous duck in a corner of the strip, is saying, "Saint Spiro??"

One of the chief targets of mockery that Nixon endured in 1972 had little to do with him but with the antics of his attorney general's wife, the inimitable Martha Mitchell. Martha was a garrulous, ebullient lady who brought the Nixon administration some of its most spontaneous moments. ("Is Richard Nixon outspoken?" asked one beltway wit. "Only by Martha Mitchell.") Martha's eccentric pronouncements, and her habit of secretly phoning Helen Thomas of the Associated Press from the seclusion of her bathroom, captured the attention and the funny bone of the public. Her declarations were quoted throughout the 1972 campaign for their humor, intentional and otherwise. Here are some of Martha Mitchell's spontaneities:

I'm little Martha Mitchell. . . . No rhyme or reason why I have to withhold my thoughts.

Man has been given his freedom to a greater extent than ever, and that's quite wrong.

Dignity and formality have completely gone from New York.

Margaret Mead caused a lot of the trouble. She advocates taking drugs and early marriage. She and those other spooks just want to get their names in the paper.

My family worked for everything we had. We even have a deed from the King of England for property in South Carolina. Now these jerks come along and try to give it to the Communists.

I have a wonderful concept of President Nixon. He'll kill me when I say it, but it's almost a fatherly love, that's how I think of him.

I love to do devilish things.

I don't think the average American realizes how desperate it is when a group of demonstrators, not peaceful demonstrators, but the very liberal Communists, move into Washington.

I can't get over saying "colored." I said it all my life. All the Negroes seem to resent it and I don't know why.

I'm calling from the bathroom upstairs so John won't hear me. . . .

Had the Democratic party or the American people realized the significance and implications of the Watergate break-in when it occurred in the midst of the 1972 presidential campaign, Nixon might not have made mincemeat of challenger George McGovern. With the virtue of 20-20 hindsight it seems manifest that when five men with electronic equipment, paid by the Republicans, were arrested at gunpoint in the dead of night in the Democratic national headquarters, it was not a matter to be dismissed with a joke and a shrug. Nonetheless, that is very nearly all that the party was able to make of it.

President Nixon dismissed it as "a bizarre incident," press secretary Ron Ziegler called it "a third-rate burglary," and America's comics laughed it away. Perhaps the Vietnam War had
created a moral exhaustion with its slaughter of naked peas-
ants, so that a break-in and a bugging met with an ethical vacuum, an attitude of "Well, that's politics." It was only after the
Democratic debacle of November 7, in which Nixon received
60.7 percent of the popular votes and swept forty-nine states,
that the disintegration of the Nixon landslide began. First,
Spiro Agnew resigned in disgrace, under attack for income
tax evasion; then came Sam Ervin, Howard Baker, Woodward
& Bernstein, and reports of bribery, perjury, forgery, and
dirty tricks.

In the midst of Nixon's Watergate shame, Al Franken
and Tom Davis of "Saturday Night Live" pilloried Nixon unmercifully. They found his sins sensational fodder for their
burn-and-slash wit. They had hammered away at Nixon all
through the 1972 campaign, and now, with Nixon on the
ropes, they delivered a satiric knockout punch. It was a sketch
based on the Woodward & Bernstein bestseller, *The Final Days.*
"Saturday Night's" producer, Lorne Michaels, had written an
introduction to the Franken-Davis sketch that he himself
would deliver. The preface ultimately remained undelivered,
but it reflects the show's distaste for Nixon so well that it de-
serves to be reproduced, at least in part. Some will find it malicious, others amusing, but for better or worse, it reflected the
counterculture's animus for Richard Nixon. Said the producer
in his undelivered introduction:

> Hi. I'm Lorne Michaels. As producer of this show, I make
> weighty decisions every day. Today I had to make the toughest
> decision of my career: whether or not to ridicule Richard
> Nixon one more time. . . . It would be too easy to make light of
> a man who hasn't slept with his wife for fourteen years . . . and
> [to suggest] that Nixon and Bebe Rebozo are having a homosex-
> ual affair has no place on network television.

The Franken-Davis sketch was presented in the form of
a Pat Nixon diary recalling the highlights of her husband's
presidential career. Dan Ackroyd played Nixon, and John Be-

lushi did a gutteral impression of Henry Kissinger. When the skit opened, Pat Nixon, played by guest host Madeline Kahn, has been nipping at the cooking sherry and is recalling the final days of her husband's presidency. In these Final Days of "Saturday's Night's" invention, Nixon is talking bitterly to a portrait of Lincoln, complaining, "Well, Abe, you were lucky. They *shot* you." Chevy Chase played the chuckleheaded David Eisenhower, and Gilda Radnor played his wife, Julie. Nixon remarks acidly to an aide that his son-in-law "looks like Howdy Doody." Nixon is obsessed with the other men who had lived in the White House. Later in the sketch he turns to a painting of Jack Kennedy and shouts, "You! Kennedy. You looked so good all the time. They're gonna find out about you too. The president having sex with women within these very walls!" says Nixon with distaste. "That's never happened when Dick Nixon was in the White House. Never! Never! Never!" It will be noted that the "Saturday Night" comic perception of Richard Nixon tended to a preoccupation with the genitals, but, in the year 1972, and the year of Nixon's disgrace that followed, the show and its youthful creators were at the center of a ribald revolution in a cynical and divided country.

Out of the unsavory revelations of Watergate, Bantam published a book which for a brief period threatened to outsell the Bible. It was called *The Watergate Follies* and served to chronicle the scandal in a more frivolous manner than did the Woodward and Bernstein books. *The Watergate Follies* consisted of a group of news photos of the felonious participants in the Watergate fiasco, with dialogic balloons putting words in the mouths of the miscreants. Here are some of them:

Nixon to the public in a televised address: "Political espionage, burglaries, wiretapping, campaigning disruption, illegal use of funds—okay, so we made a mistake."

H. R. Haldeman sits beside Nixon on Air Force One, pointing to a map in the President's lap. Says Haldeman: "This would be a good place to jump."

Nixon addresses a group of aides on the break-in: "Now, let's get our stories straight. Henry, you were in Paris—"

Nixon to the White House press corps: "Are you going to believe me or the facts?"

A stunned Frank Sinatra to Richard Nixon: "You want me to sing at the Impeachment?"

President Nixon to his economic advisers as they sit in a semicircle about his Oval Office desk: "That's very interesting, Arthur, would you mind repeating it into this inkwell?"

Queen Elizabeth to the Shah of Iran in her opulent carriage: "Yes, Mr. Nixon once visited me. He took a spoon."

Nixon to his military chiefs: "The public is clamoring for the truth about Watergate. There's only one thing to do. Start a war."

Pat Nixon to Martha Mitchell: "My husband gives his all for the people and what does he get?" Martha: "Ten to twenty."

An apparently tranquil Nixon at a state dinner, to the woman on his left: "Try the Impeach Melba."

Nixon writing solemnly in his diary: "My seventh crisis began slowly . . ."

Nixon taking the presidential oath of office: "And defend most of the Constitution . . ."

Nixon to Israeli prime minister, Golda Meir: "I've resigned in disgrace, my friends ignore me, my aides are in prison. What should I do?" Golda Meir: "Have a piece of fruit."

There was a delicious subtlety to the humor of cartoonist Garry Trudeau. When it was learned that Nixon had ordered the secret, unlawful bombing of Cambodia, Trudeau pictured a conversation between the president and White House chief of staff Al Haig:

NIXON. What is it, Haig?

HAIG. Sir, it's about the House hearings on the recent Cambodian bombings. We need to know more about the raids, sir. They say nobody but you knows about them.

NIXON. It's not true. I told everybody who had a need or a right to know.

HAIG. Yes, sir, but who? You've got to be more specific.

NIXON. Well, let me see . . . The pilots, of course.

In another fictional exchange between Nixon and Haig, the president is about to make a TV address to the nation.

NIXON. Call props and tell them to bring over some more Lincoln visuals—a bust, etchings, anything.

HAIG. Mr. President, with all due respect, sir, I think you've just about gone the limit on comparisons of yourself with Lincoln.

NIXON. You think so? Hmm. Maybe you're right, Al.

HAIG. It *would* be the fifth time, sir . . .

NIXON. It's just that I can't *get over* all the parallels.

HAIG. It *is* eerie, sir.

Like Trudeau, Jules Feiffer exposed for us the political vagaries and vulgarities of our time, and he seemed at his best during the Nixon years. "He was a turd, a wonderful turd for a cartoonist," said Feiffer. "From his Checkers speech to his 'You won't have Nixon to kick around anymore' speech to his farewell to the White House staff speech, he was a genius of the second-rate. The Mozart of mediocrity." Feiffer found Nixon a wonderful subject for his satiric pen. "His unintegrated parts invited endless comment," wrote Feiffer. "Uneasy head atop wind-up toy body. Nothing on Nixon fit right."

116

Feiffer observed that during the 1972 campaign Nixon never quite relaxed: "There were no shirtsleeve photos, even his strolls on the beach were in full dress. I am sure that, naked, he wore knee socks; in the shower, boxer shorts . . . He was our favorite Dick joke, but the joke was on us."

Certainly, the joke was on Nixon when Jules Feiffer put his talented pen to paper to illuminate Nixon's character flaws. As the election year of 1972 began, Feiffer pictured the president on Christmas Eve in a nightgown, holding a candle aloft, speaking to Santa.

NIXON. What did you buy me for '72?

SANTA. More inflation . . . Higher unemployment . . . A stagnant economy . . . The same old war . . . And a disastrous election campaign.

[Nixon bursts into tears.]

NIXON. And you call yourself Santa Claus?

SANTA. And you call yourself President?

Chapter 8
Campaign 1972
The 1000 Percent Populist

It's as if McGovern had a death wish. He makes so
many mistakes that it's hard for us to get a mistake in
edgewise.
—NIXON AIDE

When the debacle of the 1972 presidential campaign
was behind him, Senator George S. McGovern of South Da-
kota whispered in the ear of a Senate colleague: "Three things
beat me. Dirty tricks, tapped phones, and I lost forty-nine
states." At any rate, those were the words one satirist attributed to the populist campaigner.

McGovern's critical problem was reviving his eroded
reputation for honesty after the opening events of his hapless
campaign. He had chosen Senator Tom Eagleton of Missouri
as his running mate without realizing that Eagleton had undergone electric shock treatment for mental depression on numerous occasions. When the revelations came, as they inevitably did, McGovern announced that he backed his running
mate "1000 percent," which made the candidate's subsequent
turnabout doubly embarrassing. Eagleton's distress was the
subject of numberless satiric barbs, not all of them tasteless.
Said one comic: "Tom Eagleton has a lot of troubles in his
head but there's nothing in it." Said another: "A shock treatment is what Eagleton is giving McGovern." At least one Dem-

119

ocratic leader, Julian Bond, tried feebly to laugh the matter away. Casting a sardonic eye on Nixon's running mate, the bombastic Spiro Agnew, Bond said, "At least we know ours had *treatment*." But the issue would not go away. *Esquire* magazine, in its 1972 annual "Dubious Achievement Awards," pictured a glowing Tom Eagleton for its major award, which traditionally mocks egregious excess. The headline read: WE SUPPORT TOM EAGLETON ONE THOUSAND PERCENT, WE THINK. *Esquire* pointed out that Eagleton had purchased five thousand McGovern-Eagleton buttons, two thousand bumper stickers, and two thousand lapel pins, a fact to which *Esquire* responded, "Awwww." McGovern's aides came in for their share of comedic abuse for not scrupulously examining Eagleton's past. Said one Nixon aide in ridiculing McGovern's staff work: "They weren't thorough. They were the sort of guys who, if they were putting together a TV special with Ted Knight and Doris Day, would call it 'The Ted and Doris Show.'"

When Eagleton withdrew under pressure from media and party, McGovern cast about for a replacement. He settled on Sargent Shriver, who had headed the Kennedy Peace Corps and carried some of the charisma of the New Frontier. Like his presidential brother-in-law, Shriver knew the value of humor in campaigning. He launched a sardonic assault on Richard Nixon, right down to impressions of Nixon's gravelly voice. He startled and amused 1,200 students at a college in Las Vegas by doing an imitation of Nixon's acceptance speech at the GOP's Miami convention. Though the impression did not quite rival Rich Little, it brought laughter to the campus throng. Shriver straightened himself with a mock self-righteousness that was Nixon's trademark, tucked in his chin, and deepened his voice. "I believe in the American system," Shriver growled, and the young audience hooted joyously.

Many were called before Shriver was chosen. Indeed, faced with the likelihood of an ignominious loss, no one was very anxious to take up the cup that Eagleton had laid down. McGovern experienced such difficulty in finding a vice presidential stand-in for Tom Eagleton that one U.S. senator asked him, "George, does the law actually *require* that you have a Vice President?" Shriver promoted himself for the job, over the opposition of the Kennedy family, who disliked seeing the Camelot legacy squandered on a lost cause. The Kennedys are accustomed to winning. Shriver, in fact, was deep on the list of those asked to replace Eagleton, but he made a joke of his discomfort, saying, "I am not embarrassed to be George McGovern's seventh choice for Vice President. Pity Mr. Nixon— his first and only choice was Spiro Agnew." Along the campaign trail, Shriver augmented his Nixon impersonation with jokes that invoked the Kennedy years. He told one group of parents how he had motivated his own children to be more diligent students. "I told them when Lincoln was your age he walked twelve miles to school every day. But my son said, 'That's nothing. When Uncle Jack was your age, he was President.'"

In 1972 numerous democrats were straying from the party. Many saw McGovern as embracing hippies, feminists, and petulant collegians. They blanched at his views on gays, abortions, and amnesty for Vietnam deserters. With the Democratic party painfully split, Shriver tried to laugh away the schism. He quoted Will Rogers, who said, "I am not a member of an organized political party—I am a Democrat."

The great gummy issue of the Watergate caper clung to the Nixon campaign. Each day new information came to light confirming the existence of a well-organized Republican plan to defame the Democratic campaign through espionage and a variety of illegal and immoral devices. But incredibly, McGovern and Shriver were unable to turn the burgeoning scandal into votes. McGovern tried manfully to mock Nixon for the excesses of his election aides. Speaking to one audience he said, "A President who will send saboteurs inside the Democratic ranks is the kind of man who won't hesitate to wiretap your union, your law office, your university, your church or even your home." McGovern tried to turn the Watergate bugging apparatus into strategic humor. At the annual Al Smith charity dinner in New York, McGovern quipped, "I'm sorry President Nixon can't be with us tonight. But I'm sure that somewhere he's listening in."

The fumbles of the McGovern staff seemed to frustrate him more than anything the GOP could produce. Campaign director Gary Hart, who would one day see his own campaign aborted, quipped that the squabbles of the staff were "like reports of Mark Twain's death—greatly exaggerated." But the infighting was real. One of McGovern's key aides, Representative Frank Thomson, returned from a trip to learn that money he had raised for voter registration had been spent by Gary Hart for some other purpose entirely. Cracked Thomson of his diminished status: "If I had wanted to be a linebacker, I would have tried out for the Washington Redskins." There was black humor about the disarray of the hydra-headed McGovern team. "What we need," quipped a bitter campaign aide, "is one man in charge with a big black whip!"

The Miami convention that nominated Richard Nixon and Spiro Agnew had little drama or excitement. Nixon joked defensively about its utter predictability. "Those people," said Nixon, "who said that what took place in Miami was unexciting because we knew how it was going to turn out . . . well, I have never seen a John Wayne movie that was unexciting because you knew he was going to get the bad guy in the end." Yet *Newsweek* magazine called the GOP convention "The Dick & Spiro Show (Rerun)," with an eye to its planning as a scripted extravaganza. PBS covered the event with Bill Moyers, a former adviser to Lyndon Johnson. Moyers supplied a witty moment in discussing the event with *New Yorker* columnist Elizabeth Drew. When a dispute arose over allocation of delegates, Drew said, "Well, they're in power. Did you ever see anyone give up power?" "Once," said Moyers succinctly.

The Nixon nominating convention was laughably unspontaneous. The only moment of unrehearsed humor came when Sammy Davis, Jr. darted forward with a camera. A startled Nixon joshed, "Are you trying to shoot me in the back?" "No," said Davis, "I'm covering the convention for *Jet* magazine." The McGovern convention could have used a little of the Republican's stage management. Joked one party professional about McGovern's free-floating campaign staff: "That crowd could screw up a horseshoe tournament!" When Tom Eagleton refused to resign from the ticket despite revelations of his past shock therapy, it seemed to climax McGovern's opening night troubles. *Washington Post* cartoonist Herblock captured the situation with a drawing of a distraught Democratic donkey behind a desk at McGovern headquarters, head in hand. Strewn across the desk are papers covering the litany of campaign woes: POLLS, DEBTS, CONVENTION BATTLE. The Donkey is on the phone, saying, "Yeah, Tom—sure—uh-huh."

In his acceptance speech, George McGovern tried to put his problems behind him. Referring to the disintegrating Democratic ranks, he cracked, "Never underestimate the power of Richard Nixon to bring harmony to Democratic ranks." His gibe was less than prophetic. McGovern continued his grave-yard humor by declaring, "We are going to help Mr. Nixon redeem the pledge he made ten years ago—that you won't have Richard Nixon to kick around anymore." McGovern's speech was in part the product of Frank Mankiewicz, a witty member of the dynastic Mankiewicz family of Hollywood (Joe had written *All About Eve;* Herman wrote *Citizen Kane*). Frank Mankiewicz had been press secretary to Bobby Kennedy dur-ing his Senate years and played a major role in the McGovern operation. Rumpled, likable, and low-keyed, Mankiewicz de-lighted the press with his educated wit. At a meeting of Demo-crats torn into various warring factions, Mankiewicz cracked, "Every little meaning has a movement all its own." Reporters covering the McGovern campaign would needle Mankiewicz with a parody of "Twinkle, Twinkle Little Star." As the free-form politicians lurched along the campaign trail, the news-men sang:

Mankiewicz, Mankiewicz, super star,
You're not as smart as you think you are.

Though McGovern captured his party's nomination on the first ballot, thanks to the reforms in the delegate selection process that the Democrats had adopted four years before, the party had strong misgivings about McGovern's constituency. The high visibility of homosexuals, pot-smoking college boys, and black militants formed an aggressive turnoff to many tra-ditional party members. Pat Oliphant dramatized the trauma with a cartoon picturing the Democratic donkey in a Floridian shirt and shorts, hailing a Miami taxi and muttering, "Conven-tion Hall, driver . . . and don't hurry!" When it was learned that Tom Eagleton had a history of psychiatric therapy, Oliphant recalled Spiro Agnew's rise from obscurity as Nixon's vice president. He showed an embarrassed George McGovern addressing his aides on the Eagleton gaffe: "Can we get rid of whatsisname before be becomes a household word?"

McGovern's forays on the campaign trail were less than triumphal. At times his speeches were moving, but he was unable to inject the leavening of wit that might have won him points. On those occasions when he ventured into the field of humor, he produced more animus than zeal. Before a gathering of aggressive feminists, McGovern was lauded by the jovial Liz Carpenter, former resident humorist at the Johnson White House. Acknowledging McGovern's recognition of women's rights, Liz praised the candidate by saying, "We are all here because of George McGovern." The candidate smiled and said, "The credit should go to Adam." Instead of bemused laughter, the line produced angry hisses from the feminists. McGovern gasped, "Can I recover by saying Adam and Eve?"

George McGovern's chaotic campaign and catastrophic loss in the election of 1972 were largely the result of the disaffection created by the Democratic party's noisy newcomers. Speaking before Washington's Gridiron Club, when his struggle had passed into history, McGovern looked back in laughter at his electoral debacle.

"Last year," he said, "we opened the doors of the Democratic party as we promised we would, and twenty million Democrats stalked out."

Chapter 9
Campaign 1968
The Pagliacci of Politics

I can still remember the first time I ever heard Hubert Humphrey speak. He was in the second hour of a five minute talk.
—GERALD R. FORD

There was something unalterably humorous about Hubert Horatio Humphrey, even his name. He was a warm-hearted fellow, witty, spontaneous, garrulous, ebullient, and immensely likable. He wore his black hair drawn across his bulging forehead like Paul Simon playing "The Mikado." He was loquacious to a fault. Said the *New Republic*, "He is like a mad vending machine: insert dime and you get a peanut bar, and then another, and another. There is no stopping it. It rains peanut bars." Humphrey was the prototype of the Washington bureaucrat whose son asks him about Portugal. The man brings home a ton of government pamphlets about the country and his son sighs, "Dad, that's more than I want to know about Portugal." Hubert Humphrey told you more than you wanted to know about Portugal. Or anything. He was a magnet that attracted the gibes of his peers with his bombastic speech and nonstop prolixity.

For four years he had had the unenviable task, for a man so fond of words, of keeping his mouth shut and listening to the lengthy monologues of his boss, the overbearing President Lyndon Johnson. For four long years the fragrance of Lyndon's shoe polish was fresh in Humphrey's nostrils. Humphrey was probably the most maligned of vice presidents since Alexander Throttlebottom, the ineffectual Veep in *Of Thee I Sing*. In that George S. Kaufman–George Gershwin musical comedy, the president tells his vice president to stay out of sight. "Well," says Throttlebottom, "I guess I could go back to my old job." "What was that?" asks the president. "I was a hermit," says Throttlebottom.

Humphrey would have made a poor hermit. He was too gregarious. Said Mark Russell: "When the TV camera was on Hubert, he would never be caught alone. He was always shaking hands with someone. If need be he would shake hands with a plant." It often seemed that even Humphrey's most ardent admirers would end up mocking him unintentionally. When Jimmy Carter accepted the Democratic presidential nomination in 1976, he said, "We must all pay tribute to Hubert Horatio Hornblower . . . uh, Humphrey."

Humphrey was a man of considerable ability, but in the burgeoning age of television, when the electorate sought a man who was larger than life—a Kennedy, a Johnson, or a Reagan—Humphrey was no master of majesty. Ironically, Humphrey seized the presidential nomination in the very year when a TV show called "Laugh-In" seized the public fancy. They were at opposite ends of the communicative spectrum. "Laugh-In" spoke in quick, frenetic news bites, sharp and crisp, acknowledging the public's shortened attention span. Humphrey spoke in voluminous sentences that taxed the patience of the most attentive listener.

True, Humphrey's mind was exemplary, with "the retentive capacity of a sponge." Men with less imagination and liberal instincts would appropriate his ideas and assume the credit for them. Food stamps and the Peace Corps were two of the great ideas of the mid-century. Both were Humphrey's conceptions, and both were executed by other men who received the credit for their creation. Humphrey recalled to mind the hapless screenwriter in Budd Schulberg's Hollywood novel of mendacity, *What Makes Sammy Run?* Sammy Glick has the aggression and chutzpah to seize better men's ideas and ride the cyclone of success to the top. Humphrey was the victim of the political Sammy Glicks. A Washington comic remarked that Humphrey was the sort of man who would "buy a pumpkin farm the year they cancelled Halloween." Then he added, "Hubert visited the Grand Canyon, but it was closed."

This dust bowl liberal was a plain and humble soul. He would never yield to pomposity and take himself too seriously. He was able to join the throngs in laughing at himself. When he sought the presidency in 1960, running head-to-head with the moneyed aristocracy of Jack Kennedy in the primaries, Hubert was clearly outmatched—in dollars, staff and kin. As Stephen Sondheim wrote in his Broadway musical, *Merrily We Roll Along*, a takeoff on the Kennedy assault on the presidency:

> There's Bobby and Jackie and Jack
> And myriads more in the back—
> There's Ethel and Teddy and Pat alone
> Plus Eunice and Peter and Jean and Joan

Humphrey had the wit and self-deprecating humor to laugh at his travail, that being the only thing he could to do about it. With the Kennedy battalions arrayed against him, Hubert said,

> The whole Kennedy family had talent in depth. No newspaper publishers knew my father. Sargent Shriver was the head of the Merchandise Mart; I was head of Humphrey's Drug Store . . . And what's glamorous about the name Humphrey? I'm not glamorous per se. I'm not young. I'm not old. I'm like the girl next door—always available but you don't think about marriage.

Humphrey was a compulsive talker. The way an alcoholic drinks, Humphrey talked. There was not a subject on which Humphrey did not have a few thousand well-chosen words. He laughed at his own volubility. "I *like* every subject," he laughed. "I can't help it—it's *glands*."

When Lyndon Johnson tormented his Veep, as he did all his other subordinates in the White House, Humphrey had the grace to laugh off his own petty humiliations. "Hubert!" LBJ barked during one legislative breakfast. "I tried to get hold of you yesterday. Where the hell were you!" Humphrey swiveled his huge head and smiled slyly. "Try the other cheek, Mr. President," he said.

But Humphrey's self-deprecation did little to discourage others from ridiculing him. It is an unfortunate fact of political life that self-deprecation is no guarantee of insulation against the mockery of others. Jerry Ford discovered that when he kidded his own clumsiness the mockery continued. Ford was irrigating the ridicule, not drowning it. Ironically, it was Jerry Ford who was one of the most perennial gagsters with Humphrey as target. At the Gridiron Club, where Washington's newsmen pay self-proclaimed tribute to their own eminence, Humphrey and Ford once attended, representing their respective parties. Ford produced laughter at Humphrey's expense when he said:

> Nat Finney [president of the Gridiron] told me how it would go tonight. He said first he'd give a little talk, and next I'd give a little talk, and then Humphrey would follow. I said, "Who follows Humphrey?" He said, "Hardly anybody."

On another occasion, when Ford and Humphrey shared the same podium, Ford confessed to the audience, "I couldn't find my program, so I leaned over to the man sitting next to me and asked, "What follows Hubert Humphrey?" He looked at his watch, then he looked at me and said, "Christmas."

Hubert Humphrey was one of the few public figures who was so vulnerable to comic reproach that a fellow politician could devote a five-minute routine to his eccentricities and never be disappointed in the response. He was that reliable a target. At one press banquet where Ford was the guest speaker and Humphrey was not present, Ford's address was interrupted by the ringing of a telephone. Public figures rarely do "prop jokes," it being considered beneath the dignity of their office. But in this case Gerald Ford thought the subject justified the prop. A telephone had been placed by the microphone. Ford picked up the receiver. "Hello? . . . Hubert! . . . Uh-huh . . . uh-huh . . . uh-huh." Ford picked up his pipe, loaded it with tobacco, and retrieved the receiver. "Uh-huh. . . ." He lit the pipe, puffed it contentedly, and returned to the phone. "Uh-huh . . . uh-huh . . . Goodbye, Hubert . . . Goodbye, Hubert . . . Goodbye, Hubert." Ford finally hung up the receiver with a sigh and turned to the audience, which by now was convulsed with laughter. "That was Hubert," said Ford. "He just wanted to say hello."

Much of Ford's good-natured raillery at Humphrey's expense was the product of Bob Orben, Ford's resident humorist who found Humphrey's loquacity a constant source of humor. Just as novelist Herman Wouk, in his early days as a gag writer for Fred Allen, found Jack Benny's thrift a surefire source of comedy for his boss, Humphrey's tendency to gab was a golden target for Ford at the various press dinners he addressed. Speaking at the Alfalfa Club, Ford praised his hosts on their wit. "I know you haven't lost your sense of humor," he said, "just by looking at the time schedule they gave me for this dinner . . . '9:50—Candidate's acceptance speech. Hubert Humphrey responds—*briefly*.'"

But Ford recognized Humphrey's wit and acknowledged it on the occasion when he and Hubert were both invited to deliver humorous monologues before a media audience. Said Ford: "Why did I ever say I want to speak here tonight? Matching me against Hubert Humphrey for laughs is like putting Twiggy against Zsa Zsa Gabor."

The writers on "That Was the Week That Was (TW3)," the sixties TV program of political satire, found humor in Humphrey's bombastic sounding name. President Johnson had just announced in his ineffable egoism that any baby who was named after him would be given a steer from the Johnson ranch. Cracked a TW3 writer: "Any baby given the name of Hubert Horatio will also be given a prize—a choice between psychiatric therapy and boxing lessons."

Vice President Hubert Humphrey was surprised to find himself the Democratic nominee in 1968. The nomination should have gone to President Lyndon Baines Johnson, with Humphrey, at best, the loyal running mate. But Johnson's popularity had plunged as the casualty figures rose in Vietnam. Lyndon Johnson and the Democrats had squandered the huge mandate they received four years before. In 1968 the war hung over the election like a thunderclap, ultimately forcing LBJ to make his stunning declaration: "I shall not seek and will not accept the nomination of my party for another term." Johnson's abdication had been long in coming. He had turned the full force of his power, office, and earthy humor on the critics of the war. "I feel like a mongrel bitch assaulted by a pack of males," he gibed. "If I run they chew my tail off. If I hunker down they fuck me to death." Senator William Fulbright, chairman of the Foreign Relations Committee, led the flight of doves in the Congress and in the press, attacking Johnson's escalation. Cracked LBJ: "I wonder if you've seen the latest announcement from the Senate Foreign Relations Committee that it is going to hold hearings on the Viet Cong. . . . They are going to start those hearings in the editorial room of the *New York Times*."

Johnson generated angry taunts wherever he went over the unending war. There were sit-ins, marches, and noisy demonstrations all through the solemn, stormy election year of 1968. The Washington press corps were among Johnson's most strident critics. Johnson often retreated to his church, followed by a pack of newsmen. He needled them by saying, "Come on in. You need this more than I do." Worship offered no escape. LBJ's minister declared in a sermon, as his presidential parishioner squirmed, "There is a general consensus that something is wrong in Vietnam . . . We ask respectfully, why?" Johnson emerged from the church wearing a grim smile that evaporated as the minister saw him to his car. Johnson nodded curtly to the man and said, "Wonderful choir."

The press kept up a drumfire of attack on Johnson all through the election year of 1968. When he attended their Gridiron Dinner and listened to the sardonic sketches and songs aimed at his flaws and foreign policy, the thin-skinned president rose and said, "I have enjoyed the skits—I think." As the projected nominee of his party, he took the occasion to launch some darts at two of the men he thought he might be facing in the upcoming election—Richard Nixon and George Romney, president of American Motors. Said LBJ: "I've been out with the troops for the last two days, and I didn't know until I got in tonight that as a result of the automobile safety regulations, The Rambler had already called in George Romney."

Referring to Romney's auto background and the old gibe about buying a used car from Richard Nixon, LBJ continued: "Ever since I ran off to California when I was a boy, and I washed cars out there for a living, that was before I ever met either Romney or Nixon. It seems like I've always been having trouble with these used car fellers."

It was a traumatic year for LBJ. Dog owners protested when he lifted his daughter's pet beagles by their ears, causing them to yelp with pain. Cracked one Washington wise guy: "Hubert Humphrey doesn't see what all the fuss is about. Johnson's been lifting him that way for years."

1968 was a year when the power of the polls gripped America as never before. A raft of media polls mirrored the public attitude to the war, to Johnson, and to the various candidates. It became a subject of humor when Washington wit Russell Baker wrote sardonically in his *New York Times* column: "Something terrible is happening to the Presidential campaign this year. It is all settled in the press before anybody has had a chance to cast a vote." *New Yorker* cartoonist James Stevenson made an amusing point about the army of polltakers who had marched across the nation. In the cartoon, a stymied poll taker sits with pencil poised over his clipboard. The voter sits on his sofa, smiling agreeably and saying, "Nixon? He's wonderful, too. They're all wonderful—wonderful, warm people, and great great Americans!"

Elliott Reid, on "That Was the Week that Was," played a persistent polltaker who showed the deficiencies of the polling process. An exchange between a polltaker and a New Hampshire voter during that closely watched primary, went like this:

VOTER. I like Rockefeller.

POLLTAKER. What about Nixon?

VOTER. He's okay, but I like Rockefeller.

POLLTAKER. But you do like Nixon.

VOTER. Sure, but I'm for Rockefeller.

POLLTAKER. Let me get this straight. You like Rockefeller but you think Nixon is okay.

VOTER. Sure. Sure. (slams door)

POLLTAKER. (marking form) Undecided.

President Johnson often carried a copy of the latest poll in his breast pocket and would brandish it to show his popularity and that of his unpopular war. But when his ratings declined, he chose to mock them and the idea that one could rule a nation by heeding them. When the press held its Gridiron Dinner at Old Williamsburg, the recreation of the colonial city, Johnson spoke there and said, "The statesmen of Williamsburg were some of our first political analysts, and it was here that a special courier first delivered the advance release which referred to Patrick Henry's private poll from his home district: '46 percent for liberty, 15 percent for death, 15 percent undecided.'" In reading his own plummeting polls and looking ahead to the fall elections, Johnson cracked, "I've been reading a lot about my own polls in the newspapers, and I'm worried it could be I've peaked too soon."

Satirist Mason Williams bent a quizzical eye on the polls in the book, *Pat Paulsen for President*. He wrote,

The polls show that only three people in the entire country would receive more votes than LBJ if the election were held today. William Jennings Bryan, Wendell Wilkie, and Dizzy Gillespie. . . . You must admit that President Johnson always hits the nail firmly with his head, and after all, it takes 53 cowboys to run the LBJ ranch and we can't expect one cowboy to run the entire country by himself.

So uncertain was the roiling election of 1968, that Russell Baker wrote a slim, amusing volume called *Our Next President*, in which he pictured a humorous and startling scenario for the forthcoming general election. Parodying the familiar style of Theodore White's *Making of the President* series, Baker made *Our Next President* look like *Apocalypse Now*. In his version of the 1968 race, LBJ dumped Humphrey from the ticket in favor of Bobby Kennedy. The Republicans reached a convention deadlock and chose New York City's charismatic young mayor, John Lindsay, as its nominee. The summer riots gave George Wallace's third party sufficient votes to throw the election into the House of Representatives, which was stalemated in choosing a president. Meanwhile, Bobby Kennedy was selected as vice president by the Senate and moved into the Oval Office with no intention of leaving.

Russell Baker's impossible dream was not much more bizarre than the actual scenario that unfolded within the Democratic party. Johnson's popularity and credibility dropped. Martin Luther King was assassinated, triggering riots in Newark, Watts, Washington, and Detroit. Robert Kennedy was murdered after winning the California primary. The Vietnam War divided the country like a knife blade; hawks and doves were at one another's throats. An intellectual senator named Eugene McCarthy campaigned for the Democratic presidential nomination in New Hampshire, and though it seemed a laughable undertaking, it attracted the impassioned support of college students who formed a "children's crusade" that exploited America's bitterness over the war. McCarthy made a powerful showing in New Hampshire that showed Johnson how much his support had corroded.

Mason Williams, the head writer of "The Smothers Comedy Hour," wrote a witty book promoting comic Pat Paulsen's run for the presidency. Said Williams: "So far the only candidate running against President Johnson in the Democratic Party is Senator Eugene McCarthy of Minnesota. I don't believe this man has a chance to win. He has admitted that he is a peace candidate. How can he possibly win on such an anti-American platform?"

Bobby Kennedy was in a turmoil about whether to enter the lists. "To be or not to be?" asked *Newsweek* about his dilemma. As the heir of the Kennedy legacy and the leading opponent to Johnson's war, should he make the bold gamble and challenge LBJ? If he did, he might split his party and hand the election to the GOP. If he failed to act, he would endure five more years of exile in the stuffy U.S. Senate. Bobby's ambivalence was satirized by cartoonist Jules Feiffer in a strip called "THE BOBBY TWINS—EPISODE 2: IN WHICH THE GOOD BOBBY

GOES ON 'FACE THE NATION' AND THE BAD BOBBY RESPONDS."
Feiffer showed two Bobbys seated at a microphone. Lamented
the first: "We're going in there and we're killing South Viet-
namese. We're killing children, we're killing women. We're
killing innocent people . . . Do we have that right? . . . I very
seriously question whether we have that right. . . ." Whereupon the second Bobby responds: "I will back the Democratic
candidate in 1968. I expect that will be President Johnson."
The first Bobby turns a troubled face to the second Bobby and
says, "I think we're going to have a difficult time explaining
this to ourselves."

Bobby Kennedy and Lyndon Johnson had long eyed
each other with hostility and distrust. Ever since John Kennedy's death had propelled LBJ into the Oval Office, the Texan
had sensed that Bobby led a band of loyalists waiting in the
wings to succeed him. Johnson resented Bobby and the New
Frontiersmen, suspecting they were cracking cruel jokes about
him at their Georgetown dinner tables, as indeed they were.
Bobby tried to laugh the feud away. He and Lyndon were the
best of friends, he asserted. "The rumors of hostility between
us don't square with the facts," he said. "All during my brother's presidency we were the closest of friends. But then one
day, as we were leaving the inaugural stands. . . ." Bobby protested that he had no designs on the presidency. "And neither
does my wife Ethel Bird." When the 1968 edition of my elec-
tion-year perennial *Who's in Charge Here?* appeared, on the
cover was a photo of LBJ and Bobby that was less than flattering to the president. Bobby said to me with a touch of irony,
"That's going to do a lot for my relationship at the White
House."

When Gene McCarthy revealed Johnson's feet of clay in
the Granite State, Bobby waited a scant four days before he
too entered the race, declaring his own candidacy for the presidency in the very spot his brother had declared his own eight
years before. Herblock drew a cartoon for the *Washington Post*
that showed an unsettled Lyndon Johnson peering into the
Oval Office where, eerily, he sees an empty rocking chair—
and it is rocking. Such were the shock waves that Bobby's announcement produced. He began his campaign with the Indiana primary. It was the first presidential primary Bobby had

ever entered as a candidate. He knew he had to win in Indiana, and he did. His reputation for ruthlessness (Feiffer's "bad Bobby") clung to him like an albatross. He tried to dispel it with humor, speaking modestly, tentatively, and with sardonic humor turned always on himself. He told of encountering a mother superior at a primary stop. "She said she had been praying to St. Jude for me," he declared. "I thanked her, then asked somebody who St. Jude was . . . and then I learned he is the patron saint of lost causes."

At another stop, Bobby asked a sidewalk rally whether their city was going to vote for him. "Otherwise," said Bobby, "Ethel and I and our ten children will have to go on welfare. It'll be less expensive just to send us to the White House. We'll arrange it so all ten kids won't be there at once. And we won't need to expand the place. I'll send some of them away to school—and I'll make one of them Attorney General."

To those who still perceived signs of ruthlessness in Bob Kennedy from his days of fighting racketeering in the American labor movement, he had a comic disclaimer. Feigning indignation, Bobby would say, "People call me ruthless. I am *not* ruthless. And if I find the man who is calling me ruthless, I shall destroy him!"

If the humor of the 1968 campaign seemed to originate mainly in its participants—Johnson's angry jokes, Bobby's self-deprecatory cracks, Humphrey's awkward barbs—it was in part because of the morbidity of the war and the rage of the civil rights struggle, the orgies of anger and rioting. Certainly, television, that marvelous instrument for moving merchandise, offered little political humor in 1968. None of the networks wanted to offend half their audience with political positions in an overheated controversy. A comedic breakthrough called "Laugh-In" was created that year by George Schlatter and Ed Friendly. Friendly had been the NBC executive assigned to "That Was the Week That Was" four years earlier, and he brought to this new show some of the topical humor of TW3. But in place of the sometimes pretentious, heavy-handed content of TW3, the new show was devoted to fun. It was a mosaic of antic bits and pieces. Its slivers of videotape and its spectacular cast, assembled by George Schlatter, revolutionized TV comedy. But "Laugh-In" was only rarely satiric;

it's political insights were skin-deep. The Democrats should have considered themselves fortunate that "Laugh-In" was seldom ideological, since its humor might have been as conservative as TW3's was liberal. Head writer Paul Keyes was a speech writer and friend of Richard Nixon. Indeed, Nixon furthered his appeal to "Laugh-In's" vast audience by appearing on the show and proclaiming the show's trademark line, "Sock it to me." But "Laugh-In's" irreverence was in its pace and its punch lines, not in its politics.

If television comedy ever strayed into the area of political issues during this volcanic period, it was with "The Smothers Brothers Comedy Hour." Here, the subterranean anger of the young, the contempt for Nixon, the subversion of the counterculture, and the antiwar attitudes were all too visible. CBS scheduled the show opposite "Bonanza," a counter-programming plan similar to putting an animal documentary against "The Cosby Show." To everyone's shock, the Smothers Brothers' show not only survived, it prevailed. It did so with a violent assault of biting humor about Lyndon Johnson and the Vietnam War. One evening the TV audience, accustomed to the gentle inanities of "Gilligan's Island" and "The Beverly Hillbillies," was suddenly confronted by a sketch in which President Johnson transports his ranch to the White House lawn. This was impudent stuff in those days. Several CBS affiliates refused to carry the show.

Young viewers who hated the war—and perhaps felt guilty because their college status was keeping them immune to its dangers—loved the topical bite of "The Smothers Brothers Show." It was an island of satire in the vast wasteland of 1968 television. The Smothers boys, their talented producers, Ernie Chambers and Saul Ilson, and their incisive head writer, Mason Williams, constantly fought with the CBS censors to protect the comedic integrity of the show. One week Williams wrote and performed an attack on TV censorship, wielding an immense pair of scissors. The monologue was censored. A torrent of memos flowed between the apprehensive censors and the Smothers show. One memo from the censors read: "It's okay to satirize the President, as long as you do it with respect." Voltaire and Jonathan Swift take note.

The Smothers show reached an apex of pointed dissent after the Democratic convention in August, which gave Humphrey his nomination along with a hideous public relations problem. Outside the convention hall, thousands of young protesters demonstrated against the war. Mayor Richard Daley ordered his forces into the fray. There were bloody clashes—with tear gas, mace, billy clubs, and beatings. Police savaged the hippies, reporters, and pedestrians with democratic impartiality. The Smothers Brothers assembled a biting production number. Harry Belafonte sang a cheerful calypso tune called "Don't Stop the Carnival" against a background of news film of the Chicago convention riots. The taped images of bloodied youths and avenging policemen filled the screen, as Belafonte sang his cheerful ditty in black humorous counterpoint. The entire number was excised by the censors. A grim joke circulated at the Smother Brothers offices at the time:

"They held a meeting to protest police brutality."
"What happened?"
"The police broke it up with clubs and tear gas."

A wit at *Time* magazine assembled a caustic checklist of useful items to bring to the Democratic convention for the guidance of delegates. "The foresighted Democratic delegate," said *Time*, "would ideally—and intelligently—go equipped with goggles (to protect the eyes from tear gas and Mace), cyclists' crash helmet (from billy clubs, bricks, etc.), flak jacket (from snipers) . . . folding bicycle (there is a cab strike) . . . wire cutters (in case delegate is trapped inside the amphitheatre), all-purpose bail-bond credit card (if arrested) . . . chrysanthemums (for flower power if cornered by militant hippies)." Indeed, the security precautions at the convention were so elaborate, and the special barbed wire fences around the convention hall were so thick that the convention became known as "Stalag 68."

Though Hubert Humphrey—who anomalously proclaimed "the politics of joy"—received his party's prize on the first ballot, the riots, carried into America's livingrooms on national TV, made it a dubious gift. Herblock pictured a worried looking Humphrey holding the trophy that read: WINNER

DEMOCRATIC NOMINATION 1968. The cup was overflowing like a witch's cauldron.

When Humphrey took to the campaign trail with his dubious prize, he was heckled unmercifully. Wherever he went in that troubled autumn, he was met by hostile audiences. Nixon, meanwhile, who had received his nomination amidst comparative tranquility, was waging a calm, televised campaign. Humphrey poured it on, trying to contrast his passion and compassion with Nixon's callous disengagement. Humphrey resorted to sarcastic humor to diminish his opponent. He said:

> You know, every day I read about that cool, that confident, that composed and that smiling Mr. Nixon—the man who campaigns without running, the man who takes it easy and never makes a mistake . . . who either evades or straddles every issue. I'm going to send Mr. Nixon some talcum powder. He must be getting saddle sores, straddling all those issues.

Humphrey sought to give 'em hell, in the well-remembered manner of the feisty Harry Truman, who pulled off an astonishing upset in 1948 over Tom Dewey. Humphrey poured on the coals, giving a courageous, bravura performance, despite the daunting odds and the hostile hecklers. Sometimes the crowds were inspiring. Once a voice in the audience shouted, "Give 'em hell, Hubert!" And Humphrey cracked, "Well, it may be too good for them!" (Nixon remained cool and derisive. Reminded of the current Democratic war cry, Nixon sneered, "It's one thing to give 'em hell. It's another thing to give 'em Humphrey.")

Humphrey seemed unable to cope with the hecklers who taunted him. Few politicians, even those as ebullient and dauntless as Humphrey, could have been expected to maintain his aplomb in the face of such fury. (Al Smith was a memorable exception. When a heckler shouted, "Tell 'em all you know, Al," Smith responded, "I'll tell 'em all we *both* know. That won't take any longer.") When Humphrey sought to slip a punch, he was awkward and uninspired. Once, when his speech was drowned in a sea of boos, he declared that "boo" meant "I'm for you" in the language of the Sioux Indians.

Observing Humphrey's attempts to laugh his way through derision, comedian Pat Paulsen wrote in his book, *How to Wage a Successful Campaign for the President*, describing his own mock campaign of 1968, "I challenged my opponents on their home ground. I challenged Humphrey to a laughing contest during a war protest demonstration." Then, with nice impartiality, Paulsen continued, "I pursued George Wallace to debate him at a small Klan rally in Harlem. Lacking even a decent trade-in, I offered to buy a used car from Nixon."

Unfortunately for Hubert Humphrey, he was facing odds that were more formidable than those faced by any presidential candidate in memory. When doves in his audience hooted their preference for Senator Eugene McCarthy, one wag on the press bus commented, "Poor Hubert—his public career has been like one long struggle against McCarthyism." Humphrey was assailed by the ultraconservative John Birch Society on one wing, and by Rapp Brown and his activists on the other. Said Jerry Ford, with mock empathy: "Hubert has been birched red by the Old Right and rapped brown by the New Left."

Humphrey's "politics of joy" amidst the sanguinary carnage of Vietnam, drew mockery from the intellectual establishment. Wrote poet Marya Mannes, in sardonic doggerel:

Hubert the Happy
Goes yackety, yackety, yackety, yackety, yack.
If anyone tells him for God's sake to knock it,
He cheerfully yacketys back.

As election day neared, there were signs that Humphrey's campaign was escaping from the apathetic quagmire that engulfed it. He asserted his independence from Lyndon Johnson's position, declaring that he favored a halt in the bombing of North Vietnam. Given this hopeful sign, Humphrey's critics began to turn, and money started to flow into his coffers. A sign appeared in one audience proclaiming HECKLERS FOR HUMPHREY. A few days before the election, on the eve of Halloween, Lyndon Johnson called a halt to the bombing. The move was assailed as cynical politics by the Republicans. Cracked one correspondent: "Mr. Johnson gave

Richard Nixon a trick and Hubert Humphrey a treat for Halloween."

The halt in the bombing helped Humphrey as did his declaration of independence from LBJ—but it was too little too late. Humphrey lost to Nixon by a slight plurality—about 500,000 votes out of the 73 million cast. Humphrey, the Pagliacci of politics, who had been so cruelly maligned during his four years as vice president, fought a tormenting, tumultuous campaign for the presidency, only to come up a buck short.

Chapter 10
Campaign 1968
The Dead Duck

My own favorite is Richard Nixon . . . This humble
man has once again offered himself as a candidate on
the basis of his experience and I think we should accept him on that basis. After all, why go to the trouble of breaking in a new loser?
—MASON WILLIAMS

Richard Nixon ran in 1968 on the basis of experience, which made many of America's satirists smile. Back in
1960 Nixon had also run on the basis of experience, which
had promoted one observer to quip: "Experience is what he'll
have when this campaign is over." Nixon had still more experience when he lost to Pat Brown for the governorship of California in 1962. Perhaps Nixon agreed with Oscar Wilde that
"experience is the name we give to our mistakes." On that basis, by 1968 Nixon had abundant experience. But he also had
numerous political IOU's from party leaders around the country. For though he had declared after his California defeat,
"This is my last press conference . . . You won't have Nixon to
kick around anymore," he presented himself for the press's
boot in 1968. This was no mere display of masochism. Nixon
had been solidifying his relationship with the GOP brass for
six years. And so, when he entered the presidential primaries
in 1968, the public and the party responded. It seemed to
many that only Nixon could unite the Goldwater right with
the Rockefeller center.

After the debacle of Goldwater's defeat in 1964 and the scorn that Republican moderates had heaped on the Arizonan, the party could stand some unity. Jerry Ford observed that between LBJ and Bobby, Gene McCarthy and George Wallace, the Democrats were a divided party. "But we Republicans are united," quipped Ford. "We'll all rally 'round that great Republican champion, Ronald—Milhaus—Percyfeller."

As the election year began, the GOP did indeed have a number of plausible candidates in the chase. *Newsweek* chuckled that it was like a circus, "the five-count-em-five Republican elephants are lumbering into the big tent. One is showboating to the gallery [Nixon], one has to be prodded to perform at all [Reagan], another has his trunk in his mouth [Romney], the baby pachyderm is bringing up the rear [Scranton], and the scarred old lead elephant [Eisenhower] is counting the house."

Jerry Ford had a quip—sometimes rather close to the bone—about each of the GOP stalwarts. (He had no presidential ambitions himself. The presidency was still six years away for Jerry Ford, and then it would be his without the mess of a primary battle or even an election campaign.) Now Jerry Ford reviewed the Republican contenders from the secure position of House minority leader. George Romney, the Mormon president of American Motors, had dropped out of the race after his gaffe about being brainwashed on a junket to Vietnam. Said Ford: "Our Republican drag race is still exciting even with our Michigan Rambler scratched." (Said one comic of Mormon Romney: "His grandfather had four wives, 36 children, 198 grandchildren, 419 great grandchildren. One more generation and he can stampede the convention.")

Nelson Rockefeller was eyeing the convention, hoping for a draft-producing deadlock. Cracked Ford: "Rockefeller won't volunteer—but last week he installed a hot line to his draft board." Then Ford added, "Nelson is the best man to save the American dollar. It's a family habit . . . Rockefeller is the only taxpayer who can balance the Federal budget with his mad money." Ford had a few jocular remarks about Richard Nixon as well. He said of the man who would one day make him an instant President, "Dick Nixon doesn't have to stay in politics for the money. Only last week the Schick Razor Company offered him two million dollars just to do a shaving commercial . . . for Gillette." Then Ford added, "Dick is the only candidate who gets Five O'Clock Shadow on the Today Show."

Of Ronald Reagan, Ford said: "Governor Reagan says he isn't running for President. I believe him—even if his door chimes do play 'Hail to the Chief.'"

In the election year of 1968, Richard Nixon was the front-runner. He performed well in the primaries he entered that spring, but still he lacked the easy elegance of a Jack Kennedy or even the rustic charm of a Lyndon Johnson. Nixon was, in a word, stiff. He lacked the ability to behave informally, and this drew the gibes of the inveterate Nixon-haters. Reporters chuckled behind their notebooks at his habit of walking on the beach in jacket and tie. Given Nixon's humorless mind-set, even loyalist Lyn Nofziger told a symposium audience, "Every once in a while I lay awake at night trying to think of . . . something funny that Richard Nixon said."

Nixon's trademark was a counterfeit glee, which he used to laugh indiscriminately at anything that was remotely funny. (In this respect he resembled Sammy Davis, Jr., who interestingly enough was one of his most ardent supporters.) Throughout the primaries, Nixon tried to play the good sport in his public appearances. Campaigning in Burbank, he was introduced by comedians Dick Martin and Dan Rowan, whose TV farrago, "Laugh-In," was taped nearby at the NBC studios. "Laugh-In" had immortalized "beautiful downtown Burbank." In his introductory remarks, Dan Rowan cracked to Richard Nixon, "We were going to present you with the key to the city, but Burbank doesn't have any locks." "Yeah" interrupted Dick Martin, "but it does have bagels." This feeble gag produced a paroxysm of uncontrollable laughter from Nixon. The candidate's simulated sense of humor was in full flower.

Not every part of the GOP spectrum embraced Richard Nixon. The far right, which had fueled what Richard Reeves called "the Goldwater caper" four years before, would have preferred Ronald Reagan, the genial governor of California. And so, a scant two days before the convention was ready to give its imprimatur to Nixon, conservative southern legislators prevailed on Reagan to challenge the front-running Nixon. Reagan had come to the convention as a favorite son candidate. Now, at the eleventh hour, he decided to make it clear that he was in and had no intention of pulling out. "As of this moment," Reagan announced, "I am a candidate." With a mere forty-eight hours to go before the balloting would begin, Reagan's formal availability, said one journalistic wag, "was the shortest candidacy in American political history.

Reagan's demeanor was the same warm, appealing one that would win him such adoration once he entered the White House twelve years later. His approach was avuncular and amusing. He spoke of his presidential goals before thirty-five caucuses in two days. To all and sundry he said, "I have mixed emotions—like the man watching his mother-in-law drive off a cliff in his new Cadillac." Reagan's gaggery earned him laughter but few delegate votes. Indeed, his last minute lunge seemed less the product of cunning than desperation. It provoked derisive humor from some party officials. Cracked one governor about Reagan's gambit: "It's like a woman who's eight-and-a-half months pregnant announcing she's going to have a baby." Said another: "Ron's getting the cherry pickers and the flip floppers. He hasn't even got John Wayne."

Along with Reagan's hopes, Nixon buried the ambitions of other fellow Republicans. Herblock, who had been cutting through political cant and bombast for years, pictured Nixon as a grinning grave digger, wringing his hands with glee, as he studies the freshly laid gravestones marked ROMNEY, ROCKEFELLER, and RESPONSIBLE REPUBLICANISM. Herblock had won three Pulitzer Prizes with his witty work. His pen gave the most abstract issues a vivid, human face, and no face reflected more of the political sins than Herblock's Nixon. Throughout the convention and the election campaign that followed, Richard Nixon was a favorite target of much of the media. When he bowed to Pat Brown in the California gubernatorial race six years before, Nixon had been the target of a joke that was less than prophetic. It went:

"Knock-knock."
"Who's there?"
"Nixon."
"Nixon who?"
"You mean you've forgotten already?"

The anti-Nixon line of choice in the 1968 campaign accompanied a photo of a sullen Nixon staring face forward at the camera. The caption read: "Would you buy a used car from this man?"

Nixon had the capacity to engage a deep undercurrent of anger among liberals. When he chose Spiro Agnew as his running mate in 1968, a nasty bit of graffiti began to appear on subway billboards in New York City, which read: DICK AND SPIRO ADD UP TO ZERO. Nixon and Agnew often triggered a scatalogical contempt that said somewhat more about their critics than the candidates. One bit of graffiti read: NIXON IS THE FIRST PRESIDENT TO HAVE AN ASSHOLE FOR A VICE PRESIDENT. Beneath it, in another handwriting, was written: NO, EISENHOWER WAS. Written in a stall in a men's toilet at Rutgers University was the question, "How can anyone hate a President with a name like Dick?" Pat Paulsen, reflecting on the GOP convention, said: "1968 will be remembered as the campaign when the Republicans, torn between old loyalties to Barry Goldwater and the radiant promises of Herbert Hoover, chose Richard Nixon as the compromise candidate." (Alluding to the other party, Paulsen said, "The Democrats, holding a giant convention in Chicago, went through the uncontested formalities of nominating Hubert Humphrey. George Wallace's party chose the former Governor of Alabama, George Wallace. The Yippies, also meeting in Chicago, countered by nominating a pig.")

For his running mate, Nixon had available to him the very cream of the American political system—most of the Republican luminaries who had faltered on the road to the nomination. There was Romney, Rockefeller, Scranton, Percy, plus numerous other notables of the U.S. Senate and House. He chose instead to reach far beyond obscurity to pluck out the bulbous governor of Maryland, a worthy named Spiro T. Agnew. When Richard Nixon lost the presidency in 1960 to a lanky Bostonian named Jack Kennedy, *Esquire* ran a picture of Nixon roaring with laughter. Beneath it was the question: "Why is this man laughing?" In 1968, there was another question hanging in the air. "Spiro who?" Headlines sprang up, reading SPIRO AGNEW—WHO'S HE? One wit volunteered that the name rhymed with "hero," or better yet, "zero." Agnew was "a legend in his own mind," said one wag. Though Agnew was the governor of Maryland, a citizen of that state hooted, "I'm from Maryland and even I have trouble remembering his name." To demonstrate the exquisite obscurity of the man, a reporter for the *Atlanta Constitution* stopped passersby on Peachtree Street, saying: "I'm going to say two words to you. You tell me what they mean." The words were: "Spiro Agnew." Here are some of the replies:

"It's some kind of disease."
"It's some kind of egg."
"He's a Greek who owns that ship-building firm."

Agnew would generate more recognition with his campaign racism, his alliterative attacks on the press, and his resignation from the vice presidency. But at this stage in his political career, he was "Spiro who?"

Still, Agnew did have a definite appeal to border and southern states, and that, combined with his apparent probity, seemed to make him a sound choice as the vice presidential running mate. Nixon started to have second thoughts when, on the campaign trail, Agnew proved himself a loose cannon. He called a Nisei correspondent a "fat Jap" and customarily referred to Polish-Americans as "Polacks." These ethnic slurs produced a pointed bit of satire from cartoonist Pat Oliphant. The Republicans were seeking to woo black votes to the GOP banner, and Oliphant showed Agnew in a series of encounters labeled THE WORLD OF SPIRO AGNEW. The Veep candidate is greeting various offended looking ethnics. "Hi, Polack!" he says. Then, "Hi, Jap!" Then "Hi, Wop!" Then, "Hi, Wetback!" Finally, he meets a dark-skinned man. Says Agnew, "Hi . . . er . . . black Afro-American!"

Some cracked that Agnew was "Nixon's Nixon." The vice presidential candidate had charted a low-road itinerary, and a latent racist was peeking through. No one ever accused Agnew of any intellectual brilliance. One journalist gibed that Agnew's characteristic squint came from overexposure to the Baltimore Colts' football games on Sunday TV. Time after time, Agnew had to backpedal rapidly to escape the repercussions of his off-the-cuff quips. There was a venomous streak to

Agnew's humor that continued to percolate problems for the ticket. There seemed no limit to his eyebrow raisers. He called Hubert Humphrey "squishy soft on Communism," which brought an outcry from Senate Republicans who respected their patriotic colleague. Agnew promptly apologized. Since his campaign odyssey included more suburbs than inner city areas, Agnew airily dismissed his preference by saying, "When you've seen one slum you've seen them all." As Agnew's apologies and explanations piled up, some Americans laughed, while others wept. At one rally he was greeted by a poster that said, APOLOGIZE NOW, SPIRO. IT WILL SAVE TIME.

If Spiro Agnew seemed to cause more trouble than he was worth for Richard Nixon, former Alabama governor George Wallace posed a more serious threat to Nixon's electoral fortunes. He was running as head of a third party, and in the southern states he threatened to siphon votes from the Nixon column. He rivaled and even surpassed Nixon in his vehemence on the subject of law and order, or, as some called it, "lawnorder." Wallace was attacked with scathing sarcasm by the liberals. Said one columnist, "He appeared at the convention in a plain white business sheet." Said a TV satirist, "Wallace has a great deal of respect for the Negro. He feels that every man should own one." Don Wright, editorial cartoonist for the *Miami News*, pictured Wallace holding a large placard containing his party platform. It read:

1. Run over Hippies with yore car.
2. Win war—somehow.
3. Throw bureaucrats' briefcases in Potomac.
4. Run over Yippies with yore car.
5. Throw bureaucrats in Potomac.
6. Wave yore flag
7. Put crooks in jail.
8. Put Supreme Court in jail.
9. Put pink press in jail.
10. Get law and order.
11. Let police run country.

If Wallace competed vigorously with Nixon on the matter of "law and order," it was equally true that Hubert Humphrey gave significant stress to the issue. A few months before, the murder of Martin Luther King had produced outbreaks in many American cities, and all three candidates were running hard against riots. This led Mahood, the acerbic cartoonist for the *Times* of London, to sketch two blacks looking at some posters of Wallace, Nixon, and Humphrey, each placard proclaiming the candidate's devotion to law and order. One of the blacks is saying, "Well, there's the choice—which one would *you* prefer to have hitting you over the head, Alvin?" The inimitable Herblock was sharper still. He showed George Wallace fitting a Ku Klux Klansman for a respectable topcoat over his white robe. The Klansman's topcoat reads LAW AND ORDER, and the white costume beneath is labeled RACISM. Says Wallace to his customer as he pins the hem, "We'll let the overcoat out all the way, and the robe will hardly show at all."

With all the major candidates stressing the law-and-order issue, the mayor of San Francisco was moved to remark: "None of the candidates is running for President. They're all running for Sheriff!"

Whatever the American voters choice for sheriff, they chose Richard Nixon for president by a plurality of half a million voters, with Nixon carrying thirty-one states to Humphrey's fourteen and Wallace's five.

Chapter 11
Campaign 1964
The President of All the People

The stores will soon be marketing the LBJ sweater.
You get such a warm, comfortable feeling as they
pull the wool over your eyes.
—HENRY MORGAN

Every U.S. president and every candidate for the office automatically becomes a target for the witticisms—some whimsical, some cruel—of America's comics, columnists, satirists, and gadflies. And it can be fairly observed that whatever their smiles of counterfeit good fellowship, these public figures are not entirely pleased with the constant ridicule of their flaws, both personal and political. But of all the men who sought or achieved the exalted post of president, none was as sensitive to the mockery of humor as Lyndon Baines Johnson.

President John F. Kennedy used to say: "If you want to stay out of trouble, stay out of sight." And by staying out of sight during his service as Kennedy's vice president—as the constitutional system mandates—Johnson was seldom the target of wounding humor. (He was, of course, the target of beltway humor from his colleagues in the Kennedy White House, but that's another story). But when Lyndon Johnson sought the presidency in his own right, after inheriting it on the black day of Kennedy's death, he became the focus for abundant ridicule. He was an extraordinary man with extraordinary virtues

149

and extraordinary flaws, and the flaws drew most of the humorists' attention.

Johnson was more sensitive to humor and its inherent criticism than any of his predecessors in the Oval Office, primarily because of the immensity of his ego. As his friend, Speaker Sam Rayburn, once observed, "Most politicians have ample egos, but Lyndon is double dipped." Hugh Sidey, of *Time* magazine, observed that Johnson was "incapable of laughing at himself," so it was unsurprising that he would find scant humor in the witty assaults of others. LBJ was especially sensitive to the wit of columnist Art Buchwald, the dean of press humorists. On one occasion Johnson found his aide and confidant, Bill Moyers, sitting at his desk, roaring with laughter at a Buchwald column targeted on LBJ. "You find Buchwald funny?" exploded Johnson. "No sir!" snapped Moyers. On another occasion, Pierre Salinger felt the sting of Johnson's animus over Buchwald's wit. Salinger, whom LBJ inherited as his press secretary from Kennedy, was lunching with the Johnson clan at the LBJ ranch. That morning Pierre had been so imprudent as to mention that Buchwald had written a funny column on Johnson in the *New York Herald Tribune.* There were thunderclaps over the luncheon table when Salinger sat down with the president and his family and staff. "Peer," he said to Salinger with quiet menace. "Ah understand you found Art Buchwald very funny this morning." Salinger admitted he had. "Well," said the president, "will someone bring Peer a copy of this morning's *Herald Tribune.*" A copy was produced as Salinger broke into a gentle sweat. "Peer, why don't you just read the column aloud so we can all enjoy it." Salinger read the 1,250 words of Buchwald's column. When he finished, Johnson swept the table with a monarchal glare. "Well," said the president, "does anybody else find that funny?" There was utter silence.

Johnson's vanity was so thick and his skin so thin that any humor focused upon him was bound to draw blood. His predecessor had had the ability to laugh at himself, but Johnson did not. (I was the beneficiary of Jack Kennedy's taste for humor. It in fact brought me into the Kennedy circle and triggered my career as a political dilettante. In 1962 I had written a little political book called *Who's in Charge Here?* In it, I floated irreverent speech balloons over the head of President Kennedy and others in his political family. The target of my gibes was Kennedy's rocking chair, his speed reading, his wife's taste in couturier clothes, his daughter, his space program, and his cabinet. When aides brought the book to Kennedy's attention, he invited me to visit him at the White House. Needless to say, Johnson never contacted me about any of the book's sequels.)

Lyndon Johnson did not merely grin and bear it when the wags were at work. He did not bite through the stem of his pipe as Gerald Ford did when the jokesters were at play. Johnson was vindictive. Even the mildest humor or the gentlest reproach made him irate. This was an abrupt change in sophistication, taste, and wit from Kennedy. Someone observed that going from Kennedy to Johnson was like doing a slow dissolve from Noel Coward to the Dukes of Hazzard. Johnson had no taste for irony. He rarely listened to other people. His forte was the self-delivered monologue. He was a long-winded man, a Potomac Babbit, with few original ideas and little tolerance for humor at his expense.

Merriman Smith, the late dean of White House correspondents, who wrote for United Press International and who grew close to LBJ, told me that Johnson was irritated by the anti-LBJ gibes that regularly appeared on "That Was the Week That Was," the topical humor show I helped to create shortly before Johnson inherited the Oval Office. As Campaign 1964 began, the show's writers looked on candidate Barry Goldwater with skepticism, but they could see Johnson's deficiencies as well, and their doubts manifested themselves in cutting humor. For one thing, Johnson's policies were all over the political spectrum. He assumed a dizzying variety of ideological positions in attempting to lasso members of the right, left, and center. Said David Frost: "President Johnson has remolded the Democratic Party into the fresh, invigorated, cautious, conservative, liberal, radical force it is today." Johnson was doubtless not amused.

Another target of the humorists was LBJ's reputation as a wheeler-dealer. Lyndon favored the ten-gallon hats of his Texas boyhood, which led TW3 to report: "This week department stores all over America started selling the LBJ ten-gallon hat. And soon they will be marketing the LBJ Sweater. You get such a warm, comfortable feeling as they pull the wool over your eyes."

Compared to the Ivy League education of the Washington elitists and intellectuals he resented, Johnson had a second-rate education and hadn't read a book in years. He was thus sensitive to humor that mocked his cerebral gifts. Mort Sahl did not endear himself to Johnson when he remarked to one of his overflow campus audiences, "The Democratic party's ad agency also handles the Avis Rent-a-Car account. And they just came up with a new slogan for Johnson. 'He's second best but he tries harder.'"

Johnson's ability to turn the presidency to his own financial gain provoked this cutting remark from one White House correspondent: "I hear they're looking for an alternate route for a channel to replace the Panama Canal. So far, the most promising route goes through downtown Austin."

Jules Feiffer, who shares with Garry Trudeau the mantle of the wittiest cartoonist on the political scene, heaped scorn on Johnson. Said Feiffer in his retrospective of the Ike-to-Reagan years, *Jules Feiffer's America*: "LBJ was not only the first man, he had turned into the first bully, the first thief, the first credibility gap, the first war criminal, the first crack in the system, the first reason to riot in the streets, the first terrorist to the American dream." Feiffer addressed himself to Johnson's conceit, so often expressed during the 1964 campaign, as when he proclaimed that he wanted to be "the President of all the people." Liz Carpenter, who used to write jokes for LBJ's speeches, recalled the genesis of the All-the-People phrase. A roiling crowd in New Orleans had greeted the Johnson campaign train. There were tens of thousands of blacks and whites, "all mixed together," all chanting "We want Lyndon!" Said LBJ, caught up in the frenzy of the moment: "When I walked into the White House that night [after Kennedy's death] to take over the awesome responsibility that was mine, I said—as long as I am President, I am going to be President of all the people." Jules Feiffer, in a pointed series of panels, showed a group of voters looking skyward in awe at LBJ, as he hovers angelically above them.

VOTERS. Oh, what do you see, Mr. President-of-all-the-People?

LBJ. I see a land where love reigns. I see great farms and giant cities. I see men at work, children at play, women at peace.

VOTERS. O, what else do you see, Mr. President-of-all-the-People?

LBJ. I see an end of divisions and controversies. I see small men growing large and closed minds opening wide . . .

VOTERS. O, tell us more Mr. President-of-all-the-People.

LBJ. I see blacks and whites in final harmony. Rich and poor, old and young, big and little, small and large . . .

VOTERS. O, is there nothing more that you see, Mr. President-of-all-the-People?

LBJ. I see a mandate for happiness. I see the determined faces of millions—fat and skinny, tall and short, bold and shy—crying as one, "Onward to the Great Society!"

VOTERS. And how will all these things come about, Mr. President-of-all-the-People?

LBJ. I shall wheel and deal.

The contrast between Johnson's idealistic rhetoric and his manipulative techniques and vindictive rages led even his loyalists to look askance at this president-of-all-the-people. On TV he resembled, said one former Senate colleague, "a cross between Machiavelli and a riverboat gambler."

When David Frost cracked about Johnson's accomplishments in remolding the Democratic party into a variety of contradictory things, he was reflecting a fact that had long been perceived in Washington circles. As *Newsweek* pointed out, "Political parties, like house pets, have a way of coming to resemble their masters." It was certainly true that the Democratic party had been remolded in the image of Lyndon Johnson. And Lyndon Johnson was all things to all people. As the 1964 campaign began, LBJ had replicated the broadly based, widely supported party that Franklin Roosevelt had assembled thirty years before. It was a gargantuan creation, and it took a larger-than-life man to create it. It also took a man who was larger than life to manage its deterioration in four short years.

Johnson's ambitions for America and his own grand ego generated scathing humor. At a San Francisco cabaret, the actor portraying LBJ holds aloft a new book and drawls, "It's a new book all about me. It's called *LBJ: The Greatest President.* It's a fantasy." A biting, satirical play opened off-Broadway in New York and captured the public's attention. It was called *MacBird,* a Johnsonian parody of the Shakespearian tragedy, *Macbeth.* The show played to capacity houses and sold well in paperback. The Second City paid dubious tribute to Johnson's manipulations with a sketch in which LBJ is consulting with an aide:

LBJ. Goldwater's charges about my conflict of interest are getting embarrassing.

AIDE. What do you plan to do, sir?

LBJ. Well, first I'll put the White House in Lady Bird's name. . . .

Johnson's humble beginnings in the hill country of Texas sparked a gag in an early edition of a photo-cartoon book called *News Reals.* In it, Lyndon is hosting a barbecue, spreading goodwill among his guests, as the spare ribs simmer. Says Johnson: "This party on the White House lawn was a good idea. Help yourself to the food, everybody. It's out beyond the oil rig."

LBJ brought such a distinctive style to the White House, with his bullying, his manipulation, his Lincolnesque size, and his P. T. Barnum hokum, that TW3 created an entertaining fiction. Johnson, we said, had remodeled the White House from top to bottom. Said the narrator:

Johnsons's new White House bears little resemblance to the old. Gone is the imposing formality, the august dignity. In its place we have a real folksy, down-to-earth residence in the cozy Ranch House style.

The lawns surrounding the White House have been relandscaped in the picturesque Southwest mood, with live cattle grazing among the oil derricks.

Upon entering the front door of the Executive Mansion, visitors are asked to wipe their feet on the William E. Miller Memorial Welcome Mat [Miller was Goldwater's running mate]; coats are hung in the adjacent closet, which has just been enlarged to make room for various political skeletons.

Entering the Main Gallery, we see paintings depicting great moments in American history: "Lyndon Crossing the Rio Grande," and "Lyndon Signing the Declaration of Independence."

As we enter the President's office, we see the Chief Executive's desk, with its white telephone, red telephone, "hot line" telephone, intercom and—here's something new—a switch for turning on and off the United States of America.

The White House swimming pool, incidentally, is being used to store 14,000 gallons of barbecue sauce left over from the LBJ campaign picnics.

The new Game Room on the second floor . . . includes stuffed heads of Clare Boothe Luce, Strom Thurmond, and William F. Buckley.

The remodeled White House has great popular appeal; a number of families have expressed a desire to move in at any time— the Goldwaters, the Nixons, the Romneys, the Scrantons, and many others.

Sex and scandal raise eyebrows in politics, as Gary Hart discovered to his grief. Often the sexual dalliances of our past presidents remain well hidden with the help of the Secret Service and compliant journalists during the president's lifetime, but leap into print a few years after his demise. Roosevelt's mistress, Eisenhower's driver, and Kennedy's bedroom prodigies are never mentioned in their election campaigns. (Or at least that was the rule B. H., before Hart.) But the sexual proclivities of Johnson's chief protégé were an active element of the 1964 campaign.

Bobby Baker was LBJ's young man in the U.S. Senate. So great was his influence in the social and sexual life of some of the members of that distinguished club that many called Bobby Baker "the 101st Senator." Baker was extremely well connected with a tawdry minority of senators who liked their liquor straight and their women bent. (Merriman Smith once told me: "Summers are hot in Washington, so senators' wives go to Europe and the senators are left to enjoy their secretaries.") Bobby Baker helped this natural process. He was part owner of twenty-two corporations, a vending machine company, and a Washington establishment called the Carousel Motel. Senators knew that Bobby could always be depended on to provide a girl for the night, and should things go badly, an equitable solution. Johnson embraced Bobby Baker, perhaps seeing traces of his own ambitious youth. The records revealed that Bobby Baker had sent his patron an expensive gift—a Magnavox stereo set. When this gamy narrative was leaked to the press, it provoked an eruption of blue humor.

Phyllis Newman reported how often members of the U.S. Senate and their female aides had accepted Bobby Baker's hospitality at the Carousel Motel. Recalling the stereo gift to the Johnsons, Phyllis said, "The Carousel Motel is a place where senators can enjoy low fidelity with high frequency." *Newsweek* picked up the line, and Americans were laughing at it for quite a while.

The Johnson Family tried to keep Bobby Baker at arm's length throughout the campaign. In *News Reals*, Lady Bird Johnson is shown accepting a handsomely framed painting. Says the First Lady: "Oh my, it's another lovely gift from Bobby Baker. I'd better hang it in a nice place. . . . Under the rug."

Bobby Baker was Lyndon's Watergate and Iranscam, though on a lesser scale. Baker was the center of a scandal that had about it the aroma of congressional corruption and sexual

promiscuity—journalistically speaking, an unbeatable combination. The scandal spawned humor that showed Johnson
without his imperial clothes. As LBJ tried to put maximum distance between himself and his tainted protégé, Alan Alda said:
"Clearly, Mr. Johnson is the President of *all* the people—the
butcher, the baker, the candlestick maker. Oh, sorry!
. . . The butcher, the candlestick maker. . . ." Said David
Frost: "According to a Washington rumor, Bobby Baker will
receive a telegram from President Johnson on New Year's Eve
reading: 'MAY OLD ACQUAINTANCE BE FORGOT.'" Said Elliot
Reid: "They still haven't pinned anything on Bobby Baker.
The chief witness against him is too busy to testify. He's running the country." When Senator Thomas Dodd issued a report decrying all the sex and violence on television, the *Harvard Lampoon* did a satiric report on sex and violence in the
U.S. Senate:

> And now for a review of the top shows of recent Senate sea-
> sons. THE BOBBY BAKER REVIEW or POTOMAC PLACE . . . spon-
> sored by Johnson & Johnson, it features ex–Senate employee
> Robert G. Baker, with . . . a supporting cast of lobbyists in the
> Senate and Senators in the lobby. Your critic found this show
> tended to glorify sex and corruption. Furthermore, the evil-
> doers were never punished. They were re-elected.

During the summer months of 1964, when TW3 did its
annual predictions of things to come and concluded that it
would be off the air, the staff's summary included the following prophecies:

> July 26th. Bobby Baker makes a big attempt to stop Goldwater.
> He offers him a stereo set.
>
> July 27th. Goldwater refuses to accept the stereo set. Nixon
> says, "I'll take it."

Bobby Baker had started as a lowly Senate page, and
with the guidance and friendship of Lyndon Johnson, his assets had grown to a cool two million dollars; he was the Democratic party's Horatio Alger. Nancy Ames, the voluptuous

blonde TW3 girl, sang a parody of "When I Was a Boy," from Gilbert & Sullivan's *H.M.S. Pinafore,* that needled Baker and his boss. The lyrics ran in part:

> When I was a lad at an early age
> I had a position as a Senate page.
> I ran so fast on the Senate floors
> I attracted the attention of the Senators.
> I ran so fast and I did so well
> That now I am the owner of the Carousel . . .
> I schemed by night and I worked by day
> And I aimed to ingratiate Lyndon J.
> I would always please and never annoy
> And the eyes of Texas were upon me, boy . . .
> Now with what I know, if I care to try,
> I could blow the U.S. Senate seventeen miles high.

With his firsthand knowledge of the workings of the Congress, President Johnson had been able to force through more progressive legislation—Civil Rights and Medicare, for example—than his charismatic predecessor had dreamed of. Johnson's demands on the Congress brought the often lethargic legislators their share of ridicule. Said Henry Morgan: "Mr. Johnson has called on Congress to put in a six-day work-week until his 'must' legislation is passed. A lot of the congressmen resent being asked to work the extra six days."

Though Johnson's poverty program was laudable and compassionate, it too attracted its share of gibes. Said one Washington wise guy: "Next year President Johnson will announce his War on Poverty has been won, and turn his attention to a War on the Middle Class." When deep cuts in procurement by the Department of Defense idled 80,000 workers, reporters called it "Johnson's Poverty on War Campaign." And when Nelson Rockefeller sought the 1964 nomination, one wit suggested that Rockefeller could never comprehend the War on Poverty. "He's never seen the enemy." A monologist in a cabaret on Capitol Hill kidded Johnson's poverty program with a satiric song called "Poverty Pockets." Said the performer:

The President asked me to write this song about the pockets of poverty. I'm not a singer, of course. You'll have to picture this as it will be sung by Sargent Shriver. He's going to be standing on this big hill looking down on this poverty pocket where all these people are standing around starving. He'll look up and sing . . . [in rock tempo]

I'm gonna roll it
I'm gonna rock it
I'm gonna clear up each poverty pocket.
I'm gonna move on this program
And move on it fast
At least until the November
Election is past
And if there is no significant change
Won't you give it a chance?
'Cause Lyndon's War on Poverty's
Doin' all right at the ranch.

It must have been particularly galling to LBJ that despite his prodigious achievements in the interests of social justice, he was looked on with such distrust by the press and the satiric community. To reporters it was dangerous to trust anything he said. When Johnson mounted the stump on the campaign trail in 1964, surrounded by "his people," his most comfortable posture was that of the country preacher, brimming over with gospel admonitions and anecdotes about men of the cloth in the Texas hill country.

One of Johnson's favorite preacher stories concerned a clergyman who drops his sermon notes while heading for church, and before he can retrieve them his hound has chewed them to bits. In apologizing to his congregation, the preacher says, "I am very sorry. Today I have no sermon. I will have to speak as the Lord directs. But I will try to do better tomorrow." Another preacher story that embellished LBJ's 1964 campaign concerned a minister who is enraged to see a man sleeping in the front row of his congregation:

So he whispered to the congregation [said Lyndon], "All those who want to go to the Kingdom of Heaven stand up." They all got to their feet except the man sleeping in the front row.

Then the preacher shouted, "ALL THOSE WHO WANT TO WALK
WITH THE DEVIL, STAND UP!" The sleeper came awake with a
start and jumped to his feet. He saw the preacher standing tall
and angry in the pulpit, and he said, "Well, preacher, I don't
know what it is we're votin' on, but it looks like you and I are
the only ones for it."

Johnson's corn-fed brand of idealism contrasted
strangely with the horny-handed operator who knew that
force was the ultimate persuader. Johnson, after all, was the
one who didn't trust a man unless "I've got his pecker in my
pocket." This cross of the softhearted and the hard-boiled
made for an irreconcilable mix. As the campaign unfolded,
some cynical bystanders cracked that the difference between
Johnson and Goldwater was that "Goldwater preaches what
Johnson practices." One journalist predicted that the Arizonan would lose because "he's more honest and less clever."
But there is a limit to how far cleverness can take you. Lyndon
was impeded by his impatience with anything short of genuflection from the Congress and the press. When he attended
his first caucus on Capitol Hill as president and did not receive
the degree of deference he thought appropriate, he smirked
to an aide, "Now I know the difference between a caucus and
a cactus. With a cactus the pricks are on the *outside*."

Despite the alarm generated by some of Barry Goldwater's irresponsible campaign statements and fanned by Johnson's exaggerations, LBJ was finding his own critics unwilling
to be seduced by his preacher anecdotes and windy homilies.
For some, the LBJ sweet talk could decay the teeth at twenty
paces. The press was dismayed at his inability to accept even
the mildest reproach and appalled at his attempts to suppress
independent reporting. When the *Wall Street Journal* ran a
story asserting that the public was losing some of its fondness
for Lyndon, the president sneered, "I think everyone knows
how the *Wall Street Journal* reflects the views of the man on the
street—*Wall Street.* Somebody told me that the writer of that
article was free-lancing for *True Romances.*" When he learned
that a critical reporter for a New York daily had arrived in
Texas, Johnson cracked, "the price of whores is going up in
Austin." And when he heard that another unfriendly news-

man had been seen in town, Johnson gibed, "See him! I can *smell* him."

In Theodore White's observant report on the election campaign, *The Making of the President 1964*, he points out: "When Johnson thought of America, he thought of it either in primitive terms of Fourth of July patriotism or else as groups of people, forces, leaders, lobbies, pressures . . . he was ill at ease with the broad purposes and meaning of civilization." This was, as I. F. Stone wrote, "the portrait of an intellectually quite limited man. It raises the question of whether the kind of man most likely to become President is really best qualified for the job."

Johnson's own family could recognize his character flaws better than anyone. They had been exposed to them longer. Said daughter Luci: "Daddy, speaking as an outsider, what do you think of the human race?" When it was revealed that Luci Baines Johnson was taking instructions in the Roman Catholic faith because a boy whose school pin she wore was a Catholic, one sardonic reporter said: "Considering Johnson's skill at drawing support from all the divergent groups of our society, it's been rumored that his daughter Lynda Bird is dating a rabbinical student, and Mrs. Johnson is reading up on Zen Buddhism." Johnson was not so much a conversationalist as a monologist. When he was quieted for a time by surgery to remove a throat polyp, his wife said of his imposed silence, "We're going to have to make the most of it."

Lady Bird's plan to beautify America drew its share of mockery. Said one stand-up comic: "Lady Bird Johnson has asked the public for suggestions on ways to beautify America. A flood of mail came in. One of the first letters read: 'Stop hanging your stockings on the shower rod. Lyndon.'" Both of Lyndon's daughters were attractive young women who did not warrant the witticism of one Hollywood wag, who said, "President Johnson has issued the first Executive Order in his plan to beautify America. He has forbidden his daughters to drive in a convertible." Said Larry Blyden: "President Johnson has issued a statement protesting that America's countryside is begin vulgarized by billboards. He issued an order banning highway signs, and the order will be posted on a sign every one hundred yards." On TW3, Nancy Ames sang a parodic hymn to Lady Bird to the tune of "The Yellow Rose of Texas":

She's the Lady Bird of Texas
With initials L. B. J.
And she named her charming daughters
In the same delightful way.
There is L. B. this and L. B. that
And isn't it absurd?
When dear old Lyndon's angry
Why they call him Thunderbird. . . .

She's the Lady Bird of Texas
And she gives a Texas yell.
In the battle of the sexes
She comes out mighty well.
You could never ever fool 'er,
It's a certain law of life
That behind each nation's ruler
Is a most astonished wife.

It was ironic that the often egomaniacal president who would droop his head in sleep when the conversation passed to someone else, would have as his favorite motto: "You ain't learnin' nothing when you're talkin'." Perhaps it was an aphorism he urged on others.

As he campaigned across the country in what would ultimately produce one of the most overwhelming electoral mandates of the century, Johnson gave a bravura performance before massive crowds that were often as frenzied as those that greeted Jack Kennedy in 1960. But if LBJ displayed a manipulative charm of sorts, the ingredient that seemed to be missing was magnanimity. Some protested that Johnson was not a very nice person. He inflicted a gratuitous cruelty on those closest to him—the loyal aides who were serving him. Some of the humor that characterized the 1964 campaign focused on LBJ as a very tough boss. A New York cabaret presented a skit in which Johnson is meeting with a member of his subcabinet, Mennen "Soapy" Williams:

LBJ. Soapy, I've figured out a way to effect a real economy in your department.

SOAPY. What's that, sir?

LBJ. You're fired.

When Johnson called an aide early one morning and learned that he was in the shower, the president pointedly remained on the phone till the flustered fellow was out of the shower, then asked him sarcastically, "Are you all dry? I wouldn't want you to catch cold." When Johnson noticed that an assistant press secretary's desk was a sea of paper, he rasped, "I hope yore mind isn't as messed up as yore desk!" The aide promptly cleared the mess, and the next day Johnson noticed the desk's immaculate condition. Snapped the president: "I sure hope yore mind isn't as empty as yore desk." There was latent savagery to Johnson that made some congressmen fear to oppose him. Quipped Dick Shawn: "President Johnson used the money he saved by budgetary cuts to hold an enormous barbecue to which he invited all the Congressmen who are supporting him. The Congressmen who are *opposing* him were already *at* the barbecue."

Even when Johnson was being avuncular and anecdotal, his humor could carry a threat. On one occasion, he was hectoring his agency heads to reduce their departmental budgets in an attempt to reduce the deficit. Johnson told a story of a railroad that is being built right by the front door of a Texas youth. The boy has applied for a job on the line, and the foreman poses a question to test his intelligence. If the boy can answer it, he will have a job. "Suppose," says the foreman, "you're standing by the switch, you look to the east and you see a locomotive heading west at 60 miles an hour. Then you look to the west and you see another locomotive on the same track heading east at 60 miles an hour. What do you do?" The boy ponders a moment and then says, "I run into the house and get my brother." "Why on earth would you get your brother?" asks the foreman. "Because he's never *seen* a train wreck," says the boy. The anecdote held a cautionary caveat: cut your budget or you are going to be in one hell of a train wreck!

The contrast between Johnson's public warmth and private chilliness inevitably brings to mind the word "hypocrisy." Johnson certainly displayed this quality to a disturbing extent in the most controversial TV commercial ever produced in a presidential campaign. The thirty-second spot was aimed at Barry Goldwater and his verbal excesses. When Campaign 1964 began, Goldwater tried to backpedal his way to respectability. The Johnson commercial sought to remind voters of the irresponsible things Goldwater had said in the past: that the eastern seaboard should be chopped off, that Social Security should be eliminated, that we should lob a nuclear bomb into the Kremlin. The controversial TV spot addressed the latter suggestion. It showed a little girl in a sylvan setting, plucking petals from a daisy. As she counts the petals from one to ten, a more menacing voice is counting downward from ten to one—a nuclear countdown. When the deeper voice reaches zero, we see a nuclear explosion destroy our planet. The commercial ran only once but it triggered a massive reaction, mainly among Republicans injured by the fallout. They claimed it was hitting below the belt. An apparently exercised President Johnson promptly phoned Bill Moyers who had created the ad. Said Moyers in recollection:

> Johnson called me . . . And said he'd been swamped with calls . . . I could tell the moment I answered the phone that he was having a wonderful time putting on an act. He said, "What in the hell do you mean putting on that ad? I've been swamped with calls and the Goldwater people are calling it a low blow."

Johnson summoned Moyers to his office and demanded an explanation. Moyers explained that they were just reminding people that they had better put an experienced hand at the nuclear button. Besides, added Moyers, the commercial was only to be run that single time. As Moyers headed for the door, Johnson stopped him. "Bill! Bill! Just a minute. Are you sure we ought to run it just *once*?"

Said David Frost of the TV commercial flap: "The Republicans protested against the campaign commercial that showed the little girl counting the petals on the daisy." When she reached ten, declared Frost, a nuclear explosion blew up the world. "So far," said Frost dryly, "the commercial has not won a single vote for Mr. Johnson, but it has been responsible for a drastic reduction in the number of little girls picking daisies."

Some of the humor at Johnson's expense during that tumultuous campaign year flowered from the Bugs Bunny grin of Robert Kennedy, and I must confess I played a small part in it. When John F. Kennedy sat in the Oval Office, I had met with him to propose a group of books called "The New Frontier Series." Each book would deal with a different subject of what JFK called "the unfinished business of our society," and the respective editors of the books were to be the relevant members of the Kennedy cabinet. The book on Civil Rights, edited by Attorney General Robert Kennedy, was spearheading the administration's drive for civil rights—thus, my meeting with Bobby in his cavernous justice department office. Four years later, in 1964, there was much media speculation about the possibility of Bobby Kennedy as Lyndon Johnson's running mate in the presidential contest. Bobby was ambivalent. He recalled my work on "That Was the Week That Was" and my *Who's in Charge Here?* books whose irreverence his brother had enjoyed. Bobby called to ask if I had any ideas how he might respond when reporters asked him about the chance of his running with Johnson. Given the bad blood between the two, it seemed an unlikely marriage; still, Bobby did not yet want to close the door. Better to turn the matter aside with humor. I suggested two replies, which Bobby employed:

Q. How do you feel about a Johnson-Kennedy ticket?
A. I'd be willing, but I'm not sure that Mr. Johnson would accept the vice presidency.

Q. Do you think that a Johnson-Kennedy ticket is feasible?
A. I've said that a coalition government is possible in Saigon, but not in Washington.

The acrimony between LBJ and RFK had been of long standing, dating back to Bobby's attempts to persuade his brother against selecting Lyndon as his running mate in 1960. In *The Kennedy Legacy*, Ted Sorensen, the brilliant aide and speech writer who brought the glory of words to the Kennedy years, tries to explain the antagonism that sprang up between Bobby and Lyndon. Sorensen attributes it to Johnson's sense of insecurity. "Johnson had a feeling that the Kennedys were against him," writes Sorensen, "that the Kennedys were condescending to him. He wanted to emulate their graceful wit and intellectual elegance . . . but he seemed at the same time to resent the Kennedys' Eastern polish."

All through the election year of 1964, America's humorists focused on Bobby Kennedy. Predicted one press corps wag: "Bobby Kennedy is going to announce that he'll soon have another mouth to feed. I hear Arthur Schlesinger is joining his staff." When a tenth child was born to Bobby and Ethel, UPI took cognizance of the Kennedy dynasty and printed a mock story that read: "The 49th President of the United States was born yesterday to Robert and Ethel Kennedy—an eight-pound son. The baby's father will be the 38th President of the United States, the baby's brothers, the 43rd, 44th, 45th, 46th, 47th and 48th Presidents of the United States." When former presidents Eisenhower and Truman announced they had finally found a point on which they could agree—they both supported birth control—a capital wag said, "I hear Bobby Kennedy feels he's being smeared."

The perennial showman, LBJ feared that the convention that announced his nomination would be a terrible bore, and he tried to add a modicum of excitement by building suspense into the identity of his running mate. This guessing game produced its share of fun. Given the enormous popular appeal of Bobby Kennedy, there were some who anticipated a Johnson-Kennedy ticket. Said Henry Morgan: "The big question in Washington is 'Will Bobby be asked to run for Vice President?' Insiders point out that since Lyndon became President, he and Bobby have not been as close as one would expect. It seems now that the only conspicuous Democrat definitely out of the running *is* Bobby. There has been no comment on this from Mr. Baker himself."

"That Was the Week That Was" offered a summary of Johnson's possible running mates in the form of a baseball report, with actor David Doyle playing the hyperactive sportscaster:

The President of All the People

Hello there, politics fans. This is Buzzy Krankheit reporting once again on the national picture. Tonight lets recap the Democratic League. The big question is, which hurlers will Manager Johnson pick from his bullpen to face the Republicans in the all-important series in November. He may go with his Number One mound ace, Bobby "Fireball" Kennedy . . . Another possible choice for Johnson is the cagey veteran twirler Adlai "Pops" Stevenson, who has been improving his control working in the International League [at the U.N.]. You'll recall Stevenson lost two World Series by pitching over the heads of the American people. And as another possible starter don't count out Lefty Hubey Humphrey. . . ." [The lefty ultimately got the nod.]

As the possible candidates twisted slowly in the wind and Lyndon Johnson enjoyed the attention he was generating among the possible nominees, TW3 offered a sketch called "Choosing a Vice President," in which Henry Morgan and Elliot Read played two Democratic officials weighing the important decision:

REID. Let's see, Johnson is a Southerner so our V.P. should be from the North.

MORGAN. Right. And Johnson has a conservative image, so he'll have to run with a liberal.

REID. Check, and Johnson's known to be a religious man, so we'll need an atheist.

MORGAN. Johnson's for foreign aid so we need an isolationist.

REID. He's married—we need a bachelor.

MORGAN. He's a temperate man, so we need a drunk.

REID. Good. Let's add it up. What does that give us?

MORGAN. Well, what we need for Vice President is a Northern liberal isolationist who's an unmarried, atheistic alcoholic.

[There is a moment of thought.]

167

REID. Right. Now which one?

[Blackout]

During the 1964 campaign, Lyndon Johnson favored the humor of tall Texas tales. It was therefore most fitting that the election returns, when they came pouring in, resembled nothing so much as a tall tale of Bunyonesque proportions. Was it not a tall Texas tale that a southerner would walk off with 97 percent of the black vote? Or that a Protestant candidate would gather more Catholic votes than the Catholic president who preceded him? Perhaps the tallest tale of all was still to come—that three years later, this incredible man, who rolled up the biggest plurality in presidential history, would "abdicate" his office and retire to his Texas ranch to lick his wounds and write his memoirs.

Chapter 12
Campaign 1964
Mister Malaprop

Time magazine has just named Barry Goldwater Man
of the Year. 1682.
— GOODMAN ACE

A huge plurality of American voters felt that Barry
Goldwater would not make the ideal president. But the small
army of humorists, satirists, and journalistic wits who make
their living from making light of national elections found him
a wonderful source of amusement. Presidents have been chosen for various irrelevant reasons—their presidential look
(Warren Harding), their successes in war (Dwight Eisenhower), their telegenic appeal (Ronald Reagan)—but to select a
chief executive because he makes a good target for lampoonery would be a trifle frivolous. Thus, though Barry Goldwater generated some of the most searching humor in the history
of American politics, he generated few votes.

The Arizonan's words, in or out of context, were so bizarre that they lent themselves to spoofery in all the media of
the humorist—print, cartoon, sketch, blackout, song, and anecdote. And if liberals, Democrats, blacks, and moderates of
his own party did not find Goldwater very funny—he more often produced grimaces and shrugs—he did produce a good
deal of humor during his doomed campaign for the presidency.

Goldwater said he offered "a choice, not an echo," and as he stood at the podium of the GOP convention in San Francisco, his hands aloft in the traditional pose of triumph, his handsome face ruddy with the waves of cheers washing over him, Goldwater had effectively split the rock of the Republican party.

The bellicosity of the ultraconservative Goldwater was so fearsome and his pugnacity in foreign affairs so pronounced that reporters began chanting a nuclear countdown: "Ten, nine, eight, seven, six—." When Goldwater declared his controversial line, "I would remind you that extremism in the defense of freedom is no vice," one correspondent cracked incredulously, "Good Lord! He's going to run as Barry Goldwater!" The candidate's shoot-from-the-hip belligerence was so unsettling that one aide pleaded with the press: "Don't quote what he says—quote what he means."

As Goldwater started tremors running through the nation with his extremist views, moderate members of the Republican party became a source and a subject of his gallows humor. The moderates who had been trampled by Goldwater and his zealous supporters on the road to the 1964 convention included New York governor Nelson Rockefeller, Pennsylvania governor William Scranton, Senator Margaret Chase Smith, Ambassador Henry Cabot Lodge, Governor George Romney, and former Vice President Richard Nixon. The moderates tried to exercise good breeding as Goldwater's hoards crumbled them underfoot. On TW3 we simulated a tennis match between the moderate Governor Scranton, who was loathe to enter the fray, and the combative Goldwater. David Frost did the play-by-play from courtside as follows:

Good afternoon. Sixth game, second set, Mr. Goldwater leading five games to love, due mainly to the fact that during the entire set Mr. Scranton remained in the grandstand.

In the last game, Mr. Goldwater missed the first service but explained he is an Episcopalian. Ah, they're ready to begin. Mr. Goldwater is in the far court, all in white including his stand on civil rights. A great favorite in the Wightman Cup. Mr. Goldwater's serve . . .

Mr. Scranton takes it on his backhand. What's this? Someone has grabbed Mr. Scranton's racket and won't let him start. Now they're showing Mr. Eisenhower from the court. Fifteen love. Mr. Goldwater serving . . .

It's an ace! A palpable ace! Thirty love. Mr. Scranton is not doing too well. This racket doesn't seem to suit him. He's losing his grip and he's busted a gut. Here comes Mr. Goldwater's cannonball service again. . . . Another ace! And now Mr. Scranton is employing a strategy that Mr. Nixon uses whenever he's behind. He's starting to cry.

Mr. Goldwater serves . . . Scranton returns . . . Rockefeller returns . . . Romney returns . . . Nixon returns . . . Margaret Chase Smith returns . . . and now that's incredible—Lodge returns. [He chose to remain in Vietnam throughout the convention.] But there's no doubt that the biggest returns this year will *still* be Lyndon Johnson's. Good afternoon.

All the moderate Republicans were reluctant to oppose Goldwater explicitly, not wanting to antagonize his vocal backers on the far right. Even former president Eisenhower held his tongue. Said one Washington newsman of Ike, who was famed for his strangled syntax: "Eisenhower denied that his anti-Goldwater statement was an anti-Goldwater statement. But he didn't say it was a *pro*-Goldwater statement either. One thing was clear. It was obviously an Eisenhower statement."

It required no special gifts of prophecy to foresee a Goldwater debacle. Johnson had generated a broad base of support by driving Kennedy's New Frontier legislation through Congress, and Goldwater provoked trepidation with both his foreign and domestic policies. It was a case of double casino for LBJ—the affluent applauded the strength of the economy and the needy welcomed Johnson's War on Poverty. Cracked one editorialist: "We can't recall a time when a President had prosperity and poverty going for him at the same time!" Polls foreshadowed an overwhelming triumph for Johnson in November. The possibility of a Goldwater victory seemed remote. Said the *Seattle Post-Intelligencer*: "It may be that Barry Goldwater will be elected. It may also be that Chase

Manhattan will go broke . . . and that Mickey Spillane will win the Nobel Prize for literature." Chase Manhattan continued strong, and Mickey Spillane won nothing but a contract from Miller Lite and the company of John Madden.

Once the Goldwater Caper passed into history, GOP moderates looked ahead to the next election, trying to put the electoral calamity behind them. Said one Washington wit: "It has been revealed that moderate Republicans have formed an organization called The Committee of Sixty-Eight, to study ways to win the next election. It is still unclear whether The Committee of Sixty-Eight is named for the year of the next election or the number of Republicans who could be found."

The demolished moderates displayed little sympathy for their fallen candidate. Both Governor Rockefeller and Ambassador Lodge, who did little to help Goldwater during the campaign, even refused to say which presidential candidate they had voted for, on the grounds that every citizen is entitled to keep his vote a secret. Said Steve Allen: "Goldwater supporters are saying that they have nothing against the secret ballot, but this the first time they've heard of a secret campaign."

The moderates could see catastrophe coming from the day they left town after their convention. Said one GOP politician: "I'm going to have to spend the rest of the campaign explaining what Goldwater means every time he opens his mouth." Gibed another: "He's a cross between the Lone Ranger and Mr. Malaprop." This depressed moderate suggested that Goldwater suffered from foot-in-mouth disease. Observing the narrow ideological appeal of their candidate, one GOP pollster joked, "If this were China, we'd call it The Year of the Underdog." Bumper stickers sprouted that read: JOHNSON FOR PRESIDENT, GOLDWATER FOR HALLOWEEN. America's newspaper publishers have traditionally supported GOP presidential candidates, but Goldwater seemed unsupportable. Wrote *Editor and Publisher*, the weekly journal of the newspaper industry: "What [Senator Goldwater] must bear in mind when he open his mouth is that clarity begins at home."

Goldwater was no fanatic, but fanatics flew to him like filings to a magnet, extolling and embracing him. The most strident of these were members of the John Birch Society, an ultraconservative group whose views may be judged by their perception of Dwight Eisenhower as a tool of communism. The Birch Society sorely tested the capacity for humor of 1964's satirists, but they did not altogether fail. Said Henry Morgan of the society's obsession with communism: "The financial statement of the John Birch Society shows that for the fourth consecutive year, they have ended up losing money. They can't seem to stay out of the red." Said one Potomac observer: "I think the reason the John Birch Society doesn't like Communism is they feel it smacks of Socialism." And one journalist said, "Robert Welch [founder of the society] says the biggest Communist Front in America is the Communist Party. He says a Communist is just a Communist in disguise."

In my 1964 edition of *Who's In Charge Here?* I pictured a ruminative Barry Goldwater saying, "Last night I had a dream that was like a prophecy. I saw myself at the helm of the Ship of State . . . Or was it a Birch canoe?" In 1964 a bevy of groups was springing up in support of Goldwater's candidacy. They employed high-sounding, patriotic names. In my election year book, I showed Goldwater responding to a reporter who has asked what kind of organizations support him. "Well," says the candidate, "take the Christian Minuteman Crusade for Brotherhood and Americanism . . . They're a hate group." In still another photo, the Arizonan is displaying indignation as he studies a newspaper. "I wish the *New York Times* would at least get my *name* straight," he complains. "It's Goldwater. Not Backwater."

Some liberal college students regarded Goldwater as an amiable buffoon, while others took him as a danger to their survival. Goldwater's statements about nuclear weapons (for example, "I'd like to lob an A-bomb into the men's room at the Kremlin") invited ridicule or terror. California collegians greeted the candidate with signs replicating a new black comedy film: DR. STRANGELOVE, or HOW HE BECAME A CONSERVATIVE AND LEARNED TO LOVE THE BOMB.

Goldwater's domination of the GOP convention provoked the startled question, Are there enough zealots in America to put this man in the White House? Common sense said no, the polls said no, Lyndon Johnson said no, but the ferocity of his supporters gave one some doubt. After all, the people who insisted he could never be elected were the same

173

ones who had said he could never get the nomination. But how could one take him seriously? Many did not. They laughed at his assaults on big government and his wish to dismantle the whole damn business. In a cabaret skit, the actor playing Goldwater angrily declares, "This is just one more case of the federal government intruding in an area that should be left to individual initiative." And a reporter replies, "But Senator, the government has *always* run the navy." Goldwater's affection for the simplicities of an earlier age led one humorist to crack, "*Time* magazine has just named Barry Goldwater Man of the Year. 1682." Said another: "You know his favorite TV show, don't you? 'That Was the Century That Was.'" Jonas Salk had recently discovered his famous vaccine, and since Goldwater preached the merits of individual initiative, one wag remarked, "I understand Goldwater opposes the use of the Salk Vaccine. He feels a man should have the right to decide for himself whether he wants polio or not." The candidate's apparent unconcern for the poor and his generally retrogressive attitude toward social issues, led one comic to say: "For any of you who want Mr. Goldwater's views on social welfare, he'll be speaking on television tonight, from 11:00 P.M. to 10:45."

The Goldwater family owned Phoenix's largest department store, and the senator was a strong advocate of the entrepreneurial spirit. Perhaps this led him to question the motivation of the needy. Consequently, Goldwater called for an investigation of the poor. He said that such an inquiry might reveal that their indigence was the result of "low intelligence and low ambition." This led Goodman Ace to say: "I guess Mr. Goldwater figures why should the lazy loafers be supported by people like him who have had the ambition and intelligence to inherit a department store."

The family's retailing establishment came under the comic scrutiny of a Los Angeles improvisational group. Ridiculing Goldwater's position on various social issues, the performer portraying the candidate snapped, "The government should be run like we run Goldwater's Department Store. If there's something you need and we don't have it—you're a Socialist."

Goldwater had proposed giving battlefield commanders in Vietnam the authority to employ nuclear weapons. Wrote TRB in the *New Republic*, "Can you take seriously a man . . . who would delegate the incinerating nuclear weapon to bomb-rattling generals?" When former general Eisenhower gave Goldwater his grudging support, saying that he could live with a Goldwater administration, one satirist gibed: "Maybe Mr. Eisenhower could live with a Goldwater Administration. I guess he'd have as good a chance as anyone else." "With that kind of nuclear policy," said one humorist, "in this election Barry Goldwater has a good chance of losing New York . . . Twice." Said David Frost: "What are the principles of Goldwater's new-style conservatism? He's in favor of the United Nations in principle, but against it in practice. He's in favor of foreign aid in principle, but against it in practice. And of course, *everybody's* against the A-bomb in principle. But he's in favor of it in practice."

Goldwater made a striking figure with a bold, youthful charisma. True, there was none of the Kennedy rhetoric or the Johnson folksiness, but his audiences cheered his dashing pronouncements and sweeping condemnations. He infuriated those who disagreed with his simplistic views and sent them scurrying for humor with which to laugh him away, proving Oscar Wilde's epigram that the world laughs at its tragedies— that being the only thing it can do about them.

Whether it was recklessness or mere carelessness, Goldwater's campaign speeches seemed sublimely indifferent to the special interests of his audience. In ignoring this time-honored political practice, Goldwater seemed to display an unconscious death wish. Aides cringed when he attacked the Employment Opportunity Act in an impoverished area in West Virginia. Supporters winced when he assaulted public power in Knoxville, Tennessee, the home of the TVA. Detractors chortled when he proposed that Social Security be made voluntary, addressing this suggestion to the elderly of St. Petersburg. Cracked a headline in the *St. Petersburg Times:* RIGHT CITY, WRONG SPEECH.

In a satiric cartoon of the period, Goldwater is shown addressing a black tie fund-raising dinner. Says the candidate:

"I am touched by this ovation. And I am touched by this turn-out." A member of the audience responds: "I think he's touched." This sort of ridicule was triggered by Goldwater's bizarre views on a variety of subjects. Here are some of the more extreme of his utterances; they are not without their unintentional humor:

"I would turn to my Joint Chiefs of Staff and say, 'Fellows, we made the decision to win [in Vietnam], now it's your problem.'" —Goldwater in *Der Spiegel.*

"It's their baby." —Goldwater referring to segregation in the Southern states—as quoted in the *New York Herald Tribune.*

"We are told, however, that many people lack skills and cannot get jobs because they did not have an education. That's like saying that people have big feet because they wear big shoes."

"Like a three dollar bill—it's a phony." —Goldwater, on the Civil Rights Act, as quoted in *Time.*

"One Eisenhower in a generation is enough." —Goldwater, as quoted in *Time.*

"I have always favored withdrawing recognition from Russia." —Goldwater, in an interview with *U.S. News & World Report.*

"Where fraternities are not allowed, communism flourishes." —Goldwater, in a speech before The National Interfraternity Conference in Los Angeles.

"There is no way to enforce civil rights." —Goldwater, as quoted in the *Boston Globe.*

Goldwater's comments about the "phony" Civil Rights Act which, in his judgment, could not be enforced, led many black voters to feel threatened by his candidacy. One black delegate at the GOP convention slumped dolefully in his seat, intimidated by the bobbing sea of Goldwater posters. A reporter asked him what he had against Goldwater. "Nothing," grimaced the black man. "Ask him what he has against me." Said a columnist for the *New Republic*: "A foreigner traveling with Barry Goldwater in the south wouldn't know there were any blacks in it. They seem to have withdrawn from the main streets. . . . He tells reporters that 'states' rights have superceded civil rights' so there is no use bothering with them. . . . The issue is everywhere, it intrudes on everybody's thoughts, but it's like sex—it isn't mentioned."

Marvin Kitman, whose delicious satire enlivened many publications from *Harper's* to the *Saturday Evening Post*, wrote a memoir about his own mock campaign for the presidency in 1964 in a book called *The Number-One Best Seller*. Viewing the sorry state of GOP moderates in general and Goldwater's position on civil rights in particular, Kitman issued a press release, which said in part:

Leonia, N.J.—Marvin Kitman, a 34-year-old gagwriter, announced today he is planning to enter the New Hampshire Presidential primary. "I would rather be President than write," Mr. Kitman said. . . .

Mr. Kitman said he had decided to come to the aid of his party at this time to give the Republican voters a choice instead of an echo. "Rockefeller, Romney, Lodge, Stassen, Nixon, Scranton and Mrs. Smith are Franklin Roosevelt Republicans. Goldwater is a McKinley Republican. As a Lincoln Republican, I am the only reactionary in the race."

"My branch of conservatism really goes back 100 years," he added. "I will be running on the Republican Party's platform of 1864, so many of whose promises to the voters have yet to be fulfilled. I'm in favor of abolishing slavery."

Barry Goldwater ran a campaign aimed at reducing government spending, and this produced such sardonic lines as: "Goldwater in '64, Hot Water in '65, Bread and Water in '66." His slogan, which called to America from billboards and TV screens, was: "In your heart you know he's right." This produced antic variations such as: "In your heart you know he's *far* right," and the more abrasive, "In your guts you know he's nuts." Other allusions to Goldwater's position on the political spectrum were, "He'd rather be far right than President," and "He's slightly to the right of Atilla the Hun."

Despite Goldwater's extreme utterances—or because of them—he could on occasion be quite amusing. During the Los Angeles primary, as he watched the returns pouring in to give him a resounding victory, he pointed at liberal CBS correspondent Eric Sevareid. "Look at that," he shouted. "Sevareid's thinking of seven hundred reasons why this can't be happening. Eric's womb is dropping."

Goldwater's choice of a running mate produced its own peculiar levity. The unusual selection was Republican congressman William Miller, a hack politician and graduate of the House Un-American Activities Committee. Skeptics observed that in fourteen years in Congress, Miller had never managed to get a major bill named after him. His principal legislative achievement was a bill to incorporate the "Moms of America." But now it was Miller Time. Asked the reason for his improbable selection, Barry Goldwater said, "One of the reasons I chose Miller is that he drives Johnson nuts."

William Miller's vice presidential candidacy brought the sour smell of sarcasm to Goldwater's campaign (as Bob Dole had done for Gerald Ford and Richard Nixon for Dwight Eisenhower). Miller gleefully mocked the middle name of his Democratic counterpart, referring to him as "Hubert Hor-ay-ti-o Humphrey." Humphrey put the obscure congressman in his place by responding: "He thinks he has a real issue in my middle name . . . I must warn him of the hidden-middle-name vote—all those youngsters blessed with a middle name they choose to convert to an initial—may rise against him." Then, with a mischievous grin, Humphrey added, "Miller should beware of the midlash."

As the campaign progressed, allegations of corruption thickened around William Miller. Accusations of conflicts of interest covered a wide area. Said a TW3 correspondent:

Perhaps some people don't realize how fully and convincingly Mr. Miller has answered these charges. The first allegation revealed that Miller has been serving as a director and counsel of the Lockport Felt Company at an annual retainer of $7500. During the period, the Congressional Record reveals that twice on the floor of the House he spoke against legislation that would have hurt his firm, without revealing his interest. Mr.

Miller conceded that he had collected the annual retainer. Then Mr. Miller gave us a very full and complete explanation. These are his words:

MILLER. I will not be diverted into a waste of time required to answer sleazy unsubstantiated smears.

TW3. Uh-huh.

MILLER. These are left-handed attempts to embarrass me.

TW3. Yes, yes, go on.

MILLER. I will waste no further time in the rebuttal.

Herblock, who has been called "the best of our political cartoonists, not excluding Thomas Nast," brought his biting wit to bear on the Goldwater campaign. In dismissing the black vote, Goldwater had said, "We're not going to get the Negro vote as a bloc . . . so we ought to go hunting where the ducks are." Herblock responded by picturing a dismayed GOP elephant, wearing a necklace of dead albatrosses labeled: WHITE SUPREMACY VOTES—LOUISIANA, MISSISSIPPI, ALABAMA, GEORGIA, SOUTH CAROLINA. The elephant is moaning, "I met a fellow who took me hunting where the albatrosses were." When former president Eisenhower suppressed his doubts about Goldwater long enough to televise a thiry-minute conversation with the candidate for TV use, Herblock pictured the two men leaning on a fence at Ike's Gettysburg ranch. Ike is saying: "Criticism of you is tommyrot, Barry! Naturally you don't mean all those dopey things you've said." On the twentieth anniversary of D-day, Herblock needled Ike for his cautious posture in the Goldwater affair. The former president had declared he would not take part in any effort to deny Goldwater the nomination, whatever his misgivings. Herblock pictured Ike as an apprehensive old man seated before a poster showing a beaming young Ike reviewing his D-day troops. The enfeebled Ike is on the phone, saying "On second thought, forget it. I won't be a part of a cabal to stop anybody." Asked Herblock: "Is this the man who launched 1000 ships?"

Eisenhower's unwillingness to condemn Goldwater was roundly ridiculed by the nation's wits. When his cordial colloquy with Goldwater was broadcast on NBC, preempting TW3, a viewer wrote the show: "What an inspired idea, for TW3 to present those two aging comedians." When it was reported that Ike would serve as a news analyst for ABC at the Republican convention, a reporter cracked, "The only limitation Ike placed on the deal is he won't endorse any candidate, he won't criticize any candidate, and he won't identify the network." A pair of early morning radio cutups in San Francisco produced this exchange:

"I hear Ike can't involve himself in the campaign because he's working on a book."
"Oh? What's he reading?"

Goldwater's critics could not understand the zealots who heaped praise and adulation on the candidate. The positions taken in his writings seemed too extreme, too extraordinary. Goldwater seemed wedded to another century; he was too far right. He questioned the need for Social Security. He refused to recognize Red China. He labeled liberals "socialists" and worse. He accepted the endorsement of the John Birch Society. Yet, surprisingly, Goldwater's supporters were numerous and vocal.

Goldwater had even captured the support of various groups on American campuses, and this phenomenon produced one of the wittier attacks on Goldwater and his philosophy. Julius Monk was the elegant creator of a series of topical entertainments at Plaza 9, a little theater at New York's Plaza Hotel. In 1964 Monk produced a review called "Dime a Dozen" that featured a song dedicated to the college students who embraced Goldwater's views. The song was called "Barry's Boys" and was written by June Reizner. In the space of three minutes and two choruses, Ms. Reizner managed to enumerate and comically demolish most of Goldwater's excesses. Here is a sampling of the coruscating lyrics:

Mister Malaprop

We're the bright young men
Who wanta go back to 1910
We're Barry's Boys.
We're the kids with a cause
A government like grandmama's
We're Barry's boys . . .

We're the kids who agree
To be social without security
We're Barry's Boys.
Because his hat's in the ring
Where Westbrook Pegler once was king—
Now he's too left wing—
So if you don't recognize any old Red China
Or Canada, or Britain
Or South Carolina . . .
Back to Barry—back to cash and carry—
Back with Barry's Boys . . .

Roses are red, violets are blue
Walter Lippmann's a pinko too . . .
Barry Barry make your bid,
I love John Birch but oh you kid . . .
Mother mother wear a grin
And don't complain or we'll turn you in . . .

And really what's so wrong with being young and wealthy
And really when you're aged must you all be healthy?

So let's go back to the days when men were men
And start the First World War all over again . . .
Back with Barry's Boys.

Goldwater's ability to draw to his conservative colors large numbers of collegians is less surprising than the large number of senior citizens who were attracted to his credos, since Goldwater's position on Medicare and Social Security was clearly hostile to their self-interest. I addressed the irony of this seeming contradiction in a sketch written for the pilot of "That Was the Week That Was." (Broadway producer Leland Hayward had imported the audacious show from Britain where a group of precocious young Brits had created the impudent series. Hayward was producing the American counterpart on NBC.) In my Goldwater sketch, a talented comedienne named Doro Morande played an aged scrubwoman working in the Senate Office Building. We see her scrubbing the floors of Barry Goldwater's office, and she tells us of her reverence for the man—how she lovingly polished his rolltop desk and quill pen. The enfeebled old girl proudly declares that she has just resigned from Social Security. "Those social welfare programs destroy individual initiative," she says. Sketches like this led the GOP to preempt TW3 frequently through the fall election campaign, though it is my recollection that we were equally rough on the Johnson persona and policies.

One of the men who wrote with elegance of the Goldwater campaign was Richard Rovere, author of the "Letters from Washington" in the *New Yorker*. Rovere wrote with such clarity that to read a page of his prose was like examining a tray of diamonds. Rovere composed a slim volume about the campaign which he called *The Goldwater Caper,* capturing in the title the quirky qualities of the candidate's campaign. Rovere set the tone of the book by reproducing in its preface an ad whose copy exemplified the mind-set of Goldwater's supporters. The advertisement read:

BE THE FIRST IN YOUR PRECINCT TO OWN
A BARRY GOLDWATER SWEATSHIRT

You'll delight in watching liberals recoil in terror when they see you in your BARRY GOLDWATER SWEATSHIRT. You'll find your BGSS imbues you with renewed courage to suffer the slings and arrows of the extremist lunatic fringes of the ultra-left.

The Barry Goldwater Sweatshirt displays a nearly lifelike head of Barry Goldwater, with his name below to identify him to uninitiated liberals. . . .

The frequent preemption of TW3 freed me to travel as aide and resident humorist for Bobby Kennedy, who was seeking a seat in the U.S. Senate. I observed that Bobby, like many other Democrats that year, was running not so much against his opponent (a benign moderate Republican named Kenneth

Keating) but against Barry Goldwater. Bobby employed humor to mock Goldwater, winning him laughter and votes. In Syracuse Bobby invoked the name of Washington Irving, whose classic "The Legend of Sleepy Hollow" was well known to the populace. Quipped Bobby: "This community produced Rip Van Winkle, who went to sleep and woke up in another century. The only other city that can make such a claim is Phoenix, Arizona." When Bobby's airport speech in Buffalo was interrupted by the roar of a jet screaming off overhead, Bobby looked skyward and deadpanned, "He's heading back to Arizona to report."

Goldwater was soundly defeated, and the *New Republic's* TRB observed wryly that "Lyndon Johnson is the first man in history to be elected for defending the twentieth century." Goldwater's repudiation at the polls reflected the public's inability to accept his primitive political views. After his election defeat, the exhausted candidate vacationed on a Caribbean island. One comic quipped: "I understand that a TV company is filming a new 'Tarzan' series on the same island. So this week the air was filled with the cries of a man swinging from the trees on vines. However, this did not interfere with the work of the film company."

Goldwater's defeat was so stunning—he carried down with him a battalion of candidates for the Senate and state Houses—that many feared for the future of the Republican party. This question was pondered by all the leading members of the GOP. But the question of how to rebuild the Republican party in Goldwater's wake seemed too important a matter to leave to politicians alone. For this reason, TW3 conducted a poll—fictitious, of course—of leaders in other fields on the question: "What is the best way to rebuild the Republican party?"

Said Sammy Davis, Jr.: "If the Republican Party's going to start making it again, they'll have to get back on good terms with my people. And the blacks, too."

Said Leonid Brezhnev: "Of course, coming to power in the Soviet union is a little different. In the Soviet Union we have only one party . . . Well, maybe it's not so different."

Said Roy Cohn: "If the Republican Party is to become a major force again, it will need some tough hard-hitting issues. Now, I hold in my hand the names of 157 Communists . . ."

Said Max Factor: "What the cause of Republicanism needs is a creamy, more liberal complexion, with just a touch of pink."

Said Tennessee Williams: "What the Republican party needs is the sort of things I write about—alcoholism, dope addiction, and sexual promiscuity."
Q. "Will that help the party?"
A. "It usually does."

Chapter 13
Campaign 1960
The Return to Humor

I don't think that either candidate will win.
—MORT SAHL

In 1963 there would be "That Was the Week That Was" to comment satirically on the nation's politicians. In 1965 "Laugh-In" would appear with its frenetic barbs on the social and political scene. In 1967 "The Smothers Brothers Comedy Hour" would arrive with its rebellious gibes at the White House, politicians, and Pentagon. In 1975 "Saturday Night Live" would carry the comic invasion of politics further inland, making it almost subversive. But in the election year of 1960, political humor was sorely limited in the mass media. Curious to report, the most sparkling source of humor in that tumultuous, hard-fought election was one of the candidates, a lean Bostonian named John F. Kennedy.

Mort Sahl had long observed that politicians are a more reliable source of political humor "than the people we pay to amuse us." He cited Adlai Stevenson's witty way with words. Sahl quoted many of Stevenson's mots in his campus appearances, and he also cited those of John F. Kennedy, whose wit has since become legendary.

As Kennedy and Nixon joined in electoral battle that fall of 1960, there was a dearth of political humor to add leavening and perspective to the political scene. Playwrights, jour-

185

nalists, and social critics had lamented the paucity of wit during the Eisenhower years. *Time* magazine called the fifties "the silent generation," and it was most certainly silent of laughter. T. S. Eliot said our legacy would be "a thousand golf balls." And Eric Goldman gave the fifties decade a chilly farewell kiss when he wrote, "Goodbye to the fifties—and good riddance." The comics and historians alike lamented the absence of humor. It was, said Goldman, "a heavy, humorless, sanctimonious, stultifying atmosphere, singularly lacking in the self-mockery that is self-criticism." When someone challenged Mort Sahl to say something funny, he replied, "John Foster Dulles." If Ike's dour secretary of state was a sample of fifties fun, it reflected badly on the level of humor. The Eisenhower years had produced a morose self-satisfaction that was the very antithesis of humor. "Where are the guffaws in this country?" asked Eric Goldman. "Where is the purifying wit and humor? The catharsis of caricature? The outcries against all this nonsense? Sometimes I think we are just boring ourselves to death."

The boredom would cease with the arrival on the national scene of Senator John F. Kennedy and his race for the presidency. For reasons based on both personality and strategy, Kennedy injected a healthy dose of humor into his public statements. He liked the company of witty people ("he's careful to keep his wits about him," said one wag), and his chief speech writer kept him supplied with a stream of dry, subtle, pertinent wit, for those occasions when the bubbling Kennedy spontaneity failed him. Such moments were rare. Kennedy's campaign humor was ubiquitous and a part of his personality —it was wry, laconic, and germane. Kennedy told no rambling anecdotes like the presidential candidates who preceded and followed him. There were no pregnant pauses before a punch line, like a political clone of Bob Hope. There was no "I am reminded of the story . . ." to usher in a tiresome plagiarism from some ancient issue of *Reader's Digest*. Kennedy's wit was as educated as he was, and it supplied America with its most cogent humor of the 1960s campaign.

It was a campaign much in need of levity—a solemn procession to an uncertain conclusion with much at stake—for the candidates and the nation. The 1960s struggle was feral in its ferocity. Both Kennedy and Nixon were able campaigners with considerable stamina. Each had a staff of adroit professionals to chart his strategy. The Kennedy-Nixon matchup was the most fascinating presidential campaign in years and triggered the first of a series of provocative histories by Theodore H. White called *The Making of the President*. (In the comedic arena it triggered a series of humorous books called *Who's in Charge Here?* which, like White's histories, continued quadrennially for many years.

Before Jack Kennedy could undertake the bruising campaign against Richard Nixon, he first had to win the nomination from a field of Democrats who also sought the prize. It was a formidable struggle, and political observers could see in it the first signs of the emerging Kennedy wit.

"A primary fight," said Teddy White, "is America's most original contribution to the art of democracy." It is also the process that politicians most despise for its desperation, obsequity, and panic. (As this is written, six Republicans and seven Democrats are slogging through the quagmires of the 1988 primaries, each to the sound of his own uncertain trumpet.) Kennedy moved through this preconvention period with dexterity and humor. One example is particularly illuminating. In the midst of the crucial West Virginia primary, in which Kennedy faced the robust garrulity of Hubert Humphrey, he dispatched a crisis message to his brother Ted, age twenty-eight. Jack's regimen of twenty speeches a day had ravaged his throat; his vocal cords were gone, and he needed a surrogate. Teddy reached his brother's side and dutifully read Jack's speech to a large audience of miners. Here is how Ted recalled it:

> I was saying to the audience, "Do you want a man who will give the country leadership? Do you want a man who has vigor and vision?" when Jack took the microphone and said in a hoarse whisper, "I would just like to tell my brother that you cannot be selected President until you are 35 years of age."

Two of JFK's most formidable opponents in the 1960 primaries were fellow Senator Stuart Symington and Senate

Minority Leader Lyndon Johnson. The latter was particularly daunting, given his long legislative history and messianic ambition to rule. (Said one reporter who covered Johnson's doings in the Senate: "I once passed him on the Capitol steps and said, 'Lovely morning,' and Lyndon said, 'Thank you.'") Kennedy employed humor to puncture Johnson's pomposities. He told a press audience:

> I dreamed about the 1960 campaign the other night, and I told Stuart Symington and Lyndon Johnson about it in the cloakroom yesterday. I told them how the Lord came into my bedroom, anointed my head and said, "John Kennedy, I hereby anoint you President of the United States." Stu Symington said, "That's strange, Jack, because I too had a similar dream last night, in which the Lord anointed me and declared me President of the United States." And Lyndon Johnson said, "That's very interesting, gentlemen, because I *too* had a similar dream last night—and I don't remember anointing either one of you."

A less confident public man might have felt intimidated by the assembly of rivals for the Democratic nomination. Kennedy merely joked at their great number. Said JFK: "I understand there was a survey in which they asked each U.S. Senator about his preference for the Presidency—and ninety-six Senators each received one vote."

Reflecting on the internal battles being waged for power and leadership in the Democratic party, Kennedy remarked that all the infighting had "succeeded in splitting our party right down the middle—and that gives us more unity than we've had in twenty years."

When Kennedy took to the primary trail, he left behind a pregnant wife and a toddler daughter, Caroline. His schedule was so demanding that his days at home were few. Caroline was caught up in her father's pursuit of the nomination. Cracked Kennedy: "Caroline's first words were 'plane,' 'good-bye,' and 'New Hampshire.' And she recently learned to say 'Wisconsin' and 'West Virginia.' Any day now she is expected to come out with 'Oregon.'" (With the proliferation of primaries since 1960, the young daughter of one of today's candidates would develop a splendid sense of geography.)

At a primary stop in Oregon, two young women presented Kennedy with a toy donkey for his daughter. Kennedy cracked: "Caroline has the greatest collection of donkeys. She doesn't even know what an elephant looks like. We are going to protect her from that knowledge."

When the Kennedy family plane—"The Caroline"—set down in Wisconsin during Kennedy's primary imbroglio with Hubert Humphrey, JFK kidded the whole frantic primary process: "I am the first of an advancing army," he said. "By next spring the state will look like a college campus telephone booth."

Kennedy mocked the tension that he and Humphrey felt as the primaries ground down to their conclusion. At a New York gathering at which various party notables studded the podium, JFK began his address by saying:

> Senator Humphrey, Mrs. Roosevelt, Senator Lehman, Mayor Wagner, Governor Harriman, Senator Morse . . . You can tell who isn't running for office by that relaxed posture they assume up here. Hubert and I are the only ones on edge.

Kennedy's primary wit was augmented by that of the reporters who covered his efforts. One reporter penned a parody of Cole Porter's "My Heart Belongs to Daddy," in which he ridiculed the wealth of Kennedy's father, which was financing his son's campaign—purchasing a comfortable aircraft for Jack's travels so he need not depend on the vagaries of commercial airlines. The lyrics also paid dubious tribute to Bobby Kennedy, Jack's feisty kid brother, who was acting as his campaign manager. The lyrics went:

> I'll have a ball and votes this fall
> Will crown this Bostonian laddy.
> Then I will run for the top-most gun—
> And I learned it all from daddy.
> Now some hob-nob with Brother Bob,
> The boy who drove old Dave Beck batty.
> But Bob will chime that it ain't no crime
> For to take our cue from daddy . . .
> So don't try to beat this laddy,

Though your aim be perfectly swell.
For I send the bill to daddy,
'Cause my daddy he pays it so well.

Kennedy laughed away the healthy infusion of funds
that Ambassador Kennedy pumped into his primary campaign
—for advertising, staff, salaries, and transportation. He even
managed to make light of the underground slurs to the effect
that Old Joe Kennedy was actually purchasing votes. Kennedy
produced a telegram that he always carried as a prop, waved it
in the air, and said, "I have just received this wire from my father. It says 'Don't buy one vote more than is necessary—I'll
be damned if I'll pay for a landslide.'"

Once the presidential conventions do their work—with
their heroes and fools, their chaos and revelries, their climac-
tic triumphs and humbling failures—then the people must
choose. The campaign that follows, from Labor Day to Election Day, is a primitive and barbaric rite. Given the pressures
at work on the candidate (and on the staff and media that sur-
round him), it is impossible to sustain the sleepless pace without the saving grace of humor.

So many things must be done within that limited time
frame, with not enough hours or money or people to do them.
Tens of thousands must be provoked to register; voters must
be pushed from apathy to commitment; television must be
employed with cunning; rallies must be staged, and speeches
written and delivered with conviction.

"To chronicle these campaigns is like packaging fog,"
wrote Teddy White. But some men try to package it anyway,
and they are the polltakers whose measurements and projec-
tions often produce as much levity as light. In retrospect, the
pronouncements of the 1960 pollsters seem funnier than
those of Will Rogers. Ernest Dichter, oracular president of the
Institute of Motivational Research, conducted a survey on the
image of the two candidates to determine which of them projected the image of a winner. Proclaimed Dichter, "People
have been fooled by the father image. Roosevelt died, Ike got
dimmer. . . . As a result voters are settling for a brother and
son image." [Kennedy was forty-three, Nixon forty-seven.]

"Kennedy is the smoother of the two and that will undo him. He is slick, too perfect, too good-looking. . . ." (One remembers the exchange in an early Neil Simon comedy where a wife rages at her husband: "You dress right, you talk right, you're practically perfect!" and he replies, "That's a rotten thing to say.") As for Richard Nixon, Dichter declared, "He is hard angles, like a triangle." Faced with this sweeping deprecation of both candidates, Mort Sahl dourly predicted, "Neither of the candidates is going to win."

One network commentator observed that "neither candidate has a sense of humor." This reflected a startling degree of opacity. Nixon was certainly a humorless man; his mind-set was bitter and his Quaker parents had not raised him to take the world lightly. But Kennedy was the wittiest man to seek the presidency since, well, Adlai Stevenson four years before. But where Stevenson's humor had about it a whiff of arrogance—"he did not suffer fools gladly," said Hugh Sidey—Kennedy's humor reflected a sparkling personality that propelled him like a comet to the zenith of political authority and public affection.

The network expert who saw no sense of humor in either Nixon or Kennedy was not alone. Many jaded observers in 1960 saw the duo as two peas in a pod—two cool, calculating young politicians deserving neither allegiance nor power.

The matter that was most menacing to Jack Kennedy in the 1960 campaign and which, paradoxically, provided much of its humor, was neatly labeled "the religious issue." That innocent sounding appelation covered an ugly undercurrent of bias. The last time a Roman Catholic had sought the presidency—Governor Al Smith of New York in the twenties—it had produced a mocking joke in which Smith was supposed to have sent a one-word telegram to the Pope saying: "Pack!" Kennedy faced a numbing assault from the forces of the Protestant clergy. The Reverend Dr. Norman Vincent Peale joined 150 Protestant ministers and laymen in issuing a statement: "It is inconceivable that a Roman Catholic President would not be under extreme pressure by the hierarchy of his church to accede to its policies."

Kennedy responded with exquisite humor to slip the punch. He said that reporters were constantly asking him about the Pope's infallibility, and he said, he had gone to his friend Cardinal Spellman to ask how he should respond when newsmen asked him if this were true. Spellman's answer: "I don't know what to tell you, Senator. All I know is he keeps calling me Spillman."

Kennedy's Catholicism was a telling issue. It was difficult for the candidate, so skilled in the quantitative arts, to compute the emotional factor into his plans. It seemed to defy logic and analysis. Kennedy had once reflected that there were only three things that were real—God, human folly, and laughter. "Since the first two are beyond our comprehension," he said, "we will have to make the most of the third." Since the question of religion was beyond the comprehension of his pollsters, Kennedy would have to deal with it with laughter.

Norman Vincent Peale was JFK's chief adversary on the religious issue. He was best known as the author of an inspirational best-seller. So, on the heels of Dr. Peale's attack, Kennedy gibed: "We had an interesting convention in Los Angeles and ended with a strong Democratic platform which we called 'The Rights of Man.' The Republican platform has also been presented. I do not know its title but it has been referred to as 'The Power of Positive Thinking.'"

Responding to another Peale attack, Kennedy wryly declared: "Last week a noted clergyman was quoted as saying that our society may survive in the event of my election, but it certainly won't be what it was. I would like to think he was complimenting me, but I'm not sure he was."

When the drumfire of questions about Kennedy's allegiance to the Vatican continued, the candidate cracked to the press: "Now I understand why Henry the Eighth set up his own church." Campaigning in Iowa, he found himself on a ticket that bore the names O'Brien, McManus, and Kennedy. Said the candidate: "You really run a well-balanced ticket out here." Then, when the laughter subsided, JFK said, "Well, I hope you elect Congressman O'Brien, and I don't hold his name against him."

The "dirty tricks" that were a part of the Watergate scandal and that replicated similar flummery during the Johnson years, made their appearance, albeit in a more subtle form, when John Kennedy was invited to attend the Alfred E. Smith Dinner, a tribute to the late New York governor whose religion denied him the White House. The dinner, which was presided over by the senior prelate of the Catholic church in New York, Cardinal Spellman, seemed calculated to focus attention on Kennedy's religion just when the issue seemed to be in remission. Kennedy was at first wary about accepting the invitation to this strictly religious affair, fearing it would accentuate the Catholic issue. But then, at the eleventh hour, he decided to do what the Kennedys do so well—turn lemons into lemonade. Kennedy accepted the loaded invitation and delivered the wittiest, most sparkling speech of his campaign. As an example of campaign humor, crafted to ridicule an opponent, defuse an issue, and thoroughly entertain, Kennedy's Al Smith speech was an exemplar of the breed. He said:

> I am glad to be here at this notable dinner once again, and I am glad that Mr. Nixon is here also. Now that Cardinal Spellman has demonstrated the proper spirit, I assume that shortly I will be invited to a Quakers dinner honoring Herbert Hoover. [Laughter]
>
> Cardinal Spellman is the only man so widely respected in American politics that he could bring together amicably at the same banquet table, for the first time in this campaign, two political leaders who are increasingly apprehensive about the November election—who have long eyed each other suspiciously and who have disagreed so strongly both publicly and privately —Vice President Nixon and Governor Rockefeller. [Laughter]
>
> But I think the worst news for the Republicans this week was that Casey Stengel has been fired. It must show that perhaps experience does not count. [Laughter and applause]
>
> On this matter of experience, I had announced earlier this year that if successful I would not consider campaign contributions as a substitute for experience in appointing ambassadors. Ever since I made that statement, I have not received one single cent from my father.
>
> One of the inspiring notes that was struck in the last TV debate was struck by Mr. Nixon in his very moving warning to the children of the nation and the candidates against the use of profanity by presidents and ex-presidents when they are on the stump. And I know after fourteen years in the Congress with

the Vice President that he was very sincere in his views about the use of profanity.But I am told that a prominent Republican said to him yesterday in Jacksonville, Florida, "Mr. Vice President, that was a damn fine speech," and the Vice President said, "I appreciate the compliment but not the language." And the Republican went on, "Yessir, I liked it so much that I contributed a thousand dollars to your campaign." And Mr. Nixon replied, "The hell you say." [Laughter and applause]

However, I would not want to give the impression that I am taking former President Truman's use of language lightly. I have just sent him the following note: "Dear Mr. President: I have noted with interest your suggestion as to where those who vote for my opponent should go. While I understand and sympathize with your deep motivation, I think it is important that our side try to refrain from raising the religious issue. [Laughter and applause]

Reporters are a witty, rowdy bunch. Their humor can be ribald, piercing, wounding, iconoclastic, and uproarious. This may account for the relish with which journalists accepted assignment to the Kennedy campaign trail, and the stoicism of those who were assigned to travel with Nixon. The contrast between the jollity of the former and solemnity of the latter cannot be exaggerated. Kennedy, as a former reporter himself, felt a kinship with the newsmen who covered him. He often asked their advice on campaign tactics and respected their acumen. His regard for their sense of humor was also reciprocated. One of the central reasons reporters enjoyed the turmoil, wolfed sandwiches, and truncated sleep of the Kennedy campaign over similar indignities in Nixon's was that Kennedy was a vastly amusing man. His speeches were encrusted with gems of humor. The humor was topical, tasteful, and relevant. It was pointed, irreverent, and original, and it was generally subtle and self-belittling, a reflection of Kennedy's personality and private wit.

Two of the most prolific sources of humor in the Kennedy-Nixon race were not Mort Sahl and Mark Russell. They were two lesser known men—Joseph Kraft and John Bartlow Martin, a pair of journalists who handled "editorial advance" for Kennedy. That esoteric phrase meant the pair would precede Kennedy on the stump, scour the local scene, and, on his arrival, provide the candidate with humorous lines for his numberless speeches. Ted Sorensen and Dick Goodwin were Kennedy's master speech writers, the source of "the glory of words" that swept the candidate into the White House on a surge of political poetry. But Kraft and Martin supplied the relevant local humor that established an immediate rapport between JFK and his audiences. For a political rally in Rochester, New York, Kraft had given the candidate a pertinent story with which to preface his regular campaign speech. Said JFK:

> I am informed by someone with a long memory that when another presidential candidate, Mr. Thomas Dewey, came here to Rochester in 1948, he said, "It is good to be back in Syracuse." He didn't know where he was going or where he was—and I don't think the Republicans do today.

In Modesto, California, the candidate had a witty opening for his remarks provided him by the Kraft-Martin team. He said to the crowd that greeted his campaign train,

> Today we celebrate the one hundred and tenth anniversary of the admission of the State of California to the union. It seems to me that the great story of California has come about because people were not satisfied with things as they were. They liked Massachusetts and they liked Ohio and they liked Oklahoma, but they thought they could do better in California. [a pause] I don't know why they felt that way about Massachusetts.

Kraft and Martin supplied Kennedy with a repertoire of relevant jokes for his travels through the state of Texas. One of these, which had the effect of tickling the Texas vanity in a self-deprecating mode, was this:

> You remember the old story about a citizen of Boston who is visiting the Alamo and hears a Texan talking about the glories of Bowie, Davy Crocket, and the rest, and finally said, "Haven't you heard of Paul Revere?" to which the Texan replied, "Well, he's the man who ran for help."

Some of the wittiest—if scathing—humor in an election campaign is produced by the voters themselves. *Newsweek*

195

opened a floodgate of wit and malice when it invited readers to write their views on the two candidates and printed them in a special part of its Letters section, called "Taking Sides." Here are some of the caustic comments they elicited:

From Phoenix: "While Nixon talks to us about God, Kennedy talks to God about us."

From Seattle: "Thank heavens we are not electing a president for warmth, personality or charm. Kennedy should run for President of Charm, Inc."

From Akron: "Kennedy's New Frontier is just a socialist baby buggy he wants us to climb into."

From Iowa City, Iowa, came a letter kidding Kennedy's Bostonian accent: "I am quite agreed we need a national leadership with 'vigah.' The last time was with FDR."

From Dracut, Massachusetts: "Why does Mr. Kennedy always refer to the accomplishments of former Democratic Presidents? His campaign motto should be the Lost Frontier, not The New Frontier."

On election night, as the votes poured in from all over the republic, the cool, dry wit of the candidate did not desert him. As Kennedy's aides and family waited apprehensively at the TV sets, JFK took a phone call from his running mate in Texas. When Kennedy hung up the receiver, he turned to his friends and said, "That was Lyndon. He said 'I hear *you're* losing Ohio but *we're* doing fine in Pennsylvania.' "

When the grueling campaign was over and Kennedy knew he had captured the prize, he and his family adjourned to the lawn of his Hyannisport home for a game of touch football. Kennedy quarterbacked one team, his brother Bobby the other. Bobby's ebullient wife Ethel was thrilled at the outcome of the election. Said Bobby slyly: "I couldn't have done it without my brother." The Secret Service men who took up their position on the dune grass, watched uneasily as the president was assailed from all sides and went down under a pile of bodies. When Jack Kennedy dived to catch an overthrown pass and landed on his face, Bobby chuckled, "That's my brother, all guts, no brains."

Now it was over. After the rhetoric and humor, the rallies and jumpers, the hope turning to doubt and then to certainty. "Kennedy had run all the way and brilliantly," as Teddy White said. The margin of votes was razor-thin. The people had made their decision, and Jack Kennedy was the president. Never before in the century had the margin of popular votes been so slim. JFK would joke about it on a visit to Chicago early in his presidency:

> Some years ago, in the city of Fall River, Massachusetts, the Mayor was elected by one vote, and every time he went down the street, everyone would come up to him and say, "Say, Dan, I put you in office." And I feel a little like that in Chicago tonight. If all of you had voted the other way—there's about fifty-five hundred of you here tonight—I wouldn't be President of the United States."

With the coming of JFK to the White House and the arrival of the Kennedy clan in Washington, the political climate for humor changed markedly for the better. Suddenly political humor ended its long hibernation and made its appearance in nightclubs, coffeehouses, books, and record albums. The campaign of 1960 had given us a frankly witty president. Humor and whimsy had risen Phoenix-like, and it was no longer subversive to kid the president of the United States.

197

Chapter 14
Campaign 1960
The Day the Pony Died

> There are no funny stories about Richard Nixon.
> —ROSE MARY WOODS

Library shelves groan under the weight of satirical books ridiculing Richard Nixon. Philip Roth abandoned his series of novels on the Jewish-American experience long enough to write *Our Gang*, a send-up of the Nixon crowd. Gore Vidal took a sabbatical from his historical novels and elegant essays to write *An Evening With Richard Nixon*, a sardonic indictment using Nixon's own words. Vidal's political play, "The Best Man," was a thinly veiled satire of a convention battle between Nixon and Adlai Stevenson. My own *Who's In Charge Here?* books would be far duller without the quivering jowls of Richard Nixon. And John Osborne has compiled a series of wise and witty books from his reports for the *New Republic* on the Nixon years. Mockery of Richard Nixon also enriches the collected works of columnist Art Buchwald and cartoonists Herblock and Jules Feiffer.

Why has Nixon seemed such an irresistible target to America's satirists? It is for a reason that was seldom discussed in 1960, when Nixon ran as the odds-on favorite against an obscure Massachusetts senator, and that is the widespread distrust of Richard M. Nixon. In such a narrowly decided race, that amorphous ingredient of distrust was, as much as any other, the decisive one.

Politicians are not notable for their ability to generate trust. Yet, even by this waist-high criterion, Richard Nixon fell well below the mean. There was something in his mien and much in his history to support suspicions of his guile. Though other politicians were attentive to the results of polls, many observers felt that Nixon molded his words and acts more closely to the pollster's findings than was altogether healthy. Students of Nixonian oratory observed a sanctimony that raised hackles. He was heavy-handed in his name-dropping, protesting too much about his contact with world leaders. He was too ready to accuse an opponent of treason. He was uxorious in invoking his wife's name. He misstated an adversary's words and then indicted him for them. All these toxic tendencies provoked distrust; they also provoked humor.

Nixon had been ridiculed before, of course, when he ran for Congress, the Senate, and the Vice Presidency. His famous Checkers speech during the latter race was a favorite target for America's wags, for its maudlin tone and manipulative manner. But it was not until he sought the presidency in 1960 that he really mounted the humorists' bull's-eye.

The *New Republic*, that well-regarded publication whose influence far exceeds its circulation, has always been adroit in its insights and assaults on wayward politicians. During the Nixon-Kennedy campaign, it presented what it called "THE ALL-PURPOSE NIXON SPEECH," portions of which are excerpted below. In it, the magazine twitted most of Nixon's rhetorical excesses, the trivial and the wretched. The *New Republic* began by running a needle through Nixon's devotion to public relations. Said the editors:

NOTE: This universal, all-purpose speech was prepared for Vice President Nixon by a pool of public relations and advertising men who pretested each sentence in a sample of 100 cities between the population of 15,000 and 75,000. The image-meter indicated a favorable response among those Americans between 35 and 70 with an average income of $6,500, and with 1.2 barbecue pits per family.

My fellow Americans, it is good to return to _____, a town that Lincoln loved. In Washington we sometimes forget that in this nation of families, the hearth is in the cities like this, and only the chimney—with a little Democratic smoke—is in the Capital. [Pause for restrained laughter; Charlie will start]

But Chancellor Adenauer does not forget. I last saw the Chancellor shortly after I left Russia, where I had the honor of representing President Eisenhower. . . .

Chancellor Adenauer said to me: "Mr. Vice President, don't ever forget that when you saw Mr. Khrushchev you saw a man who has contempt for the little people. . . .

I am betting that the American people will turn their backs on a party that seems to share Mr. Khrushchev's contempt for little people. The Democrat Party [swallow "ic"] seems to think it can prove Abraham Lincoln wrong in saying you can't fool all the people all the time. But the party that forgot Jefferson, I pray, will not turn the people against the party that remembers Lincoln. [throb in voice]

We've got work to do, Americans! Those that love America . . . they are working day and night. The Democrats, who say they love America but who seem to think we should apologize to the man who hates America worst—they are working hard. Can I count on you to work harder? [Wait for roars of "Yes" to be started by Lew and Eddie]

Another quality that produced abundant humor during the campaign, particularly among the reporters who covered Nixon, was his capacity for self-pity. A campaign stop in Danville, Illinois, demonstrated that quality and the humor it provoked. Nixon was speaking, in a solemn, introspective tone, of his mother. It was a morose rhetoric that was replicated by Nixon on the day he resigned the presidency in disgrace. In Danville he said:

I remember my mother used to get up at five o'clock every morning in our little country grocery store to bake pies so that I and my five brothers could get the education my father didn't have. My father came from Ohio, and his mother died when he was quite young. Consequently, he went to work and he only got a sixth-grade education. . . . So they got up early in the morning and she baked pies, while my dad was going over to the market to get vegetables and put them in the store."

201

Later that day in Centralia, Illinois, Nixon returned to pick at the scab of nostalgia. He said:

> I remember that when we were growing up, my older brother very desperately wanted a pony. My father could have bought it for about seventy-five dollars and my brother, who died when I was quite young, kept saying, "Oh, I want this pony more than anything in the world. . . ." My mother and my father wanted more than anything else to give him what he wanted. It would have been easy for them to say, "Look, you can have a pony." But, you know what happened? My mother and father had a little family council and they came in and they said, "Now look, if we buy this pony we're not going to have enough money to pay the grocery bill; we're not going to have enough money to pay the clothing bill; we're not going to be able to get the shoes for your younger brother." It was an awful hard decision for my mother and father but it was the right thing.

These two speeches triggered a noisy debate on the press bus. Some reporters wanted to call that day "Maudlin Friday." Others preferred to call it simply, "The Day the Pony Died."

It should be observed that the motto of the reporters who cover presidential candidates is: "If you don't have something nice to say—let's hear it." There is a natural cynicism among correspondents continually exposed to politicians that breeds a corrosive humor. Perhaps it comes from living on the edge of irritability—stumbling off a campaign plane at two in the morning, searching for one's luggage, struggling for a few hours sleep in a strange motel room, loping after the candidate to cover an early morning breakfast. Unless you carry a sense of humor as part of your baggage, it is impossible to survive a presidential campaign. Hence the humor and its abrasive tone.

But if Nixon provoked more than his share of malicious wit from the media, the most pungent anti-Nixon humor originated with his electoral foe, John F. Kennedy. Though Nixon liked and admired Kennedy, the affection was not reciprocal. JFK once cracked to an aide in the privacy of a hotel room: "Do you realize the weight of responsibility I carry? I am the only man standing between Richard Nixon and the White House."

The growing crowds that greeted Kennedy as the campaign wound down acted like a stimulant that supplied a special kind of adrenalin. And the keenest part was the joy of needling Nixon—taunting him with humor. There is a traditional wisdom in politics that says it is reckless to use malice in one's humor. Benign humor is thought to be best. Yet in Campaign 1960, John Kennedy's taunts at Nixon's expense often had about them the whiff of malice. In the era before coffeehouses and satirical TV shows, the most amusing humorous attacks leveled at Nixon were launched from the platform of his adversary. Nixon's attacks on Kennedy were slash-and-hack; Kennedy's attacks on Nixon were more subtle. Nixon used a meat ax, Kennedy a rapier.

With his propensity for overkill, Nixon swung a club at Kennedy, calling him a "barefaced liar." In response, Kennedy pinked Nixon with his rapier. Said JFK:

> Two days ago, Mr. Nixon, in that wonderful choice of words which distinguishes him as a great national leader, asserted that I told a barefaced lie. Having seen him four times close up in this campaign, and made up [in the TV debates], I would not accuse Mr. Nixon of being barefaced.

Kennedy's humor often played off a Nixon insult. When Nixon sneeringly referred to his opponent as "another Truman," he felt the nick of Kennedy's rapier: "I regard that as a high compliment, and I have no hesitation in returning the compliment. I consider Mr. Nixon another Dewey." Nixon's name-calling generally left him with more pain than gain. When Nixon called Kennedy "an economic ignoramus" and "a Pied Piper" (because of the horde of youngsters who followed in his wake), JFK was unfazed. He responded, "Mr. Nixon, in the last seven days, has called me an economic ignoramus, a Pied Piper, and all the rest. I just confine myself to calling him a Republican, but he says that is getting low."

The Republicans had dispatched a "Truth Squad" to follow Kennedy about the country, following each of his speeches with a scathing rebuttal. When the practice was finally abandoned, Kennedy quipped, "I see the Truth Squad has been ditched. They told the truth once and they don't let them travel anymore."

Nixon suffered a lethal blow from an unexpected source, the president he had served so loyally. Asked to what decisions Richard Nixon had contributed during his eight years as vice president, President Eisenhower said he would need a week or so to think of any, and this became fodder for the Kennedy wit. He remarked: "A reporter asked President Eisenhower about a month ago what suggestions and ideas Mr. Nixon has had and the President said, 'Give me a week and I will let you know.'" Nixon protested that Ike was simply joking, but the damage was done.

Kennedy even succeeded in turning hecklers into straight men for his anti-Nixon barbs. When a group of contentious Nixon supporters tried to disrupt a Kennedy rally with a chant of "We want Nixon! We want Nixon!" Kennedy merely smiled and said, "I don't think you're going to get him."

The subtlety of Kennedy's humor at Nixon's expense was such that even when JFK vowed silence about his adversary's flaws, he was able to needle him. Early in the campaign, Nixon was hospitalized, and Kennedy declared a moratorium on criticism while his opponent was out of combat. That produced the following press conference exchange:

Q. Senator, did you say you were not going to discuss the Vice President until he is out of the hospital?

KENNEDY. That's right.

Q. But will you resume?

KENNEDY. Well, we will see what happens. I may discuss some of the Republican shortcomings but not Mr. Nixon's.

Q. You are not going to mention his part in any of them?

KENNEDY. Unless I can praise him.

Q. Do you mean as long as he stays in the hospital he has sanctuary?

KENNEDY. Yes, that's right. [thoughtfully] I may go there myself.

Eight days later Nixon was still in the hospital, and a
puckish reporter returned to the subject of Kennedy's re-
straint in attacking Nixon.

Q. Senator, when does the moratorium end on Nixon's hospi-
talization and your ability to attack him?

KENNEDY. Well, I said I would not mention him until I could
praise him, and I have not mentioned him.

Nixon made much of his meeting with General Secretary Nikita Khrushchev at a kitchen exhibit at a Moscow trade
fair. The AP photographer had sent back a picture of Nixon
shaking his finger under Khrushchev's nose, and it appeared
in newspapers all around the world. Kennedy finessed the
photo with a bit of whimsy that suggested Nixon's courage
might not have been all it appeared to be. Said JFK:

During my visit to Pittsburgh I had seen pictures of Mr. Khrushchev with Mr. Nixon's finger under his nose. Friday night,
after the TV debate, when I went over to shake hands with Mr.
Nixon and the photographers appeared, suddenly the finger
came up to my nose. I thought, here it comes; he is going to tell
me how wrong I am about the plight of America, and do you
know what he said? "Senator, I hear you have been getting better crowds than I have in Cleveland."

On another occasion Kennedy said of the Nixon-Khru-
shchev encounter: "Mr. Nixon may be very experienced in his
kitchen debates. So are a great many other married men I
know."

But whatever Nixon's success in his debate with the Soviet chairman, his first TV debate with Kennedy left his advocates badly disappointed. The sight of Kennedy and Nixon
side by side carried a powerful message. The image conveyed
the impression that the experienced Nixon and the upstart
Kennedy were actually evenly matched. And the contrast of

the cool, calm Kennedy with the tense, haggard Nixon made a telling impression. Kennedy explained the outcome of the first debate with typical grace when he told a Minnesota audience, "This week I had the opportunity to debate with Mr. Nixon. I feel I should reveal that I had a great advantage in that debate. . . . Mr. Nixon had just debated with Khrushchev and I had just debated with Hubert Humphrey, and that gave me the edge."

It is a bit puzzling why Jack Kennedy's witty assaults on Richard Nixon were so much more effective than Adlai Stevenson's witty assaults on Dwight Eisenhower in the previous two elections. Much of the difference lay in the great popular affection for Eisenhower and the latent distrust of Nixon. The latter was *vulnerable* to humor. In addition, the humor that seemed a trifle academic in Stevenson seemed like sparkling personality in Kennedy. Yet, it must be acknowledged that Stevenson made campaign humor respectable, and in the process added an extra string to Kennedy's bow.

Stevenson made a more direct contribution to Kennedy's campaign humor. Given Ike's popularity, JFK was loathe to attack him. And so he attacked the Republican party instead. He tried to show that the two parties had very different goals and, as Theodore White expressed it, "pin the Republican tag on Nixon." Kennedy sought to paint Nixon as the ideological offspring of Harding, Hoover, Coolidge, Landon, and Dewey. In doing this he was offered an effective humorous image by Adlai Stevenson. In the closing days of the Nixon-Kennedy campaign, when a razor-thin plurality separated the two, Nixon came to New York with the heavyweights of the GOP. His campaign was joined by President Eisenhower, Governor Rockefeller, and vice presidential candidate Henry Cabot Lodge. It was then that Stevenson provided Kennedy with an inspired bit of metaphorical humor. In his final series of speeches, JFK tied the GOP label to Nixon as tightly and irrevocably as possible. He said:

You have seen those elephants in the circus. [laughter] They have their heads of ivory, thick skin, no vision, long memory, and when they move around the ring they grab the tail of the elephant in front of them. [cheers] Well, Dick Nixon grabbed that tail in 1952 and 1956, but in 1960 he is running, not the President. . . . I stand tonight where Woodrow Wilson stood, and Franklin Roosevelt stood, and Harry Truman stood. [cheers] Dick Nixon stands where McKinley stood and Taft— listen to those candidates [laughter]—Harding [groans] Coolidge [groans] Landon [groans] Dewey [groans]. Where do they get those candidates? [laughter and applause]

Nixon brought a good deal of mockery down on his head with his unctuous celebrations of his wife. A typical invocation of his conjugal mate was delivered to a campaign throng on Long Island. Said Nixon in uxorious excess: "I told you I'd bring Pat out to see you, and here she is. Now I ask you, isn't she wonderful? Wasn't she worth waiting for?" Kennedy, of course, would never think of parading his wife across a political platform. Indeed, it took three weeks of campaigning just to explain Jacqueline's absence, when the candidate said simply, "My wife's home having a baby. We're having a boy in November." When his sister Pat joined him he said shyly, "She is representing my wife who is otherwise committed." Unlike his restrained opponent, Nixon often promoted and praised his wife, triggering a volley of raillery. An impressionist doing the hoarse Nixon basso had the vice president say, "Pat adores me. She always stares at me with those adoring eyes. Frankly, it's giving me the creeps."

In the battle of the 1960 campaign, the humorous front at least was the site of a rout. Kennedy was an elegantly witty man, Nixon a solemn one. Even Nixon's strongest advocates could not claim for him a sense of humor. Said Gerald Warren, Nixon's assistant press secretary: "Nixon's humor was mainly unintentional." In support of this thesis, Warren cited two major events: (1) Nixon attended Charles de Gaulle's funeral in Paris and declared, "This is a great day for France!" (2) Standing astride the Great Wall of China on his epochal China trip, Nixon proclaimed, "This is a great wall."

Chapter 15
Campaigns 1952 and 1956
Nothing to Lose but Your Yolks

> Adlai Stevenson is absolutely honest. He's passion-
> ately concerned about the welfare of his fellow man.
> Those are wonderful qualities. If only he wasn't in
> politics.
> —LELAND HEYWARD

As any precocious schoolboy learns before he is ten,
there is a large reservoir of humor in America that is devoted
to the ridicule of intellectuals. Nothing brings witticisms trem-
bling to the lips so quickly as the sight of thick bifocals, a prominent forehead, and a pile of musty books. At the other end of
the spectrum of seriousness is the military hero—his medals
sparkling, his chest emblazoned with ribbons. Thus, when an
intellectual ran against a war hero in 1952, the outcome was
preordained. America chuckled at the intellectual and
cheered the war hero. The intellectual—Illinois governor Adlai Stevenson—encouraged laughter by being the wittiest man
to run for president in this century. The hero—General
Dwight D. Eisenhower—encouraged the cheers by being avuncular, celebrated, and immensely likable.

America's political observers had some amusing things
to say about the egghead and the general. And yet, when one
compares the humorous quotient with that of any election
since, the elections of 1952 and 1956—in which the combat-
ants were the same—yield far less humor. To understand the

209

reason for this hibernation of the comic spirit, one must recall the terrors of the times. Senator Joseph McCarthy's communist-hunting powers were on the rise and political repression was increasing. In this climate, satire in all its forms went into strategic retreat. The wits and wags lacked the temerity to mock their national leaders.

Walt Kelly, creator of a popular comic strip called "Pogo," was a rare exception to the caution of America's wits. But even Kelly acknowledged that the access to ridicule in 1952 was being sharply curtailed by the times. Said Kelly: "Our recent laughter has been somewhat nervous. We have been trying to keep an eye on all sides before we laugh." Others also observed the want of humor on the political scene as Campaign 1952 began. Robert Hatch wrote that "Eisenhower was easily as laughable as Herbert Hoover, but we had lost a sense of destiny [so that all] attempts to lampoon Ike and his entourage turned rancid. Humor had become a tough business." Jules Feiffer, whose mordant sense of humor has been reliably resilient in all political crises, lamented the lack of humor during the Eisenhower years. Feiffer observed that social criticism was virtually suppressed during Ike's campaigns and incumbency. Satirists were like commandos fighting behind enemy lines. Mort Sahl had been driven underground to the intimate audiences of small clubs. One would not see him on television, and Sahl's concerts, which would overflow campus auditoriums, were still years away.

It is not as though there was nothing that merited the rapier of the satirist. Richard Nixon's cloying Checkers speech —to retain his place on the Eisenhower ticket after scandal threatened him—was a delicious target for humor. Joe McCarthy's two boyish assistants, Roy Cohn and G. David Schine, were gumshoeing their way around the world, plucking "subversive" books out of USIA libraries, and their odd odyssey was an ideal target for humor. But these sanctimonies and hypocrisies produced little satire.

There is perhaps a paradox in the lack of humor in 1952, and the fact that the Democratic candidate was a repository of abundant wit. Perhaps his landslide loss occurred, in part, as a result of this very humor. The public was in no mood to have campaign issues discussed with anything less than absolute sobriety. Indeed, when candidate Eisenhower criticized Stevenson for his levity, Adlai replied, "That reminds me of a very serious story." He said, "If I couldn't laugh, I couldn't live—especially in politics." Ike's reproaches about Adlai's quips led Stevenson to say that he now knew what GOP stood for: "Grouchy Old Pessimists." And referring to Eisenhower's detente with the notorious Joe McCarthy, Adlai added: "My opponent has been worrying about my funny bone. I'm worrying about his backbone."

If much of the humor of the 1952 campaign had its root in the Democratic candidate's mind, at least it was a quality mind and a quality humor. (A CBS executive said at the time, referring both to television's programming and to the presidential candidate: "The people will accept anything—even quality.")

Like most truly witty men, Stevenson had witty perceptions. He said that, at the Democratic convention that nominated him, he encountered a woman who was eight-months pregnant and was carrying a sign that said: STEVENSON'S THE MAN.

His famous war cry was taken up by his following of intellectuals: "Eggheads of the world, unite! You have nothing to lose but your yolks."

Stevenson was ambivalent about accepting the nomination. He did not seek it, nor did he want it. He felt the glorious burden was too much for him. When someone asked what he would do if he were nominated, he replied, "I think I'd shoot myself." He accepted the cup ruefully, telling a meeting of New York's Liberal party: "In my very brief political career I've sometimes wondered if I had any friends left. And then they suddenly nominated me for President, and I wondered if I hadn't too many."

Ted Sorensen said that, in his 1952 and 1956 campaigns for the presidency, Stevenson made political humor respectable, enabling Jack Kennedy to employ it in 1960 without pejorative effect. Stevenson did not tell jokes, as in the latter-day manner of a Lyndon Johnson or Ronald Reagan. But he expressed himself in a dry, droll, civilized way. Speaking of the rigors of the campaign trail, he said:

You must write [speeches] at every chance, think if possible . . . and ride through city after city on the back of an open car, smiling until your mouth is dehydrated by the wind, waving until the blood runs out of your arms . . . bounce gaily, confidently, masterfully into great howling halls . . . You must [read a speech] so defaced with chicken tracks that you couldn't follow it, even if the spotlights weren't blinding and even if the photographers didn't shoot you in the eye every time you looked at them.

Stevenson mocked the omniscience that is expected of the presidential candidate:

If the candidate purported to know the right answer to everything, he would be either a knave or a fool. . . . If he should arrive at election time with almost everybody satisfied, then you should, by all means, vote against him as the most dangerous charlatan of them all.

Ike was the first candidate to be elected with the forceful aide of Madison Avenue and the advertising men who were becoming increasingly visible in national politics. On the occasion that my wife and I met Stevenson at a Manhattan campaign dinner, he reproached me good-naturedly because I was working in advertising at the time. He said, "The idea that you can merchandise candidates for high office like breakfast cereal—that you can gather votes like box tops—is the ultimate indignity to the democratic process."

Stevenson rarely attacked General Eisenhower himself. Ike's popularity was too great. One of those rarities occurred in Fort Dodge, Iowa, when Adlai said, "The Republicans have a 'me too' candidate running on a 'yes but' platform, advised by a 'has been' staff." Another such rare occasion was promoted when the platform from which Ike was speaking in Richmond, Virginia, collapsed. Adlai cracked: "I'm glad the General wasn't hurt. But I wasn't surprised that it happened—I've been telling him for months that nobody could stand on that platform." Rather than attack Eisenhower—even as gently as shown above—Stevenson felt it was strategically wiser to attack the Republican party. He said, "The Republican party is the party which makes even its young men seem old. The Democratic Party is the party which makes even its old men seem young." Stevenson pinked the GOP again when he said, "I like a lot of Republicans. . . . Indeed, there are some Republicans I would trust with anything—anything, that is, except public office." When he felt his adversaries were misrepresenting his position, Stevenson cracked: "If the Republicans stop telling lies about me, I will stop telling the truth about them."

In the era of McCarthy, one of the attacks that Stevenson suffered was the charge that he favored "creeping socialism." Adlai had an adroit response. "I am no more in favor of socialism," he said, "than anybody else, and I particularly dislike things that creep. But if I don't like what they call creeping socialism, there is something else I dislike just as much, and that is galloping reaction."

Joe McCarthy was at the zenith of his power (wits called him "Low-Blow Joe"), and men as seemingly invulnerable to slander as Eisenhower himself were wary of him. (Ike deleted from a speech a defense of his old chief, General George Marshall, when McCarthy attacked Marshall's patriotism.) But Stevenson was never one to suffer knaves gladly. After McCarthy accused Roosevelt and Truman of "twenty years of treason" at a Lincoln Day dinner, Adlai snapped: "That such things are said . . . in celebration of the birthday of Abraham Lincoln adds desecration to defamation. This is the first time that politicians have sought to split the union—in Lincoln's honor." In attacking Republican lethargy, Stevenson said, "I have finally figured out what the Republican orators mean by what they call 'moderate progressivism.' All they mean is: 'Don't just do something. Stand there.'"

Stevenson found humor in the predictable election year conversion of conservative Republicans to liberal ideas. He said,

I confess that the Republican Administration has performed a minor miracle. After twenty years of incessant damnation of the New Deal, they not only haven't repealed it but they have swallowed it . . . or at least most of it. And it looks as though they might be able to keep it down until at least after the election.

When the election was history and Adlai Stevenson became the hit-and-run victim of an Eisenhower steamroller, the candidate looked back on the event and said,

Thousands wrote gracious, flattering letters, after the election, explaining why they did *not* vote for me. They seemed to feel they owed me an explanation. I was touched and flattered, but I confess the thought occurred to me that a little "x" in the right place on the ballot would have been so much easier than a long letter.

Reflecting on the tumultuous events of his ill-starred campaign, Stevenson said:

I shall not soon forget the woman in the crowd in San Francisco who reached into the car to shake hands with me, and not long after discovered that she had lost her diamond ring. Nor will I forget the warm welcome I received on a whistle stop in Bethlehem, and my thanks to "the people of Allentown." My only hope is that *they* forget it!

Stevenson talked of the pain that he felt when the votes poured in and he saw the dimensions of his defeat:

Someone asked me . . . how I felt. I was reminded of a story that Abraham Lincoln used to tell. . . . They asked him how he felt once after an unsuccessful election. He said he felt like a little boy who had stubbed his toe in the dark; that he was too old to cry, but it hurt too much to laugh.

Since brevity is said to be the soul of wit, Stevenson summed up his feeling after his unsuccessful 1952 campaign by saying: "A funny thing happened to me on the way to the White House. . . ." Then, when he was asked about his late arrival at a television studio where he was to speak, he explained that he had been delayed by a military parade. He added dryly, "Military heroes are always getting in my way." He had one final grace note. When Stevenson saw the extent of his defeat, he remarked: "The fact is that the General was far ahead of me. . . . I was happy to hear that I had even placed second."

Though the McCarthy era of communist witch-hunts cast a pall over satire in America during the Eisenhower-Stevenson campaigns, there were some wags who were willing to sink their barbs into Adlai Stevenson. A columnist for a Boston daily wrote, "I originally liked Stevenson because he was so direct and straightforward in his speeches and told you exactly what he meant. But then I lost faith in him. What I didn't like was that he was so direct and straightforward in his speeches and told you exactly what he meant."

A cartoon in the *New Yorker* showed a befuddled husband working on his income tax, leafing through his cancelled checks as his wife looks on. Says the puzzled taxpayer: "A. Stevenson, 375 dollars. That's very curious. The only A. Stevenson I know is Adlai Stevenson. And I don't know Adlai Stevenson."

The men and women who worked for Stevenson—who wrote his speeches and arranged his schedule—relished his sense of humor and knew that he valued their wit as well. They were not afraid to respond to campaign frustrations with humor, even when it was directed at the candidate. On one occasion Stevenson was studying one of the speeches that had been written for him—he preferred to write them all himself, yet this was patently impossible. Reviewing the speech draft, Adlai said to the scribe, "I'm afraid I don't like it very much. The message is cloudy, the speech is unfocused, the writing is pretentious, and the structure is disorganized." Said the speech writer: "How's the typing, Governor?"

Stevenson was anxious to know how his speeches were being received by the audiences he addressed. Knowledgeable observers were saying that "he's talking over the heads of the American people," and Stevenson was anxious to learn the reaction to his words. After one address in Buffalo, one of Stevenson's aides told him of the reaction of one member of his audience. He said, "In the back of the hall there was a cleaning woman standing and listening. She listened to you for about three minutes, then she said, 'Why should I be standing here when I could be doing the men's rooms?'"

For a man who was running against one of the century's greatest war heroes, Adlai Stevenson was not built along heroic lines. Said one of his aides to a reporter: "Let's face it, people aren't thrilled when Adlai mounts a platform. He's too damn medium. He's medium height, has medium brown hair and not much of it, medium blue eyes. . . . He could rob a bank. Nobody would be able to describe him."

Stevenson's speeches addressed the need to help the less fortunate in our society. This inspired one affluent contributor to his campaign to say: "The Governor makes people dissatisfied—makes them want more. What they don't realize is that a poor man who is unhappy is in a better position than a rich man who is unhappy. Because the poor man has hope. He thinks money would help."

The Republican party's war chest was far deeper than the Democrats', so that when the end of the campaign approached, Stevenson's finance chairman wished he had the money for an election eve burst on TV. He said, "I'd sell my soul for two hundred thousand dollars. Unfortunately, the voters aren't interested in my soul."

Hugh Sidey of *Time* magazine observed that there was about Stevenson the whiff of arrogance, which may account for the fact that his humor left the public unmoved while for John Kennedy it signaled a sparkling personality. One television executive observed this arrogance in a critical remark about the candidate. Upon hearing a Stevenson speech the executive said, "How did he get to be so *sure* of everything? He speaks as though he just got a wire from God. Somebody should ask him, 'Tell me, Adlai, how are the apostles?'"

Like most Democratic presidential candidates of this century, Adlai Stevenson campaigned on the philosophy of a growing and compassionate federal government that would offer a hand to the forgotten man. Satirists sometimes found this a subject for humor. Said one: "Adlai is always for the underdog. And if there isn't an underdog, Adlai finds a dog and puts him under."

Stevenson's love of words was also the subject of some kidding. When he addressed a group of farmers in Columbia, Missouri, the local Democratic chairman knew of the candidate's sesquipedalian tastes and decided to caution him. "Governor," he said, "would you mind using simpler language in your speech?" Said Stevenson: "I wouldn't mind, but I don't know how."

Some found an effete, elitist quality to Stevenson that did not conform to the popular image of a glad-handing politician. He was not a gut fighter like Nixon nor a war hero like Eisenhower. He seemed more aloof, like a product of academe —a Woodrow Wilson with wit. This cerebral quality generated a cabaret exchange in which a newly inaugurated President Stevenson is examining the Oval Office for the first time:

STEVENSON. What this room really needs is a great big magnificent tree, right over here.

AIDE. But Mr. President, Congress would raise the roof.

STEVENSON. Oh yes, they'd have to.

Predictably, the press was in Eisenhower's corner to an overwhelming extent. *Time* magazine marshalled their adjectives to the attack. Ike would "stride" into a room; Stevenson would "scurry." Stevenson would often direct his wit at the inequities of this journalistic arrangement. Speaking to a luncheon of newsmen, he said:

It's not honest convictions that concern me. Rather it is the tendency of many newsmen . . . to argue editorially from the personal objective, rather than from the whole truth. As the old jury lawyer said: "And these, gentlemen, are the conclusions on which I base my facts."

Stevenson expressed amusement and dismay at the great majority of the press that was against his candidacy for no reason other than that he was a Democrat. He said:

The press isn't against Democrats after a sober, considered review of the alternatives, but automatically, as dogs are against cats. As soon as a newspaper . . . sees a Democratic candidate it is filled with an unconquerable yen to chase him up an alley.

Twenty-five years before Time Inc. founded *People* magazine, the public yearned for gossip about its notables. The unmarried Stevenson found his name linked to many. Said the candidate of the press's taste for gossip:

> I have always marveled at the ingenuity of certain members of the fourth estate in creating news. They even linked my name, some time ago, with Margaret Truman's romantically . . . but that was before we had met. And since she met me, nothing else has appeared.

Stevenson's attitude toward the press was often wry and never malicious, despite the indignities he suffered at their hands. Here are some of his more pungent comments about the newsmen who covered him:

> I'm convinced that most of the press of this country follow Joseph Pulitzer's admonition—his remark that accuracy is to a newspaper what virtue is to a lady. Except, as someone pointed out, a newspaper can always print a retraction.

> I seem to spend an awful lot of time reading about myself in papers and magazines these days. The awful thing is, I can't say I mind it much either.

> I am convinced that nearly all newspaper publishers are doing their honest best, according to their lights—even if I must confess that sometimes the lights seem to be a little dim.

To the end of his days, Adlai Stevenson could never embrace an electoral process that, in the age of television, had become so much like the marketing of soap flakes. Said Stevenson: "Sometimes in the deafening clamor of political salesmanship, I've thought that the people might be better served if a party purchased a half hour of TV silence during which the audience would be asked to think quietly for themselves."

Both the 1952 and the 1956 campaigns ended in the same way—with the general overwhelming the egghead. Both campaigns were distinguished and enlivened by the eloquence of Adlai Stevenson. But he had the sagacity to acknowledge the weakness of a campaign that relied so heavily on words rather than emotion, on ideas rather than images. Years later he told the Gridiron Club, "Man does not live by words alone, in spite of the fact that sometimes he has to eat them." Stevenson may also have recognized the lack of fire in his delivery. In 1960, with typical style and magnanimity, he paid tribute to the fiery rhetoric of John F. Kennedy, saying: "Do you remember that in classical times, when Cicero finished speaking, the people said, 'How well he spoke'—but when Demosthenes finished speaking, the people said, 'Let us march.'"

Chapter 16
Campaigns 1952 and 1956
Strangled Syntax

I've just read General Eisenhower's manuscript for
"Crusade in Europe," a stirring story in 425 ungram-
matical pages.
—DOUBLEDAY EDITOR

Given the political repressions of 1952 and the dimi-
nution of satire that it caused, political humor at General Eisenhower's expense during the election of 1952 was as inoffensive as a falling leaf. There was, of course, no political satire
on radio or TV, in films, or in the slick magazines. It was primarily the young and liberal splinter groups that were occupied with political satire aimed at the popular war hero. These
youthful satirists looked behind the heroics of Ike's invasion
of Normandy and saw an older man, not unlike their grand-
fathers, mumbling folksy aphorisms, speaking a strangled syntax, and loath to take a stand on moral issues.

When John F. Kennedy ran for the presidency after
eight years of Eisenhower rule, he ran on the thesis: It's time
to get the country moving again. To many social satirists, Ike's
tenure seemed like political somnambulism. It seemed a time
when ships lay in harbor, when Americans were complacent,
self-contented, easy-going, and lulled by material prosperity.
They were gray years. Churchill had called them "the years
the locust ate." Kennedy, quoting T. S. Eliot, had said that
their legacy would be "a thousand golf balls."

But the humor leveled at Eisenhower and the Republican party that had bedecked him with its 1952 nomination was mainly at the private level. It was the kind of humor that on the national level was virtually extinct. Certainly, there was no mockery of the heroic Eisenhower by comedians on "The Ed Sullivan Show." That would have been considered blasphemy. The entertainment and media establishments—in Hollywood and New York—were solidly behind the hero of Normandy who had launched a thousand ships against Nazi Germany. Ike had served as president of Columbia University, and then, after some reflection, decided that he was a Republican rather than a Democrat and accepted the GOP's nomination in the summer of 1952.

Ike's emergence in the national political forum was prior to Mort Sahl's pounce onto the American consciousness. Irving Berlin had written a song called "We Like Ike" for the Leland Heyward Broadway musical, *Mr. President*, and the number became a theme song for the Eisenhower campaign. The lyrics were lauditory: "We like Ike/And Ike is good on a mike." Of course, Ike was not really very good on a mike, and that led to some cautious comic deprecations from some members of the community—particularly those who had become enthralled by the eloquence of Ike's opponent, Adlai Stevenson.

But political humor attacking Eisenhower was more of an underground affair. The specific target of this humor, as the campaign unfolded, was the general's mangled syntax. Every Eisenhower extemporaneous speech or press conference produced fresh evidence of this amusing strangulation of the English language.

The campaign produced an Eisenhower version of Lincoln's Gettysburg Address using the General's tortuous methods of expression. The parody was circulated by mimeograph machines in a thousand offices and schoolhouses and became a classic of sorts, like Tom Lehrer's original record album. It was called "AND NOW FOR A FEW CLOSING REMARKS BY PRESIDENT EISENHOWER." Since Ike's farm was in Gettysburg, site of the original address, the Ike version seemed especially felicitous. Here, then, is the Ike version of the Gettysburg address:

I haven't checked these figures but eighty-seven years ago I think it was, a number of individuals organized a government set-up here in this country. I believe it covered certain eastern areas, with this idea they were following up based on a sort of national independence arrangement and the program that every individual is just as good as every other individual. Well, now, of course, we are dealing with this big difference of opinion, civil disturbance you might say, although I don't like to appear to take sides or name any individuals, and the point is naturally to check up, with actual experience in the field, to see whether any governmental set-up with a basis like the one I was mentioning has any validity, whether that dedication, you might say, by those early individuals will pay off in lasting values.

Well, here we are, you might put it that way, all together at the scene where one of these disturbances between different sides got going. We want to pay our tribute to those loved ones, those departed individuals who made the supreme sacrifice here on the basis of their opinions about how this set-up ought to be handled. It is absolutely in order and one hundred percent okay to do this.

But if you look at the overall picture of this, we can't pay any tribute—we can't sanctify this area—we can't hallow according to whatever individual's creeds or faith or sort of religious outlooks are involved—like I said about this very particular area. It was those individuals themselves, including the enlisted men, very brave individuals, who have given this religious character to the area. The way I see it, the rest of the world will not remember any statements issued here but it will never forget how these men put their shoulders to the wheel and carried this idea down the fairway.

Our job, living individuals' job here, is to pick up the burden and sink the putt they made these efforts here for. It is our job to get on with the assignment—and from these deceased fine individuals to take extra inspiration, you could call it, for the same theories about the set-up for this they did such a lot. We have to make up our minds right here and now, as I see it, that they didn't put out all that blood, perspiration and —well—that they didn't just make a dry run here, and that all of us here, under God, that is, the God of our choice, shall beef up this idea about freedom and liberty and those kind of arrangements, and that government of all individuals, by all individuals, and for all individuals, shall not pass out of the world-picture.

There was no argument that Ike had a tin ear. He was tone deaf to the cadences of oratory. This became especially pronounced when contrasted with the poetry in politics of his opponent. If Jerry Ford was tone deaf to humor, Eisenhower was tone deaf to rhetoric. Thus, his statements were often bland and convoluted. When an Ike speech writer pressed him for a decision on a matter of campaign strategy and the candidate replied, "I'll sleep on it," the writer said dryly, "General Eisenhower is not only a statesman of vision, he is a natural born phrasemaker."

Eisenhower had grown to manhood in Abilene, Texas. He had a taste for Western novels, and his speech was encrusted with folksy homilies. Thus, the speech writers on his campaign train took pains to inject folksy expressions into his speeches, but Eisenhower did not enjoy having his rustic ways propagated. He once barked at an aide: "Gosh, someone around here is always feeding me all these 'folksy' phrases. Hell, I'm folksy enough as it is, without their trying to make matters worse!" Nor did he appreciate grandiose rhetoric being inserted in his speeches and once complained to his chief speech writer: "Those last couple of paragraphs are fine and ringing but I can't get away from the feeling that they make me sound like St. Peter."

Ike's supporters in the Republican party knew they had a good thing—his vast popularity—and exploited it to the hilt. Eisenhower was no fool and felt he was being patronized. "All they talk about," he carped, "is how they could win on my popularity. Nobody said I had a brain in my head."

Ike's campaign staff felt that they could win on the general's popularity alone without resorting to such irrelevancies as issues, and they proved to be right. This led them to write campaign speeches and position papers that were rich with platitudes and generalities, and it led one reporter to mock "the extremely General Eisenhower."

Eisenhower nailed down the election with a pledge to go to Korea to end the war that lingered there. The armies were stalemated at the 38th parallel in that war-ravaged nation. Ike's platitudinous campaign speeches led one journalist wag to ridicule Ike's unwillingness to talk about specific issues. As their train swept through the great Midwest, the newsman was asked, "Where are we now?" He grunted and said, "Crossing the thirty-eighth platitude."

If there was little political satire in the mass media during the 1952 and 1956 campaigns—which resembled one another except in the latter's lack of fire—there were the ubiquitous comic strip cartoon spokesmen—Al Capp's "Li'l Abner" and Walt Kelly's "Pogo" being the most prominent and politically astute. Both cartoonists were preoccupied by matters presidential. Once Ike was ensconced in the White House, his secretary of defense, Charles Wilson, came under satiric attack from the pugnacious Capp. Capp created a Dogpatch character, a cartoon replica of "Engine Charlie" Wilson, who had come to government from the presidency of General Motors. Wilson had said, "What's good for General Motors is good for the U.S.A.," and Americans were laughing at Al Capp's version of Wilson. (When the comic strip became a Broadway musical comedy, songwriter Johnny Mercer wrote a hilarious song mocking Ike's Wilson called "What's Good for General Bullmoose is Good for the U.S.A.") Al Capp and Walt Kelly had Li'l Abner and Pogo immersed in the roiling waters of the 1952 campaign. Along the way, Kelly took some pokes at Senator Joe McCarthy, depositing him in the swampland inhabited by his animal creatures.

In addition to the comic strip artists, there were the political cartoonists whose work appeared on the editorial pages of America's newspapers. Despite the generally rightward tilt of the men who owned and edited these dailies, the editorial cartoonists—most notably Herblock, whose work appeared in a few hundred papers around the country—were less idolatrous of Eisenhower, and they certainly were dubious about his battling young running mate, Senator Richard Nixon of California. Herblock always showed Nixon with a heavy growth of stubble, often burrowing in a garbage pail, as he traveled the low road of the campaign. The stubble never came off until Nixon assumed the presidency in 1968, when Herblock declared: "Every new President is entitled to one clean shave."

Since there was no mass media avenue for the humorous attacks of the young comedians of the fifties, they found their outlet in small clubs on which the young descended for their entertainment and enlightenment. The most prominent of these was the Hungry I in San Francisco, the Blue Angel in New York, Mr. Kennedy's in Chicago, and the Crescendo in Los Angeles. Deeper into the fifties, the Bitter End arrived in New York and the Troubadour in Los Angeles. All would offer a feast of political humor to assault the sanctimony of Nixon, the syntax of Eisenhower, the erudition of Stevenson, the brutality of McCarthy, and the bellicosity of the military hawks. There were also improvisational groups like the Second City in Chicago, and the Committee in San Francisco, which spawned such talents as Mike Nichols and Elaine May and a generation of gifted satirists. Meanwhile, comedians were coming of age who were politically oriented, and who were either fascinated or revolted by the machinations of our public men. There was, of course, the witty Mort Sahl, the telephone monologues of Shelly Berman, the pointed profanities of Lenny Bruce, and the humor of the black experience from Dick Gregory. There was no national publicity or mass media attention to spread their "subversive" message, but there was word of mouth, and that was enough.

One of the most outstanding of these satirists was Tom Lehrer, a Harvard mathematics professor who refused to abandon academia for the mixed pleasures of show business. I met Lehrer when he was writing a weekly song of political satire for "That Was the Week That Was" in the mid-sixties, and I was able to see at close hand the workings of his wickedly sardonic mind. In the Eisenhower years, Lehrer's songs were devoted to social satire—such subjects as the sexual proclivities of Boy Scouts, the effete Harvard football team, a lovable old dope peddler, bigotry in the Deep South, the evil beneath the surface in everyone's hometown, and the rancid loyalties of conjugal decline. But, on TW3, Lehrer's sensibility turned to political matters. He wrote a scathing song about the hypocrisy of liberal good intentions in "National Brotherhood Week," the dangers of nuclear proliferation in "Who's Next?," and the ineffectuality of folksingers who spread their ideology with guitars in "The Folk Song Army":

Join in the Folk Song Army,
Guitars are the weapons we bring
To the fight against poverty, war, and injustice,
Ready! Aim! Sing!

Lehrer also explored the dangers of pollution and the irony of our enlistment of German scientist Werner von Braun, ravager of London, in our nuclear efforts:

Gather round while I sing you
Of Werner von Braun
A man whose allegiance
Is ruled by expedience. . . .

Lehrer's device was to take a politically powerful message and marry it to a song of sentimental sweetness. Ike and Nixon and McCarthy were fortunate that he had not yet turned his talent to political knavery in the fifties.

Fortunately for us, Feiffer had. In the lavish summary of his work from Eisenhower to Reagan, Jules Feiffer described the flaws in the general that engaged his attention during that period. Feiffer observed the strangled syntax of the general, saying: "His press conferences were headlong leaps into verbal gridlocks." But Feiffer's chief complaint against the general was the fact that "he skirted moral issues." When he sent the army into Little Rock to integrate their schools, he made it clear that it was to enforce the law, not to fulfill some moral purpose. When Kennedy sent federal marshals to enroll James Meredith in Ole Miss he spoke of justice and morality. Ike talked of statutes.

Feiffer addressed this failing in a cartoon in which Ike, with his usual meandering prolixity, is explaining his views. Says Eisenhower:

Now let me make myself clear. Now we have a law and we are a country governed by law. I want you to know I feel *strongly* about that. Now there are laws we like and laws we don't like— and I want to make this clear—we must *obey* our laws or else we could aid communism. Now here is the *law of the land*. And that is that and we must enforce it. Now the rest of the world is watching—let me make that clear—and whether we like it or not—lots of them are *colored*. But that *statute's* law and we must live up with it. I can't stress that too firmly. Now let's pull together *voluntarily* and that will solve it all and whether we like it or not forge ahead. . . . And the rest of the world will respect us for our moral stand.

Shakespeare said that nature gives us one face and we make another for ourselves. Ike had made a strong, handsome, appealing face for himself out of his years of military leadership. If Feiffer tended to draw him as a sort of Daddy Warbucks, the public had a great feeling of reliance on the Eisenhower face—its determination and wisdom. I made use of photos of the Ike physiognomy in a series of photographic books called *News Reals*. In one Ike is flashing his wonderful smile at Tom Dewey, the man who had supported his nomination after losing an upset campaign to Harry Truman four years before. Ike is seated in the Oval Office speaking to his guest:

IKE. You came awfully close to being President.

DEWEY. Well, the American people don't always pick the best man.

IKE. (taken aback) They don't?

In another photo strip, Eisenhower is greeting David Ben Gurion, the prime minister of Israel, and saying: "It's a great inspiration. Despite all the anti-Semitism in the world, your country elected a Jewish President."

In another series of photos, Ike is throwing out the first ball for the opening day of the baseball season:

AIDE. I see you throw with your right hand.

IKE. You mean it suggests I'm liberal?

AIDE. No, it suggests you're conservative. *Left* is liberal.

IKE. Oh yeah, I never get that right.

Three decades before the question arose about Ronald
Reagan's hands-off style of management and his disengagement from the duties of his office, satirists were questioning
the degree of Ike's involvement. There were tales that all policy memos had to be compressed to a single page for the general. That generated the following photo-cartoon in which Ike
is addressing an audience:

> Here's how I deal with the major problems of my office. First I
> have Sherman Adams [his chief of staff] type it out on a single
> sheet of paper, never more. Then I close my eyes and count to
> ten. And when I open them—I've forgotten the problem.

Ike had a malleable face that often reflected consterna-
tion and puzzlement. In one photo, Ike is shown pensively
stroking his chin and scowling mightily in concentration, saying: "Happy, Dopey, Sleepy, Grumpy . . . ."

Despite his genial grin, those who worked closely with
Ike told of a fierce temper that belied his image of benignity.
Kennedy had mixed feelings about the man he succeeded in
the White House. He complained to one newsman: "You
know what he calls me? Kennedy. Not Jack, not Senator, just
Kennedy! How about that?" After JFK visited Ike in the Oval
Office shortly before replacing him there, he laughed with an
aide about the thing of which President Eisenhower was
proudest. "He pressed a button on his desk," said Kennedy,
"and five minutes later a helicopter landed on the lawn outside." Kennedy had a residual amusement about Eisenhower
that revealed itself on one of my visits to the White House.
President Kennedy had invited me to visit him after enjoying
the copy of my book, *Who's In Charge Here?*, that a White
House wag had baked into Kennedy's forty-fifth birthday cake
at a family party. When I met Kennedy, he asked how the
book was selling and volunteered that his favorite captioned
photo was of Ike. Said JFK: "The photo I liked best was the
one of President Eisenhower visiting de Gaulle." In that
photo, a cranky, complaining Eisenhower is shaking his finger
at the bland, imperial French president as they ride through
the streets of Paris. De Gaulle, looking aristocratic and aloof,
is saying: "You're drunk."

Ike's preoccupation with golf, often to the exclusion of his presidential responsibilities, was a subject of lampoonery among America's satirists. In one anecdote, Ike is on the links he loved so well. His running mate, Dick Nixon, comes rushing up with unsettling news. Says Nixon: "Mr. President, when you sliced that last drive, the ball hit the driver of a school bus and it swerved off the road and into a ditch, and several of the children have been hurt. What are you going to do, Mr. President?" to which Ike responds, "Well, I think I'll bring my wrist around. . . ."

Ike's face was the most famous one of his day. His grin and his scowl became as much a part of the fifties as Roosevelt's cocky cigarette holder were part of the thirties. In a Broadway comedy called "Once More With Feeling," which dealt with a temperamental symphony conductor, a violinist, whose life is music, is studying the array of framed, autographed photographs on the conductor's piano. This dialogue always brought a big laugh:

MUSICIAN. Ah—Moissivitch . . . Milsten . . . Piantigorsky . . . Solomon . . . (He picks up photograph and stares at it curiously.) And who is this?

CONDUCTOR. That's President Eisenhower.

MUSICIAN. Oh. Fine looking man.

Dwight Eisenhower and Ronald Reagan have much in common. Both were immensely likable leaders and were extremely popular with the electorate. They were the only two presidents in half a century to survive two complete terms in the White House and leave the place with most of their popularity intact. Nixon resigned in disgrace, Johnson abdicated, Ford was defeated, Carter was rejected, and Kennedy was assassinated. Only Eisenhower and Reagan managed to successfully endure two four-year terms.

When we examine the humor that was leveled at these two men during each of their two presidential campaigns, we see that public popularity is able to defuse the harsher humor normally leveled at the presidential candidate. Both Ike and

Reagan were largely immune to the biting, brutal wit that was directed to their predecessors and successors. The humor at Ike's and Reagan's expense was generally moderate and affectionate. The campaign humor that was aimed at their opponents—Stevenson, Carter, and Mondale—was often harsh and bruising. Nothing beats popular approval as an insulation to the stings of the satirist.

We hear much these days deploring the fact that the public does not pay enough attention to "issues" in presidential campaigns. The complaint is that we are too concerned with "personality" and "character." And yet, on reflection, this is not so abominable a situation as it seems. Unexpected issues arise once a nominee reaches the White House. But an individual's personality and his character—the way he manages himself under pressure and in the spotlight—can supply important insights into the performance we may expect if he is granted ultimate power.

Some complain that television has turned presidential races into beauty contests and that the print media have cheapened the political process by featuring character analysis and the cracks of our humorists. TV politics, they say, has been reduced to a series of one-liners by Johnny Carson and Mark Russell. Yet, one of the ways we can judge a potential president is by how he runs the gauntlet of these humorists of the media and show business. That too is a measurement of their confidence and modesty. Do they burst into tears at a mocking editorial? Or do they laugh it away?

American newsmen and American comedians have a long tradition of lampooning presidential candidates. None of today's practitioners, from Art Buchwald to Mort Sahl, is as strident as H. L. Mencken. Yesterday's presidential candidates suffered the attacks of far more vicious campaign humorists than do Bush and Dole and today's Democratic flock. No presidential candidate was more mocked than Franklin D. Roosevelt. In the 1944 election he was ridiculed by the press for his strategy in the war. He reacted with his usual droll humor—which showed more about his character than a dozen white papers. Said FDR: "One of the greatest American soldiers, Robert E. Lee, once remarked on the tragic fact that, in the Civil War, all the best generals were apparently working for the newspapers instead of in the Army."

Presidential campaign humor is inevitable. Most Americans have scant respect for politicians—at least until they are in the White House; then they ascribe to them a degree of wisdom and virtue that shocks us all when we posthumously learn of their feet of clay. John F. Kennedy, the wittiest of the century's presidents and candidates, knew how Americans feel about their politicians. "Mothers may still want their sons to grow up to be President," he said, "but they don't want them to become politicians in the process."

The humor that mocked Adlai and Ike in the fifties became a gushing torrent to assault Kennedy, Nixon, Johnson, Goldwater, and Humphrey in the sixties; then Ford, Carter, McGovern, and the omnipresent Nixon in the seventies; and more recently, Reagan, Carter and Mondale in the eighties. All have run the gauntlet of press and show business humor. It has usually been a cleansing and learning process for us all and shows no sign of soon abating. Let us hope it continues to flow in full stream for years to come.

The poet Dante said that the hottest places in hell are reserved for those who, in a time of great moral crisis, maintain their neutrality. It might be added that one of the more humid places is reserved for those who, in times of great electoral battle, fail to maintain their sense of humor.

Epilogue

As I conclude this informal history of presidential campaign humor and reflect on the power of such humor to illuminate and entertain, the U.S. Supreme Court is weighing a decision that could draw the needle out of campaign wit. At this moment in time, the Reverend Jerry Falwell is seeking compensation for the "emotional distress" he suffered at the hands of *Hustler* magazine and its publisher Larry Flynt. As the justices struggle to conform the First Amendment rights of our journalists to the sensibilities of a public figure, the nation's cartoonists, comics, columnists, and satirists are hoping that the high court will overturn a lower court opinion that upheld a judgment in favor of the TV evangelist.

Few of the humorists whose rights would be impinged by a ruling that favored Falwell are eager to leap to Larry Flynt's defense, since *Hustler*'s humor is often tasteless in the extreme. But a little bit of censorship in the field of political satire is as unlikely as a little bit of pregnancy or a little bit of garlic.

Jerry Falwell is seeking compensation on the basis of emotional distress. If such distress is a valid criterion for successful litigation, we shudder for the Mort Sahls, Mark Russells, Paul Conrads, Garry Trudeaus, and Jules Feiffers in the exercise of their special genius—for the emotional distress they have inflicted on presidential candidates during the electoral process is beyond measurement and beyond price. Certainly, the measurement of that distress is beyond the calipers of a Supreme Court justice.

EPILOGUE

If a presidential candidate may sue a cartoonist or comedian because of his emotional distress, he will spend more time in court than on the stump. Of course, some candidates will do better than others, based on their sensitivity to pain and the bite of the satire they provoke.

It is said by some that liberals tend to turn from liberty to license and that most journalists and satirists are liberal in their leaning. This is untrue. Indeed, our premier satirists are among our most crusted conservatives. For they believe, in the words of historian Bruce Catton, "in things like democracy, freedom, honesty . . . and elementary decency." So-called liberal humorists, says Catton, are "outraged when important people who ought to believe in these things, work to destroy them." Since this hypocrisy often occurs in the fast lane of presidential campaigning, the anger of America's satirists takes the form of waggery.

When America's comics and cartoonists speak out against political knavery, they comprise one of our most precious natural assets—and when we threaten their freedom, we toll the bell for our own.

02